❖ **The 73-volume Sud.**
This edition of _____ ized the study of
the Talmud for _____ em to understand
it for the first ti_____ olarship presented
with astounding clarity, the Schottenstein Edition of the Talmud
has been called "one of the most momentous publishing efforts
gracing the entire length of Jewish history."

❖ **The Hebrew Edition of the Schottenstein Talmud.**
Forty-one volumes of a new edition in the language of eternity are
already available. Even in the scholarly circles of Israel, it is hailed
as a monumental achievement.

❖ **The Schottenstein Edition of Talmud Yerushalmi — the Jerusalem Talmud.**
For 1650 years, this eternal classic has been a sealed book. Now
our scholars and editors are unsealing its riches.

❖ **The Edmond J. Safra French Edition of the Talmud.**
A work in progress, with ten volumes in print.

❖ **The Yad Avraham Mishnah Series.**
This series is nearly complete, with one of the finest commentaries
available in any language.

❖ **The Stone Edition of the Chumash.**
This is truly "the Chumash of choice for home and synagogue for
decades to come." A new translation and an inspiring commentary,
written with today's Jew in mind.

❖ **The Sapirstein Edition of Rashi.**
A thorough, accurate, and beautifully rendered translation and
elucidation of the "father of all commentators."

❖ **The Stone Edition of Tanach.**
A one-volume edition of all 24 books of the Bible, with translation
and capsule commentary.

❖ **The Rubin Edition of the Prophets.**
This series achieves for the Prophets what the Stone
Edition has done for Chumash. Includes the classic Hebrew
commentaries. *Joshua-Judges* and *Samuel* are in print; *Kings*
will soon follow.

(See inside back cover.)

THE SCHOTTENSTEIN EDITION

הגדה של פסח

THE INTERLINEAR

הגדה של פסח

שמחת יהושע

Published by

Mesorah Publications, ltd

THE SCHOTTENSTEIN EDITION

THE INTERLINEAR
hAGGAOAh

THE PASSOVER HAGGADAH
WITH AN INTERLINEAR TRANSLATION,
INSTRUCTIONS AND COMMENTS.

Edited by
Rabbi Menachem Davis

Contributing Editors:
Rabbi Nosson Scherman
Rabbi Meir Zlotowitz   *Designed by*
Rabbi Avie Gold   Rabbi Sheah Brander

A PROJECT OF THE

Mesorah Heritage Foundation

FIRST EDITION
First Impression . . . March 2005
Second Impression . . . March 2006

Published and Distributed by
MESORAH PUBLICATIONS, Ltd.
4401 Second Avenue
Brooklyn, New York 11232

Distributed in Europe by
LEHMANNS
Unit E, Viking Business Park
Rolling Mill Road
Jarrow, Tyne & Wear NE32 3DP
England

Distributed in Australia & New Zealand by
GOLDS WORLD OF JUDAICA
3-13 William Street
Balaclava, Melbourne 3183
Victoria Australia

Distributed in Israel by
SIFRIATI / A. GITLER — BOOKS
6 Hayarkon Street
Bnei Brak 51127

Distributed in South Africa by
KOLLEL BOOKSHOP
Shop 8A Norwood Hypermarket
Norwood 2196, Johannesburg, South Africa

Typography by CompuScribe at ArtScroll Studios, Ltd., Brooklyn, NY
Bound by **Sefercraft, Inc.**, Brooklyn, NY

This Haggadah is dedicated
to the memory of

Robert Barry Weiss ע"ה

בערל ראובן בן מנחם מענדל ע"ה

י' כסלו תשמ"א

The life of Bob Weiss was cut short at the age of 26,
when a future of fruitful accomplishment and
dedicated service to his people was still ahead of him.

He was a committed Jew who was active
throughout his life in his synagogue
and in organizations to help his fellow Jews,
in his hometown of South Bend, Indiana and beyond,
until his untimely death.

Bob aspired to better himself and his community
through education, hard work and mitzvos.
He left behind many friends and a devoted family.
He was a loving son, sibling and friend to many —
and every one of them was better for having known him.

Jay and Jeanie Schottenstein

◈§ The Interlinear Translation — How to Read it

There is a difficulty inherent in any interlinear translation of Hebrew to English: the fact that English and Hebrew are read in opposite directions. ArtScroll has developed a system of patented notations that helps the reader navigate the two languages simultaneously, without confusion.

These notations consist of the following:

1) single arrow notations ⟨ between English phrases direct the reader's eye toward the next English phrase, reading right to left, for example:

בָּרוּךְ הַמָּקוֹם, בָּרוּךְ הוּא.

《 is He. ⟨ Blessed 《   is the   ⟨   Blessed
Omnipresent;

2) Double arrow notations 《 indicate a logical break between phrases, equivalent to a period, semicolon, dash and many commas.

3) Bold double arrow notations 《 indicate the completion of a sentence at the end of a verse.

With these double arrows, the reader need not search for commas, semicolons, and periods. This was done to make the translation as user-friendly as possible; it allows the reader to continue following the Hebrew moving to the left, without the distraction of looking for English punctuation marks on the *right* side of the English words.

The arrows also identify the specific Hebrew word or words that are translated by the English phrase. This is especially useful where two or more Hebrew words are translated as a unit.

For quotations, one further convention was used: Wherever text would normally be set off by quotation marks, the quotation has been set in italics.

৵ঌ Publisher's Preface

The Schottenstein Interlinear Prayerbook Series has revolutionized the prayer experience for countless people. This new system makes it possible for people to view the original Hebrew and the English translation simultaneously, without groping for the translation on a facing page or adjoining column. Now, the Interlinear design comes to the Passover Haggadah, and it will surely make the Passover *Seder* more accessible, comprehensible and enjoyable.

There is probably no Jewish ritual more widely observed than the *Seder*. Thanks to this new Haggadah, no guest need feel at a loss to follow the text. The translation is directly under the Hebrew word, and the patented "arrow" format guides the eye along the line, avoiding the right-to-left and left-to-right confusion that might otherwise make the translation daunting for many people. The best way to appreciate the accomplishment is to try it.

Jay and Jeanie Schottenstein immediately understood what a boon this would be for untold numbers of people, and they undertook to dedicate the full series of Jewish liturgy. The Sabbath and weekday *Siddurim*, the High Holiday *Machzor*, the Book of *Tehillim*/Psalms have all been published to universal acclaim. Now, with the Passover Haggadah, they add another jewel to their crown of service to the community. The Jewish people is grateful — and the greatest expressions of this gratitude are the multitudes of people to whom these prayerbooks have become indispensable.

We are grateful to Rabbi Menachem Davis, the consummate master of the difficult art of matching the syntax of the English with the Hebrew, and to Reb Sheah Brander whose graphics artistry has created the page design that makes these volumes such a pleasure to use. So skilled are these two artists of the written and printed word that only the most discerning reader can recognize the full extent of their expertise.

Finally we thank the Almighty for enabling us to serve Him by enabling His people to bring more knowledge and feeling to their "service of the heart," and to their observance and understanding of *Pesach,* the Festival of Freedom.

Rabbi Meir Zlotowitz   Rabbi Nosson Scherman

II Adar 5765 / March, 2005

❧ The Seder /
A Celebration of Freedom and Family

The family aspect of the Seder is an integral part of the observance, for the Torah speaks frequently of the responsibility of parents to teach their children about the Exodus.

Hardly a ceremony in Jewish life is more familiar and more widely observed than the Passover *Seder*. For countless grandparents and parents, it represents an "ingathering of exiles" of sorts, as children converge from far and wide to celebrate the *Seder* together. Indeed, the family aspect of the *Seder* is an integral part of the observance, for the Torah speaks frequently of the responsibility of parents to teach their children about the Exodus.

Of no other commandment does the Torah speak about children's questions and parents' answers. So when the youngest member of the household is coaxed, bribed, and encouraged to stand before Zaidy or Daddy and say the *Mah Nishtanah*, the Four Questions, the heartwarming ritual is truly an essential part of the *Seder* — for this is a night when bonds are forged between parent and child, when the chain of generations is strengthened and new links are added. It is a night when, as we say in the Haggadah, every Jew should regard himself as though *he* were freed from Egyptian slavery, and began the march from the land of his bondage toward Sinai, where Israel would receive the gift of the Ten Commandments.

This is a night when bonds are forged between parent and child, when the chain of generations is strengthened and new links are added.

So important is that aspect of the interaction between parent and child that the Sages instituted some *Seder* customs primarily to stimulate the curiosity of youngsters. Let them ask. Let their parents answer. Let everyone inquire, think, delve, innovate, find ways to relate the adventure of old to the challenges of today. For the *Seder* and its narrative speak to every generation. Every era has its Egypt, its own brand of slavery and temptation that inhibits the development of Israel. And to every generation, the *Seder* says that this night *is* different, because it brings home lessons that can easily be drowned in the constant activity of daily life.

Every era has its Egypt, its own brand of slavery and temptation that inhibits the development of Israel. And to every generation, the Seder says that this night is different.

The Talmud lays down the dictum that our narrative of freedom must begin with the tale of our degradation, for it is only when someone recalls how bad things *were* that he can realize how good things *are*. The Haggadah's narrative of the torturous slavery of Egypt is understandable — that was bondage in its most literal sense. Surely freedom must have been sweet to the Jew whose back still smarted from the scars of the taskmaster's whip, to the mother whose child had been bricked into a pyramid or drowned in the Nile.

Surely freedom must have been sweet to the Jew whose back still smarted from the scars of the taskmaster's whip.

But the Haggadah contains a second narrative of degradation and our escape from it: *Originally our ancestors were idol worshipers, but now the Omnipresent has brought us near to His service.* There is another slavery, another degradation, one that is *not* to masters holding whips, enforcing production quotas, murdering children, separating families. Idolatry, too, is a form of enslavement, for when people choose idols that suit their own desires and concerns, they are truly slaves — to their own passions. Our ancestors were pagans. As pagans they were spiritually flawed and they would have passed on their spiritual blemish to their posterity, had not Israel been liberated from this slavery to codes of man's own creation.

Idolatry, too, is a form of enslavement, for when people choose idols that suit their own desires and concerns, they are truly slaves — to their own passions.

So the Exodus represented a twofold liberation: from physical enslavement and from spiritual degradation. The nation as a whole was cleansed of both blemishes. On the night of Passover it came to acknowledge no master but God and it began the trek to the wilderness where it would stand at Sinai and declare its willingness to accept the privilege of bearing God's message of truth and morality.

Are the enslavement of Pharaoh and the idolatry of Terach behind us? Hardly. History books and newspapers alike illustrate all too vividly that physical independence is easily lost and moral freedom easily subverted. The *Seder* is not only a celebration of past liberation but also a challenge to retain it. That is why we declare the responsibility of every Jewish man, woman and child to regard himself or herself as one of those hundreds of thousands who departed Egypt for a better life and a greater responsibility. Only by understanding the past and identifying with it can we deal intelligently with the future. Terach tried to impose idolatry on his children — so he was our enemy. Laban tried to wean his grandchildren, the first totally Jewish family, away from the faith of Abraham, Isaac and Jacob — so he was our enemy. Pharaoh tried to destroy Jewish

Are the enslavement of Pharaoh and the idolatry of Terach behind us? The Seder is not only a celebration of past liberation but also a challenge to retain it.

nationhood and tried to assimilate it into the Egyptian people — so he was our enemy. These were different kinds of challenges and one or the other is a mirror of virtually every danger — bitter or sweet — that has ever confronted Israel.

Therefore we gather our generations around the *Seder* table and transmit the message of Jewish history to our children. According to the Halachah, the *Seder* narrative must be understood; indeed, the great scholars of Jewish history made it a point to translate and simplify the Haggadah so that everyone at their tables could understand. As the Haggadah tells us, the greatest sages of their time gathered in Bnei Brak to discuss the redemption and its implications for them. And as the Haggadah tells us, the *Seder* night is the time to relate the narrative to our children — from the wisest to the simplest — encouraging them to ask, inquire, challenge, learn; for only by doing so can they become part of Jewish history and make it part of their own personal experience and perspective on the world.

According to Halachah, the Seder night is the time to relate the narrative to our children, encouraging them to ask, inquire, challenge, learn.

The *Seder* is a celebration of history — the past *and* the future. Though we Jews always learn from our past, we simultaneously look ahead to a future of spiritual perfection. This is symbolized by the *Hallel* prayer of the *Seder*. The first two chapters of *Hallel* refer to the miracles of the Exodus; they are recited just before the *Seder* feast. Following the festive meal with its many *mitzvos,* we continue with the rest of *Hallel,* the ecstatic songs of hope and prayer that allude to the prophetic visions of plowshares taking the place of swords and of Jerusalem displacing the martial capitals of the world.

Let us hear its message of the past and let it teach us how to order our present that we may build a better future.

Let us gather up our children and ourselves, to begin the *Seder.* Let us hear its message of the past and let it teach us how to order our present that we may build a better future.

✍§ Preparing for Passover

בדיקת חמץ ❏ / The Search for Chametz

Aside from the commandment to eat matzah all of Passover and the special observances of the *Seder* nights, the best-known feature of the festival is the requirement not to eat, or even to own, *chametz* all during the festival. For many Jews, one of the most vivid memories of their childhood is the seemingly endless cleaning and scrubbing of their homes during the weeks and days before Passover.

Although no household can be thoroughly cleaned in only a short while, the Talmudic Sages ordained that a search for *chametz* be made in every home and business on one night of the year.

In years when Passover begins on Saturday night, the inspection is not conducted on the evening before Passover, for this would result in a desecration of the Sabbath. Instead, it is made on Thursday night and the *chametz* is burned Friday morning.

Any *chametz* intended for that evening's supper or the next morning's breakfast must be set aside carefully. After one finishes eating, leftover *chametz* should be placed with whatever *chametz* may have been found in the evening. It will be burned the morning before Passover (except when Passover begins on Saturday night, in which case the *chametz* is burned Friday morning).

✍§ Laws of the Search

1. One must begin the search immediately at the beginning of the night of the fourteenth of Nissan. It is proper for one to begin just after *tzeis hakochavim*, even before the light of day has completely subsided, so that he not delay the search or forget about it (*Orach Chayim* 431:1 and *Mishnah Berurah* §1).

2. It is forbidden to begin a meal or to begin a bath or to do any kind of work starting from a half-hour before nighttime. However, a snack — that is, a *k'beitzah* (the size of an egg) or less of bread, or fruit in any amount — is permitted at this time. When the actual time for the search arrives one should not spend much time eating even a snack, as this would cause a delay in the start of the search (432:2 and *Mishnah Berurah* §2, 5-6).

3. It is also forbidden to engage in Torah study once the time for the search has arrived. (There are those who forbid this also during the half-hour *before* nightfall. This applies only in private, however, and not, for instance, to someone who gives a short *shiur* in a *beis midrash* after *Ma'ariv*. If someone asks a

---

Note: Source references within the laws refer to *Shulchan Aruch Orach Chayim,* unless otherwise noted.

person who is not learning to remind him about the search when the proper-time comes, he may also learn during this half-hour interval) (ibid. *Mishnah Berurah* §7).

4. Any place into which it is possible that *chametz* might have been brought must be searched. Even places not normally used for *chametz,* but where there is a reasonable possibility that *chametz* may happen to have been brought there, require a search. This includes houses, yards (except in cases where one can assume that leftover food is eaten by animals or birds), nooks and crevices as far as the hand can reach, and whatever containers might have once been used for holding *chametz.* In a situation where a search in a particular place would entail great difficulty, it is possible to be lenient and sell that place to a non-Jew, so that it would not require a search. The details of these rules may be found in *Orach Chayim* 433:3,5 and *Mishnah Berurah* §23.

5. Pockets of garments must be searched, even if one feels confident that he has never put any *chametz* in them, because one often does so without realizing it (433:11 and *Mishnah Berurah* §47).

6. One should clean up the house before the search is begun. It is customary to clean the whole house on or before the 13th of Nissan, so that the search can be started without delay at nightfall of the 14th. It is also customary to take a feather with which to dust out the *chametz* from holes and crevices (ibid. and *Mishnah Berurah* §46).

7. It is preferable to use a single-wick wax candle for the search. A search done by the light of a torch is not valid at all, but one done using a candle made of tallow is valid. The validity of a search done by the light of an oil candle is a matter of dispute between halachic authorities (433:2 and *Mishnah Berurah* §10). Contemporary authorities rule that one may use a flashlight for the search.

8. It is customary to place several pieces of bread (taking care that they should not crumble) in safe places around the house, where they may be found by the person conducting the search. (The *Arizal* wrote that *ten* pieces should be used.) Some halachic authorities write that this practice is not obligatory, and the *Taz* in fact advises against it, lest the pieces become lost. (The *Pischei Teshuvah,* however, notes that nowadays, when the entire house is rid of *chametz* before the search, there is a sound halachic basis for the practice of placing some *chametz* around the house to provide some-thing for which to search.) (432:2, *Mishnah Berurah* §13 and *Shaar Hatziun* ad loc.)

9. There is a controversy as to whether one must search those rooms which are to be sold to a non-Jew with the *chametz.* The custom is to be lenient in this regard, although it would be preferable that in this circumstance the *chametz* be sold before the search (436, *Mishnah Berurah* §32).

⋑ The *Berachah* over the Search

1. Some say that it is proper to wash the hands before reciting the *berachah* for the search, but this is only for the sake of cleanliness (432, *Mishnah Berurah* §1).

2. One must not speak between the *berachah* and the onset of the search. If he spoke about matters unrelated to the search, he must repeat the *berachah* (432:1, *Mishnah Berurah* §5).

3. One should not speak about matters unrelated to the search until he completes the search, so that one may devote his entire concentration to the task at hand. If he did, however, speak about unrelated matters after beginning the search, he need not repeat the *berachah*. Furthermore, it is altogether permitted to speak about any matters related to the search at this point (ibid.).

4. Immediately after the search one should recite the כָּל חֲמִירָא declaration, annulling all the *unknown chametz* in his possession. If one does not understand the Aramaic content of this declaration, he should say it in Hebrew or English or whatever language he does understand. If one said it in Aramaic, so long as he has a basic understanding of what the declaration means, though he may not understand the translation of every word, the annulment is valid. One who does not understand the content at all, and thinks he is reciting a prayer of some sort, has not annulled his *chametz* (434:2 and *Mishnah Berurah* §8).

⋑ Laws of *Erev Pesach*

1. Prayers are held early on *erev Pesach* in order to allow people to finish eating before the end of the fourth hour of the day (*Mishnah Berurah* 429:13).

2. אֵל אֶרֶךְ אַפַּיִם, מִזְמוֹר לְתוֹדָה, and לַמְנַצֵּחַ are not said on *erev Pesach* (*Orach Chayim* 429:2).

3. It is forbidden to eat *chametz* after a third of the halachic day has passed. The duration of the day can be calculated in various ways. One should consult a competent Halachic authority or a reliable Jewish calendar (443:1 and *Mishnah Berurah* §8).

4. The deadline for ridding one's property of *chametz* and deriving benefit from the *chametz* is at the end of the fifth hour of the halachic day (*Mishnah Berurah* §9).

5. Immediately after a third of the day has passed, one should burn the remaining *chametz* and then recite the second כָּל חֲמִירָא declaration, annulling *all* the *chametz* in his possession. This declaration must not be delayed past the start of the sixth hour, for at that time the annulment no longer has any validity (434:2). See "*Burning the Chametz*" below.

6. If *erev Pesach* falls on a Shabbos, the *chametz* should be burned on the day before *erev Pesach* (Friday) in the morning, at the same time as other years.

However, the כָּל חֲמִירָא declaration should not be said until the 14th of Nissan, i.e. Shabbos morning, after the last *chametz* meal has been eaten (444:2).

7. One should take care that all food utensils not *kashered* for *Pesach* have been thoroughly cleaned, so that they do not contain any *chametz* residue, and they should be placed out of reach for the duration of *Pesach* (440:2; end of 442, *Mishnah Berurah* 433:23).

8. Those utensils too hard to clean from *chametz* residue should be sold together with the *chametz*. (Only the residue *itself* should be sold, not the utensil, so as to avoid the necessity of immersing the utensil in a *mikveh* when it is repurchased from the non-Jew.) These utensils should also be placed in a room where they are out of reach, or together with the *chametz* that is being sold (ibid.).

9. After halachic noon it is forbidden to do any work (מְלָאכָה). If someone's clothing tore at that time, and he needs that article of clothing for *Yom Tov*, he may make a minor repair for himself, even if it involves expert workmanship. Someone else may also do it for him at no charge (*Orach Chayim* 468, *Mishnah Berurah* §5).

10. Any manner of work which is forbidden on *Chol Hamoed* is also forbidden on *erev Pesach* afternoon, although it is permissible for one to have a non-Jew do these things for him (*Mishnah Berurah* §7).

11. One should cut his nails and have his hair cut before noon. If, however, he neglected to do so, he may have his hair cut by a non-Jew even after noon, and he may cut his own nails *(Mishnah Berurah* §5).

12. Any matzah which one could use for fulfilling the mitzvah of matzah at the *Seder* may not be eaten all day on *erev Pesach,* even if that matzah has been crumbled or ground into flour and mixed with water or juices. Some people have a custom not to eat matzah from *Rosh Chodesh Nissan* (471:2, *Mishnah Berurah* §12). Some do not eat matzah from Purim (see *Igros Moshe O.C.* I:155).

13. A child who is too young to understand the story of the Exodus may be fed matzah on *erev Pesach* (471:2 and *Mishnah Berurah* §13).

14. Although we consider matzah with folds or bubbles to be unfit for *Pesach* use, these may also not be eaten on *erev Pesach* (*Mishnah Berurah* §12).

15. Matzah that has been prepared by adding juices into the dough (such as egg matzah or fruit-juice matzah) may be eaten on *erev Pesach*. (Note: It is the Ashkenazi practice to avoid such matzos whenever the eating of *chametz* is forbidden, except for the sick or elderly.)

16. From the beginning of the *halachic* tenth hour of the day, only snacks such as fruits and vegetables may be eaten. One should be careful, however, not to fill himself up on these either, to preserve one's appetite for the matzah at the *Seder* (471:1 and *Mishnah Berurah* §7).

17. The Gemara says that a small amount of wine can also cause satiety, but a large amount stimulates the appetite. *Be'ur Halachah* concludes that the amount of wine one may drink depends on his individual nature, and that a person should not drink (after the tenth hour) an amount of wine that he feels may make him feel sated (471:1 and *Be'ur Halachah* ad loc.).

◄§ Fast of the Firstborn

1. There is a custom for firstborn males to fast on *erev Pesach,* even if they are firstborn to only one of their parents. If the firstborn son is a minor, the father fasts in his place. If the father is a firstborn himself (and thus has to fast in his own right), the mother fasts for the child. (See *Orach Chayim* 270 and *Mishnah Berurah* ad loc. for the details of this law.)

2. If the firstborn has a headache or similar infirmity he does not have to fast. Similarly, if the fast is likely to cause him to be unable to fulfill the evening's mitzvos of matzah, *maror,* and the four cups of wine properly, it is better for him not to fast. In either of these cases, however, he should limit his eating to small amounts rather than eating full meals (470 and *Mishnah Berurah* ad loc.).

3. There is a controversy among the halachic authorities as to whether a firstborn may eat at a meal served in honor of a mitzvah, and this issue depends on the local custom. The generally accepted practice is to permit eating at a festive meal at the completion of a *mesechta,* even if the firstborn himself did not participate in the learning (*Mishnah Berurah* §10).

◄§ Burning the *Chametz*

1. The *chametz* should preferably not be burned until the day of the 14th of Nissan, after the last *chametz* meal has been eaten. If someone is concerned that the *chametz* found in the search may become lost or find its way back into the rest of the house if it is left too long, he should burn it at night, and he is considered to have fulfilled the Torah commandment to destroy *chametz* on *erev Pesach* (תַּשְׁבִּיתוּ) (*Orach Chayim* 445:1, *Mishnah Berurah* §6).

2. If one kept the *hoshanos* that had been used on *Succos,* he should use them to feed the flame burning the *chametz,* so that they may be used for yet another mitzvah (*Mishnah Berurah* §7).

3. The *chametz* must be burned (until it is completely charred) before the beginning of the sixth hour, and thereupon the declaration of annulment (כָּל חֲמִירָא) is recited. The annulment is ineffective if it is recited once the sixth hour has begun (*Mishnah Berurah* §1,6).

      One should not recite the annulment declaration before his *chametz* has been fully burned, so that he will be able to fulfill the mitzvah of תַּשְׁבִּיתוּ (burning the *chametz*) with *chametz* that still belongs to him (443:2).

~§ Summary of the Laws of Erev Pesach that Falls on Shabbos

1. The Fast of the Firstborn should be observed on Thursday. One fasting should not eat Thursday night until after completing the Search for *Chametz*. If it is difficult for him to fast that long and he cannot find someone to search for him, he may eat a small amount before the search (*Misnah Berurah* 470 §5).

2. If instead of fasting the firstborn participates in a *siyum,* the *siyum* should be on Thursday.

3. Many permit even those who usually do not rely on a *siyum* and fast to eat this year at a *siyum,* since the fast is not on its proper date (*Nitei Gavriel* 2:1).

4. Some have the custom of making a second *siyum* on Friday morning (ibid. 2:3). Others suggest that in lieu of a second *siyum,* one save some of the food from Thursday's *siyum* and eat it on Friday (*Mikraei Kodesh, Pesach* II, §23 and notes 2, 5, 6).

5. The Search for *Chametz* is performed on Thursday night with the usual blessing.

6. The sale of *chametz* to a non-Jew should be done on Friday, ideally before the beginning of the sixth hour.

7. The *chametz* should be burned on Friday before the beginning of the sixth hour as on other years. However, if it was not burned then it should be burned at any time before Shabbos (444:2,6).

8. The second כָּל חֲמִירָא declaration is not said until Shabbos morning, after the last *chametz* meal has been eaten (444:2,6).

9. מִזְמוֹר לְתוֹדָה and לַמְנַצֵּחַ are said in *shacharis* on Friday.

10. Work may be done after noon as on any *erev* Shabbos, including haircuts, shaving, and cutting nails. Some refrain from work in the afternoon.

11. The preparations for the *Seder* may not be done on Shabbos.

12. The *charoses* for the *Seder* must be prepared before Shabbos. If it was not prepared before Shabbos, it may be prepared on *Yom Tov* with a *shinui,* a change from normal practice, such as chopping into a dish or on a table. Only the amount needed for one Seder may be prepared before each *Seder.*

13. The *z'roa,* roasted bone, and the *beitzah,* roasted egg, must be prepared before Shabbos and used for both Sedarim. If they were not prepared before Shabbos, they may be roasted after Shabbos and eaten Sunday during the day and then roasted Sunday night for the second *Seder* and eaten Monday during the day.

14. The horseraddish should be ground on Friday. It should be placed in a sealed container to insure it retains its sharpness.

15. It is preferable to prepare the salt water on Friday. If it was not prepared then, it may be prepared on the *Seder* night; but some require that it be prepared in a different manner, such as reversing the order of adding the water and salt.

16. The matzos that are to be used at the *Seder* are considered *muktzah* by some authorities and should not be handled or moved on Shabbos.

17. If one takes a nap on Shabbos he should not *state* that the purpose of the nap is to be rested for the *Seder*.

18. Many authorities suggest that food for the Friday night and Shabbos morning meals be kosher for Pesach, prepared in Pesach pots. Just enough *chametz* bread to provide the size of an olive (according to some the size of an egg) for each person at each meal should be set aside. If necessary, a Pesach matzah — not intended for the *Seder* — can be used as the second loaf for *lechem mishneh*; however, the matzah should be in a closed bag so that it not come in contact with the *chametz* loaf. Some allow matzah for the second loaf only Friday night (*Piskei Teshuvos* 444:2).

19. It is recommended that one use disposable dishes, utensils, and tablecloths.

20. It is also recommended that the candles not be placed on the tablecloth so that it can be removed and shaken out after the *chametz* is eaten.

21. In the morning, *chametz* may not be eaten after the end of the fourth hour. Before the end of the fifth hour any remaining *chametz* should be flushed down the drain. All dishes and utensils used with *chametz* during the meal should be cleaned of any *chametz* and either thrown away or placed with the rest of the *chametz* kitchenware. One should rinse his mouth and clean his teeth after the meal.

22. Before the end of the fifth hour, once all *chametz* has been removed and disposed of, the second כָּל חֲמִירָא, (nullification of *chametz*) declaration is said. The Shabbos meal can continue with non-*chametz* food.

23. The third Shabbos meal, *Seudah Shelishis*, may be satisfied with meat, fish, or fruits.

See the ArtScroll *Pesach* for additional laws and information regarding *erev Pesach* that falls on Shabbos.

⹂⫷ THE SEARCH FOR CHAMETZ / בדיקת חמץ ⫸⹂

ON THE NIGHT PRECEDING 14 NISSAN, THE NIGHT BEFORE THE PESACH *SEDER*, THE SEARCH FOR *CHAMETZ* (LEAVEN) IS MADE. IT SHOULD BE DONE WITH A CANDLE AS SOON AS POSSIBLE AFTER NIGHTFALL. [WHEN THE FIRST *SEDER* IS ON SATURDAY NIGHT, THE SEARCH IS CONDUCTED ON THURSDAY NIGHT (13 NISSAN).] BEFORE THE SEARCH IS BEGUN, THE FOLLOWING BLESSING IS RECITED. IF SEVERAL PEOPLE ASSIST IN THE SEARCH, ONLY ONE RECITES THE BLESSING FOR ALL.

בָּרוּךְ אַתָּה יהוה, אֱלֹהֵינוּ מֶלֶךְ הָעוֹלָם,

‹‹ of the universe, ‹ King ‹ our God, ‹ HASHEM, ‹ are You, ‹ Blessed

אֲשֶׁר קִדְּשָׁנוּ בְּמִצְוֹתָיו, וְצִוָּנוּ עַל בִּעוּר חָמֵץ.*

‹‹ of ‹ the ‹ concerning ‹ and has ‹ with His com- ‹ has sanctified ‹ Who
chametz. * removal   commanded us   mandments   us

⹂⫷ BURNING THE CHAMETZ / ביעור חמץ ⫸⹂

UPON COMPLETION OF THE *CHAMETZ* SEARCH, THE *CHAMETZ* IS WRAPPED WELL AND SET ASIDE TO BE BURNED THE NEXT MORNING AND THE FOLLOWING DECLARATION IS MADE. THE DECLARATION MUST BE UNDERSTOOD IN ORDER TO TAKE EFFECT; ONE WHO DOES NOT UNDERSTAND THE ARAMAIC TEXT MAY RECITE IT IN ENGLISH, YIDDISH, OR ANY OTHER LANGUAGE. ANY *CHAMETZ* THAT WILL BE USED FOR THAT EVENING'S SUPPER OR THE NEXT DAY'S BREAKFAST OR FOR ANY OTHER PURPOSE PRIOR TO THE FINAL REMOVAL OF *CHAMETZ* THE NEXT MORNING IS NOT INCLUDED IN THIS DECLARATION.

כָּל חֲמִירָא וַחֲמִיעָא* דְּאִכָּא בִּרְשׁוּתִי,*

‹ in my possession* ‹ that there is ‹ or chametz* ‹ leavening ‹ Any

דְּלָא חֲזִתֵּה (נ׳׳א: דְּלָא חֲמִתֵּה) וּדְלָא בִּעַרְתֵּה

‹ removed, ‹ and that (‹ observed, ‹ that I) ‹ seen, ‹ that I
    I have not   have not   have not

⹂⫷ בְּדִיקַת חָמֵץ / THE SEARCH FOR CHAMETZ ⫸

⹂§ בִּעוּר חָמֵץ — *The removal of chametz.* Since the Torah forbids a Jew to have *chametz* in his possession during Pesach, the Rabbis ordained a search of all homes, shops, and any other places where *chametz* may have been brought in during the year. The Talmud derives from Scriptural implications that the search be made by candlelight and therefore it should be done at night when a candle's flame is effective (*Pesachim* 2a). The primary mitzvah is the destruction of the *chametz* that will take place on the next morning, but the blessing is made now because the search is in preparation for, and part of the mitzvah of, the destruction. It is customary that ten bits of bread be hidden so that the searcher will truly search and the quest for *chametz* will not be in vain.

כָּל חֲמִירָא וַחֲמִיעָא — *Any leavening or chametz.*

All *chametz* must be declared ownerless so that one not be in possession of *chametz* without knowing it. The evening declaration carefully omits any *chametz* that one wishes to retain for the next day's breakfast, the *chametz* that will be burned the next morning, and the *chametz* that will be sold to a non-Jew in the morning.

This is a *legal* declaration, not a prayer; therefore it must be understood. If one does not understand the Aramaic, he should recite it in a language he understands. It should be recited by all members of the family.

דְּאִכָּא בִּרְשׁוּתִי — *That there is in my possession.* If one has appointed an agent to conduct the search or to burn his *chametz*, the agent should say, "... *that there is in So-and-so's possession* ..." Nevertheless, it is preferable that the owner of the *chametz* recite the declaration, wherever he may be.

וּדְלָא יְדַעְנָא לֵהּ, לִבָּטֵל וְלֶהֱוֵי הֶפְקֵר כְּעַפְרָא

⟨ like the dust ⟨ ownerless ⟨ and shall ⟨ shall hereby ⟨⟨ know about, ⟨ and that
become be annulled I do not

דְאַרְעָא.

⟨⟨ of the earth.

THE FOLLOWING DECLARATION, WHICH INCLUDES ALL *CHAMETZ* WITHOUT EXCEPTION, IS TO BE
MADE AFTER THE BURNING OF LEFTOVER *CHAMETZ*. IT SHOULD BE RECITED IN A LANGUAGE WHICH
ONE UNDERSTANDS. WHEN *PESACH* BEGINS ON *MOTZAEI SHABBOS*, THIS DECLARATION IS MADE ON
SHABBOS MORNING. ANY *CHAMETZ* REMAINING FROM THE *SHABBOS* MORNING MEAL IS FLUSHED
DOWN THE DRAIN BEFORE THE DECLARATION IS MADE.

כָּל חֲמִירָא וַחֲמִיעָא דְּאִכָּא בִרְשׁוּתִי,

⟨ in my possession, ⟨ that there is ⟨ or *chametz* ⟨ leavening ⟨ Any

דַּחֲזִתֵּהּ וּדְלָא חֲזִתֵּהּ (נ״א דַּחֲמִתֵּהּ וּדְלָא חֲמִתֵּהּ),

(⟨⟨ observed ⟨ or whether ⟨ whether I have) ⟨⟨ seen it, ⟨ or whether ⟨ whether I
it, I have not observed it I have not have seen it

דְּבַעֲרִתֵּהּ וּדְלָא בַעֲרִתֵּהּ, לִבָּטֵל וְלֶהֱוֵי הֶפְקֵר

⟨ ownerless, ⟨ and shall ⟨ shall hereby ⟨⟨ removed it, ⟨ or whether ⟨ whether I have
become be annulled I have not removed it

כְּעַפְרָא דְאַרְעָא.

⟨⟨ of the earth. ⟨ like the dust

❧ ERUV TAVSHILIN / עֵרוּב תַּבְשִׁילִין ❧

WHEN A FESTIVAL FALLS ON FRIDAY, AN *ERUV TAVSHILIN* IS MADE ON *EREV YOM TOV*.
THE *ERUV*-FOODS ARE HELD WHILE THE FOLLOWING BLESSING AND DECLARATION ARE RECITED.

בָּרוּךְ אַתָּה יהוה אֱלֹהֵינוּ מֶלֶךְ הָעוֹלָם, אֲשֶׁר

⟨ Who ⟨⟨ of the universe, ⟨ King ⟨ our God, ⟨ HASHEM, ⟨ are You, ⟨ Blessed

קִדְּשָׁנוּ בְּמִצְוֹתָיו, וְצִוָּנוּ עַל מִצְוַת עֵרוּב.

⟨⟨ of eruv. ⟨ the ⟨ concerning ⟨ and has ⟨ with His ⟨ has
mitzvah commanded us commandments sanctified us

בְּהֲדֵין עֵרוּבָא יְהֵא שָׁרֵא לָנָא לַאֲפוּיֵי

⟨ to bake, ⟨ for us ⟨ permitted ⟨ it will be ⟨ eruv ⟨ Through this

---

❧ עֵרוּב תַּבְשִׁילִין / **ERUV TAVSHILIN** ❧

Although it is forbidden on the Festival to
prepare food for another day even if that day is
the Sabbath, if, however, Sabbath preparations
were started before the Festival began, they may

be continued on the Festival. Therefore, the
Sages instituted the mechanism known as *Eruv
Tavshilin*, to permit preparation of fresh food
for the Sabbath: On the day before the Festival,
one takes a matzah along with a cooked food

וּלְבַשּׁוּלֵי וּלְאַטְמוּנֵי וּלְאַדְלוּקֵי שְׁרָגָא וּלְתַקָּנָא

⟨ and to prepare, ⟨ a flame, ⟨ to kindle ⟨ to insulate, ⟨ to cook,

וּלְמֶעְבַּד כָּל צָרְכָּנָא, מִיּוֹמָא טָבָא לְשַׁבַּתָּא

⟨⟨ for [the sake of] ⟨ on the Festival ⟨ necessary ⟨ anything ⟨ and to do
the Sabbath

[לָנָא וּלְכָל יִשְׂרָאֵל הַדָּרִים בָּעִיר הַזֹּאת].

⟨⟨ in this city]. ⟨ who live ⟨ Jews ⟨ and for all ⟨ [for ourselves

❧ KINDLING LIGHTS / הדלקת הנרות ❧

ON THE FIRST TWO NIGHTS OF PESACH TWO BLESSINGS ARE RECITED. WHEN PESACH COINCIDES
WITH THE SABBATH, LIGHT THE CANDLES, THEN COVER THE EYES AND RECITE THE BLESSINGS. UN-
COVER THE EYES AND GAZE BRIEFLY AT THE CANDLES. WHEN PESACH FALLS ON A WEEKDAY, SOME
FOLLOW THE ABOVE PROCEDURE, WHILE OTHERS RECITE THE BLESSINGS BEFORE LIGHTING THE
CANDLES. WHEN PESACH COINCIDES WITH THE SABBATH, THE WORDS IN BRACKETS ARE ADDED.

ON THE SECOND NIGHT OF *YOM TOV* (AND ON THE FIRST NIGHT WHEN EREV PESACH FALLS ON THE
SABBATH) THE CANDLES ARE LIT AFTER NIGHTFALL.

[IT IS FORBIDDEN TO CREATE A NEW FLAME — FOR EXAMPLE, BY STRIKING A MATCH — ON *YOM TOV*.
THEREFORE, WHEN THE CANDLES ARE LIT ON *YOM TOV* THEY MUST BE LIT FROM A FLAME THAT HAS
BEEN BURNING FROM BEFORE *YOM TOV* (OR THE SABBATH).]

בָּרוּךְ אַתָּה יהוה אֱלֹהֵינוּ מֶלֶךְ הָעוֹלָם,

⟨⟨ of the universe, ⟨ King ⟨ our God, ⟨ HASHEM, ⟨ are You, ⟨ Blessed

אֲשֶׁר קִדְּשָׁנוּ בְּמִצְוֹתָיו, וְצִוָּנוּ לְהַדְלִיק נֵר שֶׁל

⟨ of ⟨ the ⟨ to kindle ⟨ and has com- ⟨⟨ with His ⟨ has ⟨ Who
light manded us commandments, sanctified us

[שַׁבָּת וְשֶׁל] יוֹם טוֹב.

⟨⟨ the Festival. ⟨ and of] ⟨ [the Sabbath

IN MANY COMMUNITIES THE FOLLOWING IS ADDED (EXCEPT ON THE LAST TWO DAYS OF PESACH):

בָּרוּךְ אַתָּה יהוה אֱלֹהֵינוּ מֶלֶךְ הָעוֹלָם,

⟨⟨ of the universe, ⟨ King ⟨ our God, ⟨ HASHEM, ⟨ are You, ⟨ Blessed

שֶׁהֶחֱיָנוּ וְקִיְּמָנוּ וְהִגִּיעָנוּ לַזְּמַן הַזֶּה.

⟨⟨ to this season. ⟨ and has ⟨ and has ⟨ Who has kept
brought us sustained us, us alive,

(such as fish, meat, or an egg), and sets them
aside to be eaten on the Sabbath.

❧ הַדְלָקַת הַנֵּרוֹת / KINDLING LIGHTS ❧
The Sabbath and Festival lights are kindled
approximately eighteen minutes before sunset.

Since women generally look after household
matters, the mitzvah of kindling the lights has
devolved upon the mistress of the house
(*Rambam*). Nevertheless, a man living alone is
required to kindle the lights. Similarly, if a

IT IS CUSTOMARY TO RECITE THE FOLLOWING PRAYER AFTER KINDLING THE LIGHTS.

יְהִי רָצוֹן לְפָנֶיךָ, יהוה אֱלֹהַי וֵאלֹהֵי אֲבוֹתַי, שֶׁתְּחוֹנֵן אוֹתִי

〈 to me 〈 that You 《 of my 〈 and God 〈 my God 〈 Hashem, 《 before 〈 the will, 〈 May
show favor　forefathers,　　　　　　　　　　　　　　　　　　You,　　　　　　　　　it be

———————— THE WORDS THAT APPLY ARE INCLUDED: ————————

וְאֶת אִישִׁי, וְאֶת בָּנַי, וְאֶת בְּנוֹתַי, וְאֶת אָבִי, וְאֶת אִמִּי

〈 and to my mother 〈 and to my father, 〈 and to my daughters, 〈 and to my sons, 〈 and to my husband,

וְאֶת כָּל קְרוֹבַי; וְתִתֵּן לָנוּ וּלְכָל יִשְׂרָאֵל חַיִּים טוֹבִים וַאֲרוּכִים;

《 and long; 〈 that is 〈 a life 〈 Israel 〈 and all 〈 us 〈 and [that] 《 my 〈 and to all
　　　　good　　　　　　　　　　　　　　　　　You grant relatives;

וְתִזְכְּרֵנוּ בְּזִכְרוֹן טוֹבָה וּבְרָכָה; וְתִפְקְדֵנוּ בִּפְקֻדַּת יְשׁוּעָה

〈 of 〈 with a 〈 [that] You 《 and 〈 of 〈 with a 〈 [that] You
salvation consideration consider us　blessing; goodness memory remember us

וְרַחֲמִים; וּתְבָרְכֵנוּ בְּרָכוֹת גְּדוֹלוֹת; וְתַשְׁלִים בָּתֵּינוּ; וְתַשְׁכֵּן

〈 [that] You 《 our 〈 [that] You make 《 that are 〈 with 〈 [that] You 《 and
cause to dwell households; complete great; blessings bless us compassion;

שְׁכִינָתְךָ בֵּינֵינוּ. וְזַכֵּנִי לְגַדֵּל בָּנִים וּבְנֵי בָנִים חֲכָמִים וּנְבוֹנִים,

《 and 〈 who are 〈 and 〈 children 〈 to 〈 Privilege 《 among 〈 Your
understanding, wise grandchildren　raise　me　us.　Presence

אוֹהֲבֵי יהוה, יִרְאֵי אֱלֹהִים, אַנְשֵׁי אֱמֶת, זֶרַע קֹדֶשׁ, בַּיהוה

〈 who to 《 that 〈 offspring 《 of truth, 〈 people 《 God, 〈 and fear 〈 Hashem 〈 who love
Hashem　are holy,

דְּבֵקִים, וּמְאִירִים אֶת הָעוֹלָם בַּתּוֹרָה וּבְמַעֲשִׂים טוֹבִים, וּבְכָל

〈 and with 《 that are 〈 and with 〈 with 〈 the world 〈 [who] 《 are
every　good,　deeds　Torah　　　illuminate　attached,

מְלֶאכֶת עֲבוֹדַת הַבּוֹרֵא. אָנָּא שְׁמַע אֶת תְּחִנָּתִי בָּעֵת הַזֹּאת,

《 at this time, 〈 my supplication 〈 hear 〈 Please, 《 of the 〈 in the 〈 labor
　　　　　　　　　　　　　　　　　　Creator.　service

בִּזְכוּת שָׂרָה וְרִבְקָה וְרָחֵל וְלֵאָה אִמּוֹתֵינוּ, וְהָאֵר נֵרֵנוּ

〈 our 〈 and 《 our matriarchs, 〈 and Leah, 〈 Rachel, 〈 Rebecca, 〈 of Sarah, 〈 in the
light　shine　　　　　　　　　　　　　　　　　　　　　merit

שֶׁלֹּא יִכְבֶּה לְעוֹלָם וָעֶד, וְהָאֵר פָּנֶיךָ וְנִוָּשֵׁעָה. אָמֵן.

《 Amen. 《 so that we 〈 Your 〈 and 《 and 〈 forever 〈 be 〈 that it
　　　shall be saved. countenance shine　ever,　　extinguished　not

woman is too ill to light, her husband should light the candles (*Magen Avraham*).

Although there should be some light in every room where it will be needed, the blessing is recited upon the flames that are kindled in the dining room (*Mishnah Berurah*). A brightly lit festive table represents one form

of fulfillment of the prophet's instructions: *If you proclaim the Sabbath a delight, [proclaim] the holy one of* HASHEM *honored ... then you shall be granted delight with* HASHEM *...* (*Isaiah 58:13-14*). The lights honor the Sabbath by brightening, and thereby imparting dignity and importance to, the festive meal (*Rashi*).

הַהֲכָנוֹת לַסֵּדֶר / Preparing for the Seder

Preparing Wine for the Four Cups

1. It is preferable to use red wine, if it is not inferior in quality to the white wine available (472:11).

2. One may use boiled wine or wine to which flavoring has been added, although it is preferable to use pure, unboiled wine so long as it is not of inferior quality (472:2 and *Mishnah Berurah* §39-40).

Karpas

1. One should use the vegetable called *karpas,* because this word is an anagram of the words 's = 60 (referring to the 600,000 Jews), and פֶּרֶךְ, *worked hard.* However, any vegetable may be used other than those which may be used for *maror.*

2. One should prepare salt water or Kosher for *Pesach* vinegar in which to dip the *karpas.* (If the *Seder* night falls on Shabbos, the salt water should be made beforehand. If one forgot to do so, he may prepare the minimum amount of salt water on Shabbos, immediately prior to the meal, making sure that he puts less than 66 percent salt in the mixture.) (473:4 and *Mishnah Berurah* §19,21).

Maror

1. There are five vegetables which the Mishnah (*Pesachim* 2:6) mentions which may be used for maror: *chazeres* (lettuce), *ulshin* (endives), *tamcha* (horseradish), *charchavinah* and *maror.* One may use either the leaves or the stalks of these species. While one may not use their roots, the thick, hard part of the root (as the horseradish root) has the same status as the stalk. The leaves may not be used after they have dried out, but the stalk may be used when dry. Neither may be used if it has been soaked in water or any other liquid for 24 hours.

    Since the Mishnah lists the varieties in order of preference, and *chazeres* precedes *tamcha,* it should be preferable to use lettuce rather than horseradish. However, since lettuce is extremely hard to rid of all the bugs that infest it, if one is unable to check and cleanse the lettuce thoroughly he should use horseradish instead (473:5, *Mishnah Berurah* ad loc.).

2. The horseradish should be ground, as eating a whole piece of horseradish constitutes a danger to one's health and is not a fulfillment of the mitzvah. However, the ground horseradish should not be left open for a long time, as this causes all its bitterness to dissipate (ibid.).

3. The *Mishnah Berurah* records that the *Gra* used to leave the grinding of the horseradish until after he came home from shul on the *Seder* night, and then left it covered until the beginning of the *Seder.* (Note: The grinding of these

vegetables on *Yom Tov* should be done differently from the usual way. See *Orach Chayim* 504.) When the *Seder* night comes out on Shabbos, when such grinding is forbidden, the horseradish should be prepared before Shabbos and left covered until the beginning of the *Seder* (ibid.). (Nowadays many people prepare the horseradish before *Yom Tov* even when it is not Shabbos, since its sharpness can be preserved quite well in a closed container. This was the practice of *Maran R' Schach* as well.)

4. If someone is too ill or sensitive to eat the entire *k'zayis* of horseradish at one time, he may spread it out over a period of *Kedei Achilas Peras* (approx. 2-9 minutes).

·◊§ *Charoses*

1. *Charoses* should be prepared with fruits which are used in Tanach as metaphors for Israel — such as figs (see *Shir Hashirim* 2:13), nuts (ibid., 6:11) and apples (ibid., 8:5). It is also customary to use almonds, because the Hebrew word for almond (שָׁקֵד) also means *swift,* and is thus a reminder of God's speedy deliverance of the Jews from Egypt. One should also put in pieces of ginger and cinnamon, to symbolize the straw that was used by the Jewish slaves to prepare bricks. The *charoses* should have a thick consistency, as a reminder of the mortar that the Egyptians forced the Jews to prepare. However, just before it is used (to dip the *maror*) some wine should be poured into it, as a remembrance of the blood that played an important role in the Exodus (and also to make it more usable as a dip). When the *Seder* is held on Shabbos the wine should be put into the *charoses* before Shabbos. If one forgot to do so, he may do it differently than usual, and should add enough wine to made a loose consistency (473:5, *Mishnah Berurah* and *Be'er Heitev* ad loc.).

·◊§ Two Cooked Foods

1. After the destruction of the Temple the Sages instituted the practice of placing two kinds of cooked foods on the *Seder* tray, one to commemorate the meat of the *pesach* offering and the other to commemorate the meat of the *chagigah* offering — both of which were sacrificed in the Temple on the fourteenth of Nissan and eaten at the *Seder.* The custom has developed that one of the two foods should be meat, customarily a shankbone (corresponding to the human arm, symbolizing the "outstretched arm" of Hashem) that has been roasted on the fire (as the *pesach* meat was). The second food is customarily an egg, because the Aramaic word for egg (בֵּיעָא) is related to the Aramaic word for *desire* — God *desired* (בָּעָא) to take us out of Egypt with an outstretched arm. The egg can be cooked or roasted in any way (as the *chagigah* was), although some have the custom to roast it specifically.

   Rema writes that many have the custom to eat eggs at the *Seder.* He explains that eggs are traditionally eaten by mourners, and they are eaten at this time as a commemoration of the destruction of the Temple. The *Mishnah Berurah*, citing *Gra*, says that we eat the egg of the *Seder* plate, since, as noted above, it symbolizes the *chagigah* offering. (According to this explanation, only the egg on the *Seder* plate needs to be eaten, but this custom subsequently became popularly extended to include the eating of eggs in general.) (473:4, *Mishnah Berurah* ad loc.; 476:2, *Mishnah Berurah* §11.)

2. It is best to boil or roast these two foods before *Yom Tov*. If this was neglected, they may be prepared on *Yom Tov*. If they were prepared on *Yom Tov*, the foods must be eaten on that day of *Yom Tov*, as one may only cook food on *Yom Tov* if it will be eaten that same day. The two foods will thus have to be prepared anew for the second *Seder* (ibid.).

❧ Making Arrangements for Reclining

1. The seats of those who must recline while drinking the wine and eating the matzah should be prepared in a manner that will enable comfortable reclining on one's left side (472:2).

❧ Preparing the Cups

1. The cups should be whole (not chipped or broken) and clean, and should be able to hold at least a *revi'is*. Since it is preferable to drink a majority of the wine in the cup for each of the four cups, it is advisable not to use a very large cup. This applies to the cups used by all the participants in the *Seder*, including women and children (who have reached the age of training in mitzvos). (472:14, 15; *Mishnah Berurah* §33.)

❧ Preparing the Table

1. The table should be set with elegant and luxurious articles according to one's means. Although it is usually proper to use moderation in this regard out of mourning for the Temple, on *Pesach* it is encouraged, as this serves as yet another demonstration of our freedom. The table should be set in advance so that the *Seder* can get underway without delay (so the children should not become too tired) (472:1,2; *Mishnah Berurah* §6).

❧ The Beginning of the Seder

1. Although, as mentioned above, the *Seder* should begin as promptly as possible, *Kiddush* should not be said before dark (*tzeis hakochavim*) (472:1).
2. It is customary for the leader to wear a *kittel* for the *Seder* (ibid., *Mishnah Berurah* §12).
3. Only one *Seder* plate is set, before the leader of the *Seder*.
4. The children should be kept awake at least until after reciting עֲבָדִים הָיִינוּ, so that they should hear the basic story of the Exodus. Children who have reached the age of training in mitzvos must participate in all the practices of

the entire *Seder*. (However they must only consume a cheekful of wine, according to the size of their own mouths, for each required cup. Furthermore, there is an opinion that holds that they need not drink the four cups of wine at all.) (472:15; *Mishnah Berurah* §46, 47.)

◆§ Reclining

1. One should not recline on his back or stomach, but only on his left side. This applies to left-handed people as well (472:3, *Mishnah Berurah* ad loc.).

2. Someone who is in mourning for a relative should also recline, although he should do so in a less luxurious manner than usual. It is also customary for a mourner not to wear a *kittel* for the *Seder*, although some opinions permit it (*Mishnah Berurah* §13).

3. The custom is that women do not recline (472:4).

4. A student in the presence of his *rebbi* — or any person in the presence of a great, recognized rabbinical figure — should not recline. This holds true only if they are seated at the same table. (According to some opinions, a student in the presence of his rebbi should ask for permission to recline even if he is sitting at a separate table.) (472:5, *Mishnah Berurah* §18.)

5. A son must recline in the presence of his father, even if his father is also his *rebbi* (472:5).

6. If one forgot to recline for any of the places in the *Seder* which call for reclining, he has not fulfilled that mitzvah, and it must be performed again. *Raaviah* maintains, however, that since eating in a reclining position is not a sign of freedom and leisure in our culture, the practice need not be followed. Although we do not follow the *Raaviah's* opinion, when redoing one of the mitzvos might lead to a halachic complication, this opinion is adopted and the mitzvah in question is not done over. These exceptions will be noted in appropriate places in the Haggadah (472:7, *Mishnah Berurah* §20).

◆§ Drinking the Four Cups

1. Even if one dislikes wine or suffers discomfort when drinking it, he should force himself to drink the four cups (unless it will actually make him ill). The wine may be diluted, as long as it remains fit to be used as *Kiddush* wine.

2. It is preferable to drink the entire cup of wine each time. The minimum amount that *must* be consumed is a majority of a *revi'is,* although there is an opinion that one must drink most of the wine in the cup, if the cup is larger than a *revi'is.* The requisite amount of wine should be drunk all at once, or at the very most within a time span of *kedei achilas pras* (approx. 2-9 minutes) (472:9, *Mishnah Berurah* §30, 33, 34).

3. The four cups must be drunk in their appropriate places in the *Seder*: one for *Kiddush,* one after *Maggid,* one for *Birkas Hamazon,* and one for *Hallel* (472:8).

◈§ The Seder Plate

The *Seder* preparations should be made in time for the *Seder* to begin as soon as the synagogue services are finished. It should not begin before nightfall, however. Matzah, bitter herbs and several other items of symbolic significance are placed on the *Seder* plate in the arrangement shown.

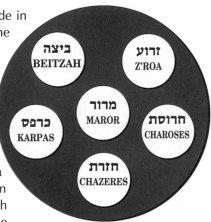

ג' מצות – 3 MATZOS

◈§ **Matzah** — Three whole matzos are placed one atop the other, separated by a cloth or napkin. Matzah must be eaten three times during the *Seder*: by itself, with maror, and as the *afikoman*. Each time, the minimum portion of matzah for each person should have a volume equivalent to half an egg. Where many people are present, enough matzos should be available to enable each participant to receive a proper portion.

◈§ ***Maror* and *Chazeres*** — Bitter herbs are eaten twice during the *Seder,* once by themselves and a second time with matzah. Each time a minimum portion, equal to the volume of half an egg, should be eaten. The Talmud lists several vegetables that qualify as *maror,* two of which are put on the *Seder* plate in the places marked *chazeres* and *maror*. Most people use romaine lettuce (whole leaves or stalks) for *chazeres,* and horseradish (whole or grated) for *maror,* although either may be used for the mitzvah of eating *maror* later in the *Seder*.

◈§ ***Charoses*** — The bitter herbs are dipped into *charoses* (a mixture of grated apples, nuts, other fruit, cinnamon, and other spices, mixed with red wine). The *charoses* has the appearance of mortar to symbolize the lot of the Hebrew slaves, whose lives were embittered by hard labor with brick and mortar.

◈§ ***Z'roa*** — [Roasted Bone] and ***Beitzah*** [Roasted Egg] — On the eve of Passover in the Holy Temple in Jerusalem, two sacrifices were offered and their meat roasted and eaten at the *Seder* feast. To commemorate these two sacrifices we place a roasted bone (with some meat on it) and a roasted hard-boiled egg on the *Seder* plate. The egg, a symbol of mourning, is used in place of a second piece of meat as a reminder of our mourning at the destruction of the Temple — may it be rebuilt speedily in our day.

◈§ ***Karpas*** — A vegetable (celery, parsley, boiled potato) other than bitter herbs completes the *Seder* plate. It will be dipped in salt water and eaten. (The salt water is not put on the *Seder* plate, but it, too, should be prepared beforehand, and placed near the *Seder* plate.)

✍ The Order of the Seder

The *Seder* ritual contains fifteen observances, which have been summarized in the familiar rhyme **Kaddesh, Urechatz, Karpas, Yachatz** and so on. Aside from its convenience as a memory device, the brief formula has been given various deeper interpretations over the years. Accordingly, many people recite the appropriate word from the rhyme before performing the mitzvah to which it applies — קַדֵּשׁ, *Kaddesh*, before Kiddush, וּרְחַץ, *Urechatz*, before washing the hands, and so on.

KADDESH	**Sanctify** the day with the recitation of Kiddush.	קַדֵּשׁ
URECHATZ	**Wash** the hands before eating Karpas.	וּרְחַץ
KARPAS	Eat a **vegetable** dipped in salt water.	כַּרְפַּס
YACHATZ	**Break** the middle matzah. Put away larger half for Afikoman	יַחַץ
MAGGID	**Narrate** the story of the Exodus from Egypt.	מַגִּיד
RACHTZAH	**Wash** the hands prior to the meal.	רָחְצָה
MOTZI	Recite the blessing, **Who brings forth,** over matzah as a food.	מוֹצִיא
MATZAH	Recite the blessing over **Matzah.**	מַצָּה
MAROR	Recite the blessing for the eating of the **bitter herbs.**	מָרוֹר
KORECH	Eat the **sandwich** of matzah and bitter herbs	כּוֹרֵךְ
SHULCHAN ORECH	The **table prepared** with the festive meal.	שֻׁלְחָן עוֹרֵךְ
TZAFUN	Eat the afikoman which had been **hidden** all during the Seder.	צָפוּן
BARECH	Recite Bircas Hamazon, the **blessings** after the meal.	בָּרֵךְ
HALLEL	Recite the **Hallel** Psalms of praise.	הַלֵּל
NIRTZAH	Pray that God **accept** our observance and speedily send the Messiah.	נִרְצָה

⊰{ KADDESH / קדש }⊱

KIDDUSH SHOULD BE RECITED AND THE SEDER BEGUN AS SOON AFTER SYNAGOGUE SERVICES
AS POSSIBLE — HOWEVER, NOT BEFORE NIGHTFALL.
EACH PARTICIPANT'S CUP SHOULD BE POURED BY SOMEONE ELSE TO SYMBOLIZE
THE MAJESTY OF THE EVENING, AS THOUGH EACH PARTICIPANT HAD A SERVANT.

SOME RECITE THE FOLLOWING BEFORE KIDDUSH:

הֲרֵינִי מוּכָן וּמְזוּמָּן לְקַדֵּשׁ עַל הַיַּיִן, וּלְקַיֵּם מִצְוַת

⟨ the ⟨ and to ⟪ wine, ⟨ over ⟨ to recite ⟨ and ⟨ am ⟨ I now
mitzvah perform   the Kiddush ready   prepared

כּוֹס רִאשׁוֹן מֵאַרְבַּע כּוֹסוֹת. לְשֵׁם יְחוּד קֻדְשָׁא בְּרִיךְ הוּא

⟪ is ⟨ Blessed ⟪ of the ⟨ of the ⟨ For the ⟪ Cups. ⟨ of the Four ⟨ of the first cup
He,   Holy One, unification sake

וּשְׁכִינְתֵּיהּ, עַל יְדֵי הַהוּא טָמִיר וְנֶעְלָם, בְּשֵׁם כָּל יִשְׂרָאֵל.

⟪ Israel. ⟨ of ⟨ –[I pray] ⟪ and Who is ⟨ Who is ⟨ Him ⟨ through ⟪ and His
          all   in the name inscrutable hidden   Presence,

KADDESH / קַדֵּשׁ

Although the night's proceedings focus on the Exodus, the Sabbath Kiddush takes precedence for it is the more common occurrence, and it commemorates an earlier event, the Creation.

⊷§ Laws of *Kiddush*

1. If someone forgot to say שֶׁהֶחֱיָנוּ in *Kiddush* he may say it at any time during the duration of the holiday, until the end of the last day of Pesach. (If one remembered after he has said שֶׁהֶחֱיָנוּ in *Kiddush* on the second night in *Chutz La'aretz* he should not say it again.) (*Mishnah Berurah* 473:1.)

2. If someone forgot to say *Havdalah* in *Kiddush* when the Seder is on *Motzaei Shabbos*, he should say *Havdalah* on the second cup of wine (after *Maggid*). If he remembered his mistake only after the second cup, see the details in *Mishnah Berurah* 473:5.

3. When drinking the *Kiddush* wine, one should have in mind that he is doing so for the sake of fulfilling the mitzvah of drinking the first of the four cups of wine of the Seder. Many people have the custom to recite a verbal declaration to this effect before *Kiddush* (הֲרֵינִי מוּכָן וּמְזוּמָּן) (*Mishnah Berurah* 473:1).

4. Even those who have the custom to wash their hands for *Hamotzi* before saying *Kiddush* during the rest of the year should not do so on the Seder night. Similarly, the washing for the *karpas* should not be done before *Kiddush*, even if this is more convenient for some reason (*Mishnah Berurah* 473:6).

5. The master of the house should not pour his own wine, but should be served by someone else, as an expression of freedom and nobility (473:1). Some extend this practice to everyone.

6. One must drink the wine while reclining on his left side (see above, p. 25). If he forgot to recline, the *Rema* writes that he should drink another cup of wine while reclining. The *Mishnah Berurah*, however, notes that others contend that a new *berachah* would have to be recited over this additional cup of wine, and this would thus give the appearance of adding on to the ordained number of four cups. According to them, then, another cup of wine should not be drunk (see above, p. 25).

   There are differing opinions as to whether one may drink between the first and second cup, so this should be avoided unless absolutely necessary. This, however, applies only to wine or other alcoholic beverages; other kinds of drinks may be drunk at this point (473:3, *Mishnah Berurah* §16).

קַדֵּשׁ וּרְחַץ כַּרְפַּס יַחַץ מַגִּיד רָחְצָה מוֹצִיא מַצָּ

ATZAh MOTZI RAChTZAh MAGGID YAChATZ KARPAS UREChATZ KADDESh

וִיהִי נֹעַם אֲדֹנָי אֱלֹהֵינוּ עָלֵינוּ, וּמַעֲשֵׂה יָדֵינוּ כּוֹנְנָה

⟨ establish ⟨ of our ⟨ the work ⟨⟨ be upon us; ⟨ our God, ⟨ of the ⟨ the ⟨ May
hands, Lord, pleasantness

עָלֵינוּ, וּמַעֲשֵׂה יָדֵינוּ כּוֹנְנֵהוּ.¹

⟨⟨ establish it. ⟨ of our hands, ⟨ the work ⟨⟨ for us;

ON FRIDAY NIGHT BEGIN HERE:

(וַיְהִי עֶרֶב וַיְהִי בֹקֶר) – Silently)

⟨ morning ⟨ and ⟨ evening ⟨ And
there was there was

יוֹם הַשִּׁשִּׁי. וַיְכֻלּוּ* הַשָּׁמַיִם וְהָאָרֶץ* וְכָל צְבָאָם.

⟨⟨ their ⟨ and ⟨ and the ⟨ the heaven ⟨ Thus were ⟨⟨ The sixth day.
legion. all earth,* finished*

וַיְכַל אֱלֹהִים בַּיּוֹם הַשְּׁבִיעִי מְלַאכְתּוֹ אֲשֶׁר עָשָׂה,

⟨⟨ He had done, ⟨ which ⟨ His work ⟨ on the Seventh Day ⟨ did God ⟨ Finish

וַיִּשְׁבֹּת בַּיּוֹם הַשְּׁבִיעִי מִכָּל מְלַאכְתּוֹ אֲשֶׁר עָשָׂה.

⟨⟨ He had ⟨ which ⟨ His work ⟨ from all ⟨ on the Seventh Day ⟨ and He
done. abstained

וַיְבָרֶךְ אֱלֹהִים אֶת יוֹם הַשְּׁבִיעִי, וַיְקַדֵּשׁ אֹתוֹ, כִּי בוֹ

⟨ on it ⟨ because ⟨⟨ it, ⟨ and sanctify ⟨ the Seventh Day ⟨ did God ⟨ Bless

שָׁבַת מִכָּל מְלַאכְתּוֹ, אֲשֶׁר בָּרָא אֱלֹהִים לַעֲשׂוֹת.²

⟨⟨ to make. ⟨ God created ⟨ which ⟨ His work ⟨ from all ⟨ He had
abstained

סַבְרִי מָרָנָן וְרַבָּנָן וְרַבּוֹתַי:

⟨⟨ and gentlemen: ⟨ rabbis, ⟨ distinguished ⟨ By your leave,
people

בָּרוּךְ אַתָּה יהוה אֱלֹהֵינוּ מֶלֶךְ הָעוֹלָם,

⟨⟨ of the universe, ⟨ King ⟨ our God, ⟨ HASHEM, ⟨ are You, ⟨ Blessed

(אָמֵן.) – All respond) בּוֹרֵא פְּרִי הַגָּפֶן.

⟨⟨ (Amen.) ⟨⟨ of the vine. ⟨ the fruit ⟨ Who creates

---

(1) *Psalms* 90:17. (2) *Genesis* 1:31-2:3.

וַיְכֻלּוּ — *Thus were finished.* The Midrash interprets וַיְכֻלּוּ and וַיְכַל homiletically as *longing,* as
we find כָּלְתָה נַפְשִׁי, *my soul longed* (*Psalms* 84:3).
Heaven and earth, and God Himself, long for
the coming of the Sabbath, because it infuses all

of creation with holiness (*Tzror HaMor*).

וַיְכֻלּוּ הַשָּׁמַיִם וְהָאָרֶץ — *Thus were finished the
heaven and the earth.* The verse uses the passive
form *were finished* rather than the active *and
HASHEM finished.* This implies that, despite the

NIRTZAh hALLEL BARECh TZAFUN shULChAN ORECh KORECh MARO

ON FRIDAY NIGHT INCLUDE ALL THE WORDS IN BRACKETS:

בָּרוּךְ אַתָּה יהוה אֱלֹהֵינוּ מֶלֶךְ הָעוֹלָם,

‹‹ of the universe, ‹ King ‹ our God, ‹ Hashem, ‹ are You, ‹ Blessed

אֲשֶׁר בָּחַר בָּנוּ מִכָּל עָם, וְרוֹמְמָנוּ מִכָּל לָשׁוֹן,

‹‹ tongues, ‹ above all ‹ exalted us ‹‹ peoples, ‹ from all ‹ us ‹ has chosen ‹ Who

וְקִדְּשָׁנוּ בְּמִצְוֹתָיו. וַתִּתֶּן לָנוּ* יהוה אֱלֹהֵינוּ

‹ our God, ‹ Hashem, ‹ us,* ‹ And You gave ‹‹ with His commandments. ‹ and sanctified us

בְּאַהֲבָה [שַׁבָּתוֹת לִמְנוּחָה וּ]מוֹעֲדִים* לְשִׂמְחָה

‹ for gladness, ‹ appointed Festivals* ‹ for rest,] ‹ [Sabbaths ‹‹ with love

חַגִּים וּזְמַנִּים לְשָׂשׂוֹן, [אֶת יוֹם הַשַּׁבָּת הַזֶּה וְ...]

‹ and] ‹‹ [this day of Sabbath ‹‹ for joy, ‹ and times ‹ Festivals

אֶת יוֹם חַג הַמַּצּוֹת הַזֶּה, זְמַן חֵרוּתֵנוּ

‹‹ of our freedom ‹ the time ‹‹ this Festival of Matzos, ‹ the day of

[בְּאַהֲבָה*] מִקְרָא קֹדֶשׁ,* זֵכֶר לִיצִיאַת מִצְרָיִם. כִּי

‹ For ‹‹ from Egypt. ‹ of the Exodus ‹ a remembrance ‹ a holy convocation,* ‹‹ [with love],*

בָנוּ בָחַרְתָּ וְאוֹתָנוּ קִדַּשְׁתָּ מִכָּל הָעַמִּים, [וְשַׁבָּת]

‹ [and the Sabbath] ‹‹ the nations, ‹ from all ‹ did You sanctify ‹ and us ‹ did You choose ‹ us

וּמוֹעֲדֵי קָדְשֶׁךָ [בְּאַהֲבָה וּבְרָצוֹן] בְּשִׂמְחָה

‹ in gladness ‹ and in favor,] ‹ [in love ‹‹ of Your holiness ‹ and the appointed Festivals

---

magnitude of the task, God expended only minimal effort in the creation of the universe (*Tzror HaMor*).

וַתִּתֶּן לָנוּ — *And You gave us.* Having chosen us, God gave us this special day. If the Festival falls on a Sabbath, that day, too, is mentioned here specifically. The difference in description between the Sabbath and the Festivals expresses a major difference between them. Although there is rest on the Festivals and gladness on the Sabbath, their primary features are, as we say here, Sabbath for *rest* and Festivals for *gladness*.

מוֹעֲדִים — *Appointed Festivals.* This term has the connotation of meeting; God has designated times when Israel can greet His Presence.

בְּאַהֲבָה — *With love.* The extra expression of love referring only to the Sabbath denotes the particular affection with which Israel accepted the Sabbath commandments. Whereas the Festival observance represents our acknowledgment of God's kindness to our ancestors, the Sabbath shows our desire to honor Him as the Creator.

מִקְרָא קֹדֶשׁ — *A holy convocation.* On these days, the nation is called upon to gather for the pursuit of holiness, and to sanctify the Festival through prayer and praise to God (*Ramban; Sforno*).

קַדֵּשׁ וּרְחַץ כַּרְפַּס יַחַץ מַגִּיד רָחְצָה מוֹצִיא מַצָּ...

...TZAh MOTZI RAChTZAh MAGGID YAChATZ KARPAS URECHATZ KADDESH

וּבְשָׂשׂוֹן הִנְחַלְתָּנוּ. בָּרוּךְ אַתָּה יהוה, מְקַדֵּשׁ
‹ Who ‹‹ HASHEM, ‹ are You, ‹ Blessed ‹‹ did You give us ‹ and in joy
sanctifies   as a heritage.

[הַשַּׁבָּת וְ]יִשְׂרָאֵל וְהַזְּמַנִּים.   (אָמֵן.–All)
‹‹ (Amen.)   ‹‹ and the [festive] seasons. ‹ and] Israel ‹ [the Sabbath

ON SATURDAY NIGHT, TWO CANDLES OR WICKS WITH FLAMES TOUCHING ARE HELD AND THE FOLLOWING BLESSINGS ARE RECITED. AFTER THE FIRST BLESSING, HOLD THE FINGERS UP TO THE FLAMES TO SEE THE REFLECTED LIGHT.

בָּרוּךְ אַתָּה יהוה אֱלֹהֵינוּ מֶלֶךְ הָעוֹלָם, בּוֹרֵא מְאוֹרֵי הָאֵשׁ.
‹‹ of fire. ‹ the illumi- ‹ Who ‹‹ of the ‹ King ‹ our God, ‹ HASHEM, ‹ are You, ‹ Blessed
nations   creates   universe,

(אָמֵן.–All)
‹‹ (Amen.)

בָּרוּךְ אַתָּה יהוה אֱלֹהֵינוּ מֶלֶךְ הָעוֹלָם, הַמַּבְדִּיל בֵּין
‹ between ‹ Who ‹‹ of the ‹ King ‹ our God, ‹ HASHEM, ‹ are You, ‹ Blessed
distinguishes   universe,

קֹדֶשׁ לְחוֹל, בֵּין אוֹר לְחֹשֶׁךְ, בֵּין יִשְׂרָאֵל לָעַמִּים, בֵּין
‹ between ‹‹ and the ‹ Israel ‹ between ‹‹ and ‹ light ‹ between ‹‹ and the ‹ the
nations,   darkness,   secular, sacred

יוֹם הַשְּׁבִיעִי לְשֵׁשֶׁת יְמֵי הַמַּעֲשֶׂה. בֵּין קְדֻשַּׁת שַׁבָּת
‹ of the ‹ the sanctity ‹ Between ‹‹ of labor. ‹ days ‹ and the six ‹ the Seventh Day
Sabbath

לִקְדֻשַּׁת יוֹם טוֹב הִבְדַּלְתָּ, וְאֶת יוֹם הַשְּׁבִיעִי מִשֵּׁשֶׁת
‹ from among ‹ and the Seventh Day ‹‹ You have ‹ of the holidays ‹ and the
the six   distinguished,   sanctity

יְמֵי הַמַּעֲשֶׂה קִדַּשְׁתָּ, הִבְדַּלְתָּ וְקִדַּשְׁתָּ אֶת עַמְּךָ יִשְׂרָאֵל
‹ Israel ‹ Your people ‹ and You have ‹ You have ‹‹ You have ‹ of labor ‹ days
sanctified distinguished sanctified

בִּקְדֻשָּׁתֶךָ. בָּרוּךְ אַתָּה יהוה, הַמַּבְדִּיל בֵּין קֹדֶשׁ לְקֹדֶשׁ.
‹‹ between [one level] of holiness ‹ Who ‹‹ HASHEM, ‹ are ‹ Blessed ‹‹ with Your
and [another level of] holiness. distinguishes You,   holiness.

(אָמֵן.–All)
(Amen.)

⋅⋅⋅ Havdalah

If a Festival day falls on Sunday, we must mark the end of the Sabbath with הַבְדָּלָה, *Havdalah*, the ceremony by which we separate the Sabbath with its greater holiness from the rest of the week.

We are permitted certain activities on Yom Tov, such as baking or cooking, that are forbidden on the Sabbath; therefore, it is necessary to declare the Sabbath as ended. For this purpose,

NIRTZAh hALLEL BAREch TZAFUN shULchAN OREch KOREch MARO

THE FOLLOWING BLESSING IS OMITTED ON THE LAST TWO NIGHTS OF PESACH:

בָּרוּךְ אַתָּה יהוה אֱלֹהֵינוּ מֶלֶךְ הָעוֹלָם,
‹‹ of the universe, ‹ King ‹ our God, ‹ Hashem, ‹ are You, ‹ Blessed

שֶׁהֶחֱיָנוּ* וְקִיְּמָנוּ וְהִגִּיעָנוּ לַזְּמַן הַזֶּה. (אָמֵן. —All)
‹‹ (Amen.) to this season. ‹ and brought ‹ sustained ‹ Who has kept
us, us alive,*

THE WINE SHOULD BE DRUNK WITHOUT DELAY WHILE RECLINING ON THE LEFT SIDE. IT IS PREFERABLE
TO DRINK THE ENTIRE CUP, BUT AT THE VERY LEAST, MOST OF THE CUP SHOULD BE DRAINED.

❧ URCHATZ / *וּרְחַץ ❧

THE HEAD OF THE HOUSEHOLD — ACCORDING TO MANY OPINIONS, ALL PARTICIPANTS IN THE SEDER
— WASHES HIS HANDS AS IF TO EAT BREAD, [POURING WATER FROM A CUP, TWICE ON THE RIGHT
HAND AND TWICE ON THE LEFT] BUT WITHOUT RECITING A BLESSING.

❧ KARPAS / *כַּרְפַּס ❧

ALL PARTICIPANTS TAKE A VEGETABLE OTHER THAN MAROR AND DIP IT INTO SALT WATER. A PIECE
SMALLER IN VOLUME THAN HALF AN EGG SHOULD BE USED. THE FOLLOWING BLESSING IS RECITED
[WITH THE INTENTION THAT IT ALSO APPLIES TO THE MAROR WHICH WILL BE EATEN DURING THE
MEAL] BEFORE THE VEGETABLE IS EATEN.

בָּרוּךְ אַתָּה יהוה אֱלֹהֵינוּ מֶלֶךְ הָעוֹלָם,
‹‹ of the universe, ‹ King ‹ our God, ‹ Hashem, ‹ are You, ‹ Blessed

בּוֹרֵא פְּרִי הָאֲדָמָה.
‹‹ of the ground. ‹ the fruit ‹ Who creates

we pronounce the blessing, *Who creates the illuminations of fire,* and also the blessing of *Havdalah,* which distinguishes between the greater holiness of the Sabbath and the lesser holiness of Yom Tov.

שֶׁהֶחֱיָנוּ — *Who has kept us alive.* This blessing is called בִּרְכַּת הַזְּמַן, *the blessing of the time,* or simply זְמַן, *time.* It is recited: on the Festivals; over fruits of a new season, provided they ripen at recurring intervals and are not always available; upon *mitzvos* that are performed at seasonal intervals such as *succah, lulav,* and others connected with the annual Festivals; upon seeing a friend whom one has not seen for a significant interval; upon purchasing a new garment of significance; and upon benefiting from a significant event [see *Orach Chaim* 225].

URECHATZ / וּרְחַץ

The *Taz* (473 §6) explains that the purpose of

our washing our hands is to observe the rabbinic enactment that before eating wet foods one must wash, just as before eating bread. But, he asks, why is this followed only on the night of Pesach? *Chock Yaakov* §28 answers that it is an additional change instituted so that the children will ask. R' Reuven Margulies suggests that it was included as part of the Seder practice since meticulousness about cleanliness is a sign of freedom and refinement.

According to all views, though, if one uses a fork or spoon to dip the *Karpas* in the salt water, one has, in effect, eliminated the custom of washing, since most authorities hold that the sages did not require washing hands when the hands do not get wet and do not touch the food.

כַּרְפַּס / KARPAS

The vegetable used for *Karpas* is of lowly origin, from beneath the earth. Yet, it develops

⊰ YACHATZ / יחץ ⊱

THE HEAD OF THE HOUSEHOLD BREAKS THE MIDDLE MATZAH IN TWO. HE PUTS THE SMALLER PART BACK BETWEEN THE TWO WHOLE MATZOS, AND WRAPS UP THE LARGER PART FOR LATER USE AS THE AFIKOMAN. SOME BRIEFLY PLACE THE AFIKOMAN PORTION ON THEIR SHOULDERS, IN ACCORDANCE WITH THE BIBLICAL VERSE RECOUNTING THAT ISRAEL LEFT EGYPT CARRYING THEIR MATZOS ON THEIR SHOULDERS, AND SAY בְּבְהִלוּ יָצָאנוּ מִמִּצְרַיִם, *IN HASTE WE WENT OUT OF EGYPT.*

⊰ MAGGID / מגיד ⊱

SOME RECITE THE FOLLOWING BEFORE MAGGID:

הִנְנִי מוּכָן וּמְזוּמָּן לְקַיֵּם הַמִּצְוָה לְסַפֵּר בִּיצִיאַת מִצְרָיִם.

≪ from ⟨ about the ⟨ of ⟨ the ⟨ to ⟨ and ⟨ am ⟨ I now
Egypt. Exodus telling mitzvah perform ready prepared

לְשֵׁם יִחוּד קֻדְשָׁא בְּרִיךְ הוּא וּשְׁכִינְתֵּיהּ, עַל יְדֵי הַהוּא

⟨ Him ⟨ through ≪ and His ≪ is ⟨ Blessed ≪ of the ⟨ of the ⟨ For the
Presence, He, Holy One, unification sake

טָמִיר וְנֶעְלָם, בְּשֵׁם כָּל יִשְׂרָאֵל. וִיהִי נֹעַם אֲדֹנָי אֱלֹהֵינוּ

⟨ our ⟨ of the ⟨ the ⟨ May ≪ Israel. ⟨ of ⟨ – [I pray] ≪ and Who is ⟨ Who is
God, Lord, pleasantness all in the name inscrutable hidden

עָלֵינוּ, וּמַעֲשֵׂה יָדֵינוּ כּוֹנְנָה עָלֵינוּ, וּמַעֲשֵׂה יָדֵינוּ כּוֹנְנֵהוּ:[1]

≪ establish ⟨ of our ⟨ the work ≪ for us; ⟨ establish ⟨ of our ⟨ the work ≪ be
it. hands, hands, upon us;

---

(1) *Psalms* 90:17.

into an integral part of a sacred feast. So the lowly slave-nation grew to become the Chosen People. And so must each and every Jew strive for ever greater spiritual heights.

⊰ Laws of Maggid

1. Men and women alike are obligated to recite the Haggadah (or hear it recited by someone else). The absolute minimum requirement in this regard is listening to *Kiddush* (and drinking the wine, as well as the other three cups of wine) and the recitation of the passage רַבָּן גַּמְלִיאֵל הָיָה אוֹמֵר וכו' (*Mishnah Berurah* 473:64).

2. The main parts of the Haggadah should be translated or explained in the vernacular if there are people present who do not understand Hebrew (473:6).

3. One should not recite the Haggadah in the reclining position assumed for the wine and matzah; rather, it should be recited with a feeling of reverence and awe.

4. The matzah should be at least partly visible during the recitation of the Haggadah. The Gemara explains that matzah is called לֶחֶם עֹנִי (*Devarim* 16:3) because it is the bread over which many words are recited (עוֹנִין) (473:7, *Mishnah Berurah* §76).

5. While reciting the Haggadah, one should bear in mind that he is doing so in order to fulfill the Torah's mitzvah to recount the story of the Exodus. Many people have the custom to recite a verbal declaration to this effect before *Maggid* (הִנְנִי מוּכָן וּמְזוּמָּן) (*Mishnah Berurah* 473:1).

6. The second cup of wine, which follows *Maggid*, must be consumed while reclining. If one forgot to recline while drinking it, he should drink another cup afterwards (without a *berachah*) (472:7).

NIRTZAh hALLEL BARECH TZAFUN ShULCHAN ORECH KORECH MARO

AS THE HEAD OF THE HOUSEHOLD BEGINS WITH THE FOLLOWING BRIEF EXPLANATION OF THE
PROCEEDINGS, THE SEDER PLATE (IF IT CONTAINS THE MATZOS) OR THE MATZOS ARE LIFTED FOR ALL
TO SEE. (CONTEMPORARY PRACTICE IS TO RAISE ONLY THE BROKEN MATZAH.)

הָא לַחְמָא* עַנְיָא דִי אֲכָלוּ אַבְהָתָנָא בְּאַרְעָא

⟨ in the land ⟨ by our fathers ⟨ was ⟨ that ⟨ of ⟨ is the ⟨ This
eaten afiction bread*

דְמִצְרָיִם. כָּל דִּכְפִין יֵיתֵי וְיֵכוֹל, כָּל דִּצְרִיךְ

《 is in need ⟨ whoever 《 and eat; ⟨ — let 《 is hungry ⟨ Whoever 《 of Egypt.
him come

יֵיתֵי וְיִפְסַח. הָשַׁתָּא הָכָא, לְשָׁנָה הַבָּאָה

⟨ to come ⟨ in the year ⟨ [we are] ⟨ Now, 《 and celebrate ⟨ — let him
here; the Pesach festival. come

בְּאַרְעָא דְיִשְׂרָאֵל. הָשַׁתָּא עַבְדֵי, לְשָׁנָה הַבָּאָה

⟨ to come ⟨ in the year 《 [we are] ⟨ Now, 《 of Israel! ⟨ [may we be]
slaves; in the Land

בְּנֵי חוֹרִין.

《 [may we be] free men!

THE FOUR QUESTIONS

THE SEDER PLATE IS REMOVED AND THE SECOND OF THE FOUR CUPS OF WINE IS POURED.
THE YOUNGEST PRESENT ASKS THE REASONS FOR THE UNUSUAL PROCEEDINGS OF THE EVENING.

מַה נִּשְׁתַּנָה*[1] הַלַּיְלָה הַזֶּה מִכָּל הַלֵּילוֹת?

《 [other] nights? ⟨ from all ⟨ — this night 《 is it different* ⟨ Why

1.

שֶׁבְּכָל הַלֵּילוֹת אָנוּ אוֹכְלִין חָמֵץ וּמַצָּה,

《 and matzah, ⟨ chametz ⟨ [may] eat ⟨ we ⟨ nights ⟨ For on all [other]

הַלַּיְלָה הַזֶּה כֻּלוֹ מַצָּה.

《 matzah. ⟨ — only 《 [but] on this night

---

(4) Alternate: *How different is this night . . .!* (*Aruch HaShulchan* 473:21)

הָא לַחְמָא — *This is the bread.* The redemption is at this moment incomplete, we are free from Egypt, but we still look forward to have a future redemption when we will celebrate Passover, as of old, in the Holy Temple in a rebuilt Jerusalem.

מַה נִּשְׁתַּנָה — *Why is it different.* The Story of the

Exodus opens with a child's questions, for Scripture often mentions this narrative in the form of a father's reply to his child's questions. The Four Questions note the contradictory observances of the Seder. We eat matzah and bitter herbs, which symbolize oppression and slavery, but at the same time we dip our vegetables and recline

2.

שֶׁבְּכָל הַלֵּילוֹת אָנוּ אוֹכְלִין שְׁאָר יְרָקוֹת,
« vegetables, ⟨ other ⟨ eat ⟨ we ⟨ nights ⟨ For on all [other]

הַלַּיְלָה הַזֶּה מָרוֹר.*
« — [we must eat] « [but] on this night
maror [bitter herbs].*

3.

שֶׁבְּכָל הַלֵּילוֹת אֵין אָנוּ מַטְבִּילִין אֲפִילוּ
⟨ even ⟨ dip ⟨ we do not ⟨ nights ⟨ For on all [other]

פַּעַם אֶחָת, הַלַּיְלָה הַזֶּה שְׁתֵּי פְעָמִים.
« times. ⟨ — two « [but] on this night « one time,

4.

שֶׁבְּכָל הַלֵּילוֹת אָנוּ אוֹכְלִין בֵּין יוֹשְׁבִין וּבֵין
⟨ or ⟨ sitting ⟨ either ⟨ eat ⟨ we ⟨ nights ⟨ For on all [other]

מְסֻבִּין, הַלַּיְלָה הַזֶּה – כֻּלָּנוּ מְסֻבִּין.
« recline. ⟨ — we all « [but] on this night « reclining,

THE SEDER PLATE IS RETURNED. THE MATZOS ARE KEPT UNCOVERED AS THE HAGGADAH IS RECITED
IN UNISON. THE HAGGADAH SHOULD BE TRANSLATED, IF NECESSARY,
AND THE STORY OF THE EXODUS SHOULD BE AMPLIFIED UPON.

עֲבָדִים* הָיִינוּ לְפַרְעֹה בְּמִצְרָיִם, וַיּוֹצִיאֵנוּ
⟨ but take us out « in Egypt, ⟨ to Pharaoh ⟨ we were ⟨ Slaves*

יהוה אֱלֹהֵינוּ מִשָּׁם בְּיָד חֲזָקָה וּבִזְרוֹעַ
⟨ and an arm ⟨ that is mighty ⟨ with a hand ⟨ from there ⟨ our God, ⟨ did HASHEM,

נְטוּיָה. וְאִלּוּ לֹא הוֹצִיא הַקָּדוֹשׁ בָּרוּךְ הוּא
« is He – ⟨ Blessed ⟨ – the Holy « He had not ⟨ And if « that is
One, taken out outstretched.

on couches, which indicate opulence and freedom!

מָרוֹר — *Maror*. The reason we eat *maror* at the Seder — when we should be celebrating Israel's freedom — is that the perception that their existence in Egypt was insufferably bitter was the first step towards their salvation.

עֲבָדִים — *Slaves*. The child is first answered with a brief summary of the entire epoch "We were slaves, and then God freed us." Subsequently, more and more details will be added to the narrative.

מָרוֹר כּוֹרֵךְ שֻׁלְחָן עוֹרֵךְ צָפוּן בָּרֵךְ הַלֵּל נִרְצָה
NIRTZAh hALLEL BARECh TZAFUN shULChAN ORECh KORECh MAROR

אֶת אֲבוֹתֵינוּ מִמִּצְרַיִם, הֲרֵי אָנוּ וּבָנֵינוּ וּבְנֵי

‹ and the ‹ our ‹ we, ‹ then ⟪ from Egypt, ‹ our fathers
children children,

בָּנֵינוּ מְשֻׁעְבָּדִים הָיִינוּ לְפַרְעֹה בְּמִצְרָיִם.

⟪ in Egypt. ‹ to Pharaoh ‹ would have ‹ subservient ⟪ of our
remained children,

וַאֲפִילוּ כֻּלָּנוּ חֲכָמִים, כֻּלָּנוּ נְבוֹנִים, כֻּלָּנוּ

‹ we all ‹ people of ‹ we all ‹ people of ‹ we all ‹ Even if
were understanding, were wisdom, were

זְקֵנִים, כֻּלָּנוּ יוֹדְעִים אֶת הַתּוֹרָה, מִצְוָה עָלֵינוּ

‹ upon ‹ it would [still] ⟪ of the Torah, ‹ had [full] ‹ and we ‹ people of
us be an obligation knowledge all experience,

לְסַפֵּר* בִּיצִיאַת מִצְרָיִם. וְכָל הַמַּרְבֶּה לְסַפֵּר*

‹ in telling* ‹ who elaborates ‹ And ⟪ from Egypt. ‹ about the ‹ to tell*
anyone Exodus

בִּיצִיאַת מִצְרַיִם, הֲרֵי זֶה מְשֻׁבָּח.

⟪ praiseworthy. ‹ he is ‹ certainly ⟪ from Egypt, ‹ about the Exodus

מַעֲשֶׂה* בְּרַבִּי אֱלִיעֶזֶר וְרַבִּי יְהוֹשֻׁעַ וְרַבִּי

‹ Rabbi ‹ Yehoshua, ‹ Rabbi ‹ Eliezer, ‹ involving ‹ There was
Rabbi an occurrence*

אֶלְעָזָר בֶּן עֲזַרְיָה וְרַבִּי עֲקִיבָא וְרַבִּי טַרְפוֹן

‹ Tarfon ‹ and Rabbi ‹ Akiva, ‹ Rabbi ‹ Azaryah, ‹ son of ‹ Elazar

שֶׁהָיוּ מְסֻבִּין בִּבְנֵי בְרַק, וְהָיוּ מְסַפְּרִים בִּיצִיאַת

‹ the Exodus ‹ recounting ‹ They ⟪ in Bnei Brak. ‹ gathered ‹ who
were (at the Seder) were

מִצְרַיִם כָּל אוֹתוֹ הַלַּיְלָה. עַד שֶׁבָּאוּ תַלְמִידֵיהֶם

‹ their students came ‹ until ⟪ night, ‹ that ‹ all ‹ from Egypt

מִצְוָה עָלֵינוּ לְסַפֵּר — *It would [still] be an obligation upon us to tell.* The two Hebrew words הַגָּדָה and סִיפּוּר, both translated as telling or recounting, differ in that הַגָּדָה is used to tell the story to someone who does not know it — וְהִגַּדְתָּ לְבִנְךָ, *You shall tell your son,* (*Exodus* 13:8), while סִיפּוּר is used even where the story is well-known, as in the story of the sages in Bnei Brak (*R' Reuven Margulies*).

מַעֲשֶׂה — *There was an occurrence.* Even great sages, who surely know the story, must recount it at great length. The most venerable sages of that time spend the entire night of Pesach recounting the story of the Exodus.

וְאָמְרוּ לָהֶם, רַבּוֹתֵינוּ הִגִּיעַ זְמַן קְרִיאַת שְׁמַע
< of < for the < [daybreak,] < it is < Our teachers, << to them: < and said
Shema   reading   time   now

שֶׁל שַׁחֲרִית.
<< the morning. < of

אָמַר רַבִּי אֶלְעָזָר בֶּן עֲזַרְיָה, הֲרֵי אֲנִי
< I am < Indeed << Azaryah: < son of < Elazar < Rabbi < Said

כְּבֶן שִׁבְעִים שָׁנָה, וְלֹא זָכִיתִי שֶׁתֵּאָמֵר יְצִיאַת
< of the   < in [requiring] <   but I did   << seventy years old, < like one
Exodus   the mentioning   not succeed

מִצְרַיִם בַּלֵּילוֹת, עַד שֶׁדְּרָשָׁהּ בֶּן זוֹמָא,
< by Ben Zoma, < it was expounded < until << every night, < from Egypt

שֶׁנֶּאֱמַר, לְמַעַן תִּזְכֹּר אֶת יוֹם צֵאתְךָ מֵאֶרֶץ
< the land < you left < the day < that you may < In order << as it says:
remember

מִצְרַיִם כֹּל יְמֵי חַיֶּיךָ.[1] יְמֵי חַיֶּיךָ הַיָּמִים, כֹּל
< [the addi- << [indicates < of your < [The << of your < the days < all < of Egypt
tion of the   only]   life   phrase]   life.
word] all   the days;   the days

יְמֵי חַיֶּיךָ הַלֵּילוֹת. וַחֲכָמִים אוֹמְרִים, יְמֵי חַיֶּיךָ
< of your < the days << declare: < But the Sages << [includes] the << of your < [to] the
life   nights [as well].   life   days

הָעוֹלָם הַזֶּה, כֹּל יְמֵי חַיֶּיךָ לְהָבִיא לִימוֹת
< the days < includes << of your < [to] the < [the addi- << [indicates only]
life   days   tion of] all   the present world;

הַמָּשִׁיחַ.
<< of Mashiach.

בָּרוּךְ הַמָּקוֹם, בָּרוּךְ הוּא. בָּרוּךְ שֶׁנָּתַן תּוֹרָה
< the < is the One < Blessed << is He. < Blessed << is the < Blessed
Torah   Who has given   Omnipresent;

---

(1) *Deuteronomy* 16:3.

לְעַמּוֹ יִשְׂרָאֵל, בָּרוּךְ הוּא. כְּנֶגֶד* אַרְבָּעָה בָנִים

> sons < four < Concerning* > is He. < Blessed > Israel; < to His people

דִּבְּרָה תוֹרָה: אֶחָד חָכָם, וְאֶחָד רָשָׁע, וְאֶחָד

> one < is wicked, < one < is wise, < — one > in the < there is
                         Torah   a reference

תָּם, וְאֶחָד שֶׁאֵינוֹ יוֹדֵעַ לִשְׁאוֹל.

> how to ask. < know < who does not < and one < is simple,

חָכָם מָה הוּא אוֹמֵר? מָה הָעֵדֹת וְהַחֻקִּים

< decrees, < are the < What > say? < does he < — what > The wise
          testimonies,   [son]

וְהַמִּשְׁפָּטִים אֲשֶׁר צִוָּה יהוה אֱלֹהֵינוּ אֶתְכֶם?[1]

> to you? < our God, < by < were < which < and ordinances
               HASHEM, commanded

וְאַף אַתָּה אֱמָר לוֹ כְּהִלְכוֹת הַפֶּסַח, אֵין

< [until] one > of the pesach < [all] the laws < to him < explain > You as well,
  may not   offering,

מַפְטִירִין אַחַר הַפֶּסַח אֲפִיקוֹמָן.[2]

> anything < of the pesach < after [the < eat
  as a dessert.   offering   final taste]

רָשָׁע* מָה הוּא אוֹמֵר? מָה הָעֲבֹדָה הַזֹּאת

< is this service < Of what > say? < does he < — what > The
             purpose   wicked [son]*

לָכֶם?[3] לָכֶם וְלֹא לוֹ, וּלְפִי שֶׁהוֹצִיא אֶת עַצְמוֹ

< himself < he has < Since > to < but > — [implying] > to you?
         excluded   him. not   to you,

---

(1) Deuteronomy 6:20. (2) Pesachim 10:8. (3) Exodus 12:26.

כְּנֶגֶד — Concerning. From the various shades of expression in Scripture's description of the father-son dialogue, four types of offspring can be discerned:

1. The wise son seeks knowledge.

2. The wicked son looks down on the beliefs of his people and scoffs.

3. The simple son asks a simple question.

4. If the child does not ask, the parent must teach.

רָשָׁע — The wicked son. The question of the wicked son is presented in the Torah not as a question, but as a statement: וְהָיָה כִּי יֹאמְרוּ .... אֲלֵיכֶם בְּנֵיכֶם, And it shall be that when your children say to you ...(Exodus 12:26). The wicked son is dictating his position to you and is

מִן הַכְּלָל, כָּפַר בְּעִקָּר – וְאַף אַתָּה הַקְהֵה

‹ blunt ‹ You as well, ‹‹ the basic principle ‹ he ‹‹ the community ‹ from
[of Judaism]. denies [of believers],

אֶת שִׁנָּיו וֶאֱמָר לוֹ, בַּעֲבוּר זֶה עָשָׂה יהוה לִי

‹ for ‹ that Hashem did so ‹ of ‹ It is ‹‹ him: ‹ and tell ‹‹ his teeth
me this because

בְּצֵאתִי מִמִּצְרָיִם.¹ לִי וְלֹא לוֹ, אִלּוּ הָיָה שָׁם

‹ there, ‹ he ‹ – had ‹‹ for ‹ but not ‹ For ‹‹ of Egypt. ‹ when
been him me, I went out

לֹא הָיָה נִגְאָל.

‹‹ redeemed. ‹ have ‹ he would
been not

תָּם מָה הוּא אוֹמֵר? מַה זֹּאת? וְאָמַרְתָּ

‹ You shall say ‹ is this? ‹ What ‹‹ say? ‹ does he ‹ – what ‹‹ The
simple [son]

אֵלָיו, בְּחֹזֶק יָד הוֹצִיאָנוּ יהוה מִמִּצְרַיִם מִבֵּית

‹ from the ‹ from Egypt, ‹ Hashem took us out ‹ of ‹ With ‹‹ to him:
house hand strength

עֲבָדִים.²

‹‹ of bondage.

וְשֶׁאֵינוֹ יוֹדֵעַ* לִשְׁאוֹל, אַתְּ פְּתַח* לוֹ.

‹‹ for ‹ must initiate* ‹ you ‹‹ to ask, ‹ know* ‹ And as for [the son]
him, [the discussion] [enough] who does not

שֶׁנֶּאֱמַר, וְהִגַּדְתָּ לְבִנְךָ בַּיּוֹם הַהוּא לֵאמֹר,

‹‹ saying: ‹ on that day, ‹ your son ‹ You shall tell ‹‹ as it says:

בַּעֲבוּר זֶה עָשָׂה יהוה לִי בְּצֵאתִי מִמִּצְרָיִם.³

‹‹ Egypt.' ‹ when I left ‹ on my ‹ that Hashem acted ‹ of this ‹ 'It is
behalf because

---

(1) Exodus 13:8. (2) 13:14. (3) 13:8.

---

not interested in your answers (Yaavetz).
וְשֶׁאֵינוֹ יוֹדֵעַ . . . אַתְּ פְּתַח — Who does not know . . .
you initiate (lit. open). The Divrei Chayim ex-

pounds that to one who truly knows that he
does not know, to such a person everything
from א, aleph to ת, tav is opened for him.

NIRTZAh   hALLEL   BARECh   TZAFUN   shULChAN OReCh   KOReCh   MAROR

יָכוֹל מֵראשׁ חֹדֶשׁ, תַּלְמוּד לוֹמַר בַּיּוֹם הַהוּא.[1]

‹‹ [You shall tell your son] on that day. ‹ saying: ‹ [but] the [Torah] teaches ‹‹ commences with the first day of the month [of Nissan], ‹ One might think [that the obligation to discuss the Exodus]

אִי בַּיּוֹם הַהוּא, יָכוֹל מִבְּעוֹד יוֹם, תַּלְמוּד לוֹמַר

‹‹ saying: ‹ [therefore] the [Torah] teaches ‹‹ daytime; while it is still ‹ [only] one might think it means ‹‹ on that day, ‹ But if [we learn from]

בַּעֲבוּר זֶה.[1] בַּעֲבוּר זֶה לֹא אָמַרְתִּי אֶלָּא בְּשָׁעָה

‹ at the time ‹ except ‹ could not be said ‹ of this ‹ Because ‹‹ of this. ‹ [You shall tell your son . . .] It is because

שֶׁיֵּשׁ מַצָּה וּמָרוֹר מֻנָּחִים לְפָנֶיךָ.

‹‹ before you [at the Seder]. ‹ placed ‹ and maror ‹ matzah ‹ when there are

מִתְּחִלָּה,* עוֹבְדֵי עֲבוֹדָה זָרָה הָיוּ אֲבוֹתֵינוּ,

‹‹ our forefathers, ‹ were ‹ of idols ‹ worshipers ‹ Initially*

וְעַכְשָׁו קֵרְבָנוּ הַמָּקוֹם לַעֲבוֹדָתוֹ. שֶׁנֶּאֱמַר,

‹‹ as it says: ‹‹ to His service, ‹ by the Omnipresent ‹ we have been brought near ‹ but now

וַיֹּאמֶר יְהוֹשֻׁעַ אֶל כָּל הָעָם, כֹּה אָמַר יהוה

‹ HASHEM, ‹ says ‹ 'So ‹‹ the people, ‹ all ‹ to ‹ Yehoshua said

אֱלֹהֵי יִשְׂרָאֵל, בְּעֵבֶר הַנָּהָר יָשְׁבוּ אֲבוֹתֵיכֶם

‹ did Your fathers live ‹ the [Euphrates] River ‹ beyond ‹‹ of Israel: ‹ God

מֵעוֹלָם, תֶּרַח אֲבִי אַבְרָהָם וַאֲבִי נָחוֹר, וַיַּעַבְדוּ

‹ and they worshipped ‹‹ of Nachor, ‹ and the father ‹ of Avraham ‹ the father ‹ Terach ‹‹ from ancient times,

אֱלֹהִים אֲחֵרִים. וָאֶקַּח אֶת אֲבִיכֶם אֶת אַבְרָהָם

‹ Avraham ‹ your father ‹ Then I took ‹‹ other gods.

---

(1) Exodus 13:8.

מִתְּחִלָּה — Initially. The spiritual greatness of our lofty Abrahamitic heritage is contrasted with the moral decay of our earliest ancestors.

קַדֵּשׁ וּרְחַץ כַּרְפַּס יַחַץ מַגִּיד רָחְצָה מוֹצִיא מַצָּ...

ATZAh   MOTZI   RAChTZAh   MAGGID   YAChATZ   KARPAS   URECHATZ   KADDESH

מֵעֵבֶר הַנָּהָר, וָאוֹלֵךְ אוֹתוֹ בְּכָל אֶרֶץ כְּנָעַן,

‹‹ of Canaan. ‹ the land ‹ through all ‹ him ‹ and I led ‹ the river ‹ from beyond

וָאַרְבֶּה אֶת זַרְעוֹ, וָאֶתֶּן לוֹ אֶת יִצְחָק. וָאֶתֵּן

‹ I gave ‹‹ Yitzchak. ‹ him ‹ and gave ‹ his offspring ‹ I multiplied

לְיִצְחָק אֶת יַעֲקֹב וְאֶת עֵשָׂו, וָאֶתֵּן לְעֵשָׂו

‹ to Esav ‹ I gave ‹‹ and Esav; ‹ Yaakov ‹ to Yitzchak

אֶת הַר שֵׂעִיר לָרֶשֶׁת אוֹתוֹ, וְיַעֲקֹב וּבָנָיו יָרְדוּ

‹ went ‹ and his ‹ but Yaakov ‹‹ it, ‹ to inherit ‹ Seir ‹ Mount
down   children

מִצְרָיִם.¹

‹‹ to Egypt.'

בָּרוּךְ שׁוֹמֵר* הַבְטָחָתוֹ לְיִשְׂרָאֵל, בָּרוּךְ הוּא.

‹‹ is He! ‹ Blessed ‹‹ to Israel; ‹ His pledge ‹ Who keeps* ‹ Blessed is He

שֶׁהַקָּדוֹשׁ בָּרוּךְ הוּא חִשַּׁב אֶת הַקֵּץ, לַעֲשׂוֹת

‹ in order ‹ the End ‹ calculated ‹‹ is He, ‹ Blessed ‹‹ For the
to do   [of the bondage]   Holy One,

כְּמָה שֶׁאָמַר לְאַבְרָהָם אָבִינוּ בִּבְרִית בֵּין

‹ Between ‹ at the ‹ our father ‹ to Avraham ‹ He said ‹ as
Covenant

הַבְּתָרִים, שֶׁנֶּאֱמַר, וַיֹּאמֶר לְאַבְרָם, יָדֹעַ תֵּדַע כִּי

‹ that ‹ 'Know with ‹‹ to Avram, ‹ He said ‹‹ as it says: ‹‹ the Parts,
certainty

גֵר יִהְיֶה זַרְעֲךָ בְּאֶרֶץ לֹא לָהֶם, וַעֲבָדוּם וְעִנּוּ

‹ and they ‹ they will ‹‹ their ‹ not ‹ in a land ‹ will your ‹ aliens
will oppress enslave them own;   offspring be

אֹתָם, אַרְבַּע מֵאוֹת שָׁנָה. וְגַם אֶת הַגּוֹי אֲשֶׁר

‹ which ‹ the nation ‹ upon ‹ But also ‹‹ years. ‹ hundred ‹ four ‹ them

---

(1) *Yehoshua* 24:2-4.

בָּרוּךְ שׁוֹמֵר — *Blessed is He Who keeps.* Despite Israel's descent to Egypt, God's promise to Abraham was not forgotten. Indeed, that promise has stood by us in all generations, through countless persecutions. Even before the Exodus, that promise protected us from Laban, whose evil was, in a sense, more potent that Pharoah's.

יַעֲבֹדוּ דָן אָנֹכִי, וְאַחֲרֵי כֵן יֵצְאוּ בִּרְכֻשׁ גָּדוֹל.¹

《 with great wealth.' 〈 they shall leave 〈 that 〈 and after **《** will I execute judgment, 〈 they shall serve

THE MATZOS ARE COVERED AND THE CUPS LIFTED AS THE FOLLOWING PARAGRAPH IS PROCLAIMED JOYOUSLY. UPON ITS CONCLUSION, THE CUPS ARE PUT DOWN AND THE MATZOS ARE UNCOVERED.

וְהִיא שֶׁעָמְדָה* לַאֲבוֹתֵינוּ וְלָנוּ, שֶׁלֹּא

〈 For it is not **《** and us. 〈 our fathers 〈 that has sustained* 〈 And it is this

אֶחָד בִּלְבַד עָמַד עָלֵינוּ לְכַלּוֹתֵנוּ. אֶלָּא שֶׁבְּכָל

〈 that in every 〈 but rather **《** to annihilate us, 〈 against us 〈 [who] has risen 〈 isolated 〈 one [enemy]

דּוֹר וָדוֹר עוֹמְדִים עָלֵינוּ לְכַלּוֹתֵנוּ, וְהַקָּדוֹשׁ

《 But the Holy One, **《** to annihilate us. 〈 against us 〈 they rise 〈 after generation 〈 gener-ation

בָּרוּךְ הוּא מַצִּילֵנוּ מִיָּדָם.*

《 from their hand.* 〈 rescues us **《** is He, 〈 Blessed

צֵא וּלְמַד* ² מַה בִּקֵּשׁ לָבָן הָאֲרַמִּי לַעֲשׂוֹת

〈 attempted to carry out 〈 the Aramean 〈 Lavan 〈 was the scheme 〈 what 〈 and learn* 〈 Go

לְיַעֲקֹב אָבִינוּ, שֶׁפַּרְעֹה לֹא גָזַר אֶלָּא עַל

〈 against 〈 only decreed 〈 For Pharaoh **《** our father! 〈 against Yaakov

הַזְּכָרִים, וְלָבָן בִּקֵּשׁ לַעֲקוֹר אֶת הַכֹּל. שֶׁנֶּאֱמַר:

《 as it is said: **《** everything, 〈 to uproot 〈 attempted 〈 while Lavan **《** the males,

---

(1) *Genesis* 15:13-14. (2) Cf. *Sifri Devarim* 301, *Midrash Tanaim* 26:5-8, *Midrash Lekach Tov, Ki Tavo* (45b-46a).

וְהִיא שֶׁעָמְדָה . . . מַצִּילֵנוּ מִיָּדָם — *And it is this that has sustained . . . rescues us from their hand.* Once God's mercy was aroused for Him to miraculously save Israel from an enemy who sought to annihilate them, the same arousal of mercy remains to effect the salvation of Israel from all similar attacks in the future (*Noam Elimelech*). In the same manner, the *Tiferes Shlomo* explains the promise בְּנִיסָן נִגְאֲלוּ, בְּנִיסָן עֲתִידִים לִיגָּאֵל, *In Nissan, they were redeemed; in Nissan they will be redeemed in the future* (*Rosh Hashanah* 11a), that the first divine redemption

will provide the basis for the final one.

צֵא וּלְמַד — *Go and learn.* Details of Israel's descent, oppression, prayers, and deliverance are now added in a word-by-word exposition of four verses in *Deuteronomy*. The first verse, . . . אֲרַמִּי, *An Aramean . . .*, speaks of the descent to Egypt; the second verse, . . . וַיָּרֵעוּ, *Evil intentions were attributed . . .* describes the oppressiveness of the Egyptians; the third verse, . . . וַנִּצְעַק, *We cried out . . .*, speaks of our prayers and God's response; the fourth verse, . . . וַיּוֹצִאֵנוּ ה׳, *Hashem took us out . . .*, tells of the deliverance.

קַדֵּשׁ וּרְחַץ כַּרְפַּס יַחַץ מַגִּיד רָחְצָה מוֹצִיא מַצָּה
ATZAh MOTZI RACHTZAh MAGGID YACHATZ KARPAS URECHATZ KADDESH

אֲרַמִּי אֹבֵד אָבִי,* וַיֵּרֶד מִצְרַיְמָה וַיָּגָר

‹ and he sojourned ‹ to Egypt ‹ he descended ‹‹ my father;* ‹ attempted to destroy ‹ An Aramean

שָׁם בִּמְתֵי מְעָט, וַיְהִי שָׁם לְגוֹי גָּדוֹל

‹ — great, ‹‹ a nation ‹ there ‹ and he became ‹‹ who were few; ‹ with people ‹ there

עָצוּם וָרָב. [1]

‹‹ and numerous. ‹ mighty,

וַיֵּרֶד מִצְרַיְמָה — אָנוּס עַל פִּי הַדִּבּוּר.

‹‹ the word [of God]. ‹ by ‹ — compelled ‹‹ to Egypt ‹ He descended

וַיָּגָר שָׁם — מְלַמֵּד שֶׁלֹּא יָרַד יַעֲקֹב אָבִינוּ

‹‹ our father — ‹ — Yaakov ‹‹ descend ‹ that he did not ‹ — this teaches ‹‹ there ‹ And he sojourned

לְהִשְׁתַּקֵּעַ בְּמִצְרַיִם, אֶלָּא לָגוּר שָׁם. שֶׁנֶּאֱמַר,

‹‹ as it is said. ‹‹ there, ‹ to stay temporarily ‹ but only ‹‹ in Egypt, ‹ to settle

וַיֹּאמְרוּ אֶל פַּרְעֹה, לָגוּר בָּאָרֶץ בָּאנוּ, כִּי אֵין

‹ there is no ‹ for ‹‹ have we come, ‹ in the land ‹ 'To sojourn ‹‹ Pharaoh: ‹ to ‹ They (the sons of Yaakov) said

מִרְעֶה לַצֹּאן אֲשֶׁר לַעֲבָדֶיךָ, כִּי כָבֵד הָרָעָב

‹ is the famine ‹ severe ‹ because ‹‹ belong to your servants, ‹ which ‹ for the flocks ‹ pasture

בְּאֶרֶץ כְּנָעַן, וְעַתָּה יֵשְׁבוּ נָא עֲבָדֶיךָ בְּאֶרֶץ

‹ in the land ‹ of your servants ‹ please, ‹ allow the dwelling, ‹ and now ‹‹ of Canaan; ‹ in the land

גֹּשֶׁן. [2]

‹‹ of Goshen.'

---

(1) *Deuteronomy* 26:5. (2) *Genesis* 47:4.

אֲרַמִּי אֹבֵד אָבִי — *An Aramean attempted to destroy my father.* As *Mahari Bei Rav* points out, Lavan's actions can be blamed for Yaakov's descent to Egypt: Because of Lavan's switching Leah for Rachel, Yosef was not Yaakov's firstborn. Had Yosef been the firstborn, his primacy would have been accepted by his brothers. It was their jealousy of Yosef that led to the exile in

בְּמְתֵי מְעָט – כְּמָה שֶׁנֶּאֱמַר, בְּשִׁבְעִים

‹ With people ‹‹ who were few ‹ — as ‹‹ it is said: ‹ With seventy

נֶפֶשׁ יָרְדוּ אֲבֹתֶיךָ מִצְרָיְמָה, וְעַתָּה

‹ persons, ‹ your forefathers descended ‹ to Egypt, ‹‹ and now,

שָׂמְךָ יהוה אֱלֹהֶיךָ כְּכוֹכְבֵי הַשָּׁמַיִם לָרֹב.¹

‹‹ HASHEM, your God, has established you ‹ as the stars ‹ of heaven, ‹‹ vast in number.

וַיְהִי שָׁם לְגוֹי – מְלַמֵּד שֶׁהָיוּ יִשְׂרָאֵל

‹ And he became ‹ there ‹ a nation ‹‹ — this teaches ‹ that the Israelites were

מְצֻיָּנִים שָׁם.

‹ distinctive ‹‹ there.

גָּדוֹל עָצוּם – כְּמָה שֶׁנֶּאֱמַר, וּבְנֵי יִשְׂרָאֵל פָּרוּ

‹‹ Great, ‹ mighty ‹‹ — as ‹ it says: ‹‹ And the Children ‹ of Israel ‹ were fruitful,

וַיִּשְׁרְצוּ וַיִּרְבּוּ וַיַּעַצְמוּ בִּמְאֹד מְאֹד, וַתִּמָּלֵא

‹ increased greatly, ‹ multiplied, ‹ and became mighty ‹‹ — exceedingly so; ‹‹ and filled

הָאָרֶץ אֹתָם.²

‹ was the land ‹‹ with them.

וָרָב – כְּמָה שֶׁנֶּאֱמַר, רְבָבָה כְּצֶמַח הַשָּׂדֶה

‹‹ And numerous ‹ — as ‹ it says: ‹‹ A myriad, ‹ as the plants ‹ of the field

נְתַתִּיךְ, וַתִּרְבִּי וַתִּגְדְּלִי וַתָּבֹאִי בַּעֲדִי עֲדָיִים,

‹‹ did I inaugurate you; ‹ you grew ‹‹ and you developed, ‹‹ and you came to be ‹ a beauty ‹ of beauties,

שָׁדַיִם נָכֹנוּ וּשְׂעָרֵךְ צִמֵּחַ, וְאַתְּ עֵרֹם וְעֶרְיָה;

‹ mature in figure, ‹ your hair, ‹‹ sprouted; ‹ but you were ‹ naked ‹‹ and bare.

---

(1) Deuteronomy 10:22. (2) Exodus 1:7.

Egypt (Chukas HaPesach).

SOME ADD THE VERSE'S CONCLUSION:

וָאֶעֱבֹר עָלַיִךְ וָאֶרְאֵךְ מִתְבּוֹסֶסֶת בְּדָמָיִךְ, וָאֹמַר
‹ and I said ‹ in your blood ‹ wallowing ‹ and saw you ‹ over you ‹ And I passed

לָךְ, בְּדָמַיִךְ חֲיִי, וָאֹמַר לָךְ, בְּדָמַיִךְ חֲיִי.¹
« shall ‹ 'Through « to ‹ and « shall ‹ 'Through « to
you live.' your blood you: I said you live'; your blood you:

וַיָּרֵעוּ אֹתָנוּ הַמִּצְרִים, וַיְעַנּוּנוּ, וַיִּתְּנוּ
‹ and they ‹ and they « [by] the ‹ to us ‹ Evil intentions
imposed afflicted us, Egyptians were attributed

עָלֵינוּ עֲבֹדָה קָשָׁה.²
« that was grueling. ‹ labor ‹ upon us

וַיָּרֵעוּ אֹתָנוּ הַמִּצְרִים – כְּמָה שֶׁנֶּאֱמַר, הָבָה
‹ Let us « it says: ‹ – as « [by] the ‹ to us ‹ Evil intentions
Egyptians were attributed

נִתְחַכְּמָה לוֹ, פֶּן יִרְבֶּה, וְהָיָה כִּי תִקְרֶאנָה
‹ there ‹ that if ‹ and it ‹ they ‹ lest « with ‹ deal shrewdly
should be would be multiply them,

מִלְחָמָה, וְנוֹסַף גַּם הוּא עַל שֹׂנְאֵינוּ, וְנִלְחַם
‹ and they « our enemies, ‹ with ‹ would they ‹ joined « a war,
will fight also be

בָּנוּ, וְעָלָה מִן הָאָרֶץ.³
« the land. ‹ from ‹ and go up ‹ against us

וַיְעַנּוּנוּ – כְּמָה שֶׁנֶּאֱמַר, וַיָּשִׂימוּ עָלָיו שָׂרֵי
‹ officers ‹ over ‹ They « it says: ‹ – as « And they
in charge them appointed afflicted us

מִסִּים, לְמַעַן עַנֹּתוֹ בְּסִבְלֹתָם, וַיִּבֶן עָרֵי מִסְכְּנוֹת
‹ for the ‹ cities ‹ and they « with the ‹ to afflict ‹ in order « of the
treasure built [Egyptian's] burdens; them work tax,

לְפַרְעֹה, אֶת פִּתֹם וְאֶת רַעַמְסֵס.⁴
« and Raamses. ‹ Pisom « 'of Pharaoh,

---

(1) *Ezekiel* 16:7,6. (2) *Deuteronomy* 26:6. (3) *Exodus* 1:10. (4) 1:11.

NIRTZAH HALLEL BARECH TZAFUN SHULCHAN ORECH KORECH MAROR

וַיִּתְּנוּ עָלֵינוּ עֲבֹדָה קָשָׁה – כְּמָה שֶׁנֶּאֱמַר,

And they imposed ⟩ upon us ⟩ labor ⟩ that was grueling ⟩ – as ⟩ it says:

וַיַּעֲבִדוּ מִצְרַיִם אֶת בְּנֵי יִשְׂרָאֵל בְּפָרֶךְ.[1]

The Egyptians subjugated ⟩ the Children ⟩ of Israel ⟩ with crushing labor.

וַנִּצְעַק אֶל יהוה אֱלֹהֵי אֲבֹתֵינוּ,

We cried out ⟩ to ⟩ HASHEM, ⟩ the God ⟩ of our fathers;

וַיִּשְׁמַע יהוה אֶת קֹלֵנוּ,* וַיַּרְא אֶת עָנְיֵנוּ,

and HASHEM heard ⟩ our cry* ⟩ and He saw ⟩ our affliction,

וְאֶת עֲמָלֵנוּ, וְאֶת לַחֲצֵנוּ.[2]

our travail, ⟩ and our oppression.

וַנִּצְעַק אֶל יהוה אֱלֹהֵי אֲבֹתֵינוּ – כְּמָה

We cried out ⟩ to ⟩ HASHEM, ⟩ the God ⟩ of our fathers ⟩ – as

שֶׁנֶּאֱמַר, וַיְהִי בַיָּמִים הָרַבִּים הָהֵם, וַיָּמָת מֶלֶךְ

it says: ⟩ It happened ⟩ [after] the many days ⟩ that [Moses was away], ⟩ the death ⟩ of the king

מִצְרַיִם, וַיֵּאָנְחוּ בְנֵי יִשְׂרָאֵל מִן הָעֲבֹדָה, וַיִּזְעָקוּ,

of Egypt; ⟩ and the Children of Israel groaned ⟩ because of ⟩ the work ⟩ and cried out;

וַתַּעַל שַׁוְעָתָם אֶל הָאֱלֹהִים מִן הָעֲבֹדָה.[3]

rise up ⟩ did their cry ⟩ to ⟩ God ⟩ because of ⟩ the work.

וַיִּשְׁמַע יהוה אֶת קֹלֵנוּ – כְּמָה שֶׁנֶּאֱמַר,

And HASHEM heard ⟩ our cry ⟩ – as ⟩ it says:

וַיִּשְׁמַע אֱלֹהִים אֶת נַאֲקָתָם, וַיִּזְכֹּר אֱלֹהִים

God heard ⟩ their groaning, ⟩ and God recalled

(1) Exodus 1:13. (2) Deuteronomy 26:7. (3) Exodus 2:23.

— וַנִּצְעַק אֶל יהוה אֱלֹהֵי אֲבֹתֵינוּ, וַיִּשְׁמַע יהוה אֶת קֹלֵנוּ We cried out to HASHEM, the God of our fathers and HASHEM heard our cry. Rabbi Yochanan (Berachos 10b) states that כָּל הַתּוֹלֶה בִּזְכוּת אֲחֵרִים תּוֹלִין לוֹ בִּזְכוּת עַצְמוֹ, If one depends in prayer upon the merit of others, the fulfillment of his prayer will be based on his own merit. Although Israel invokes the merit of their fathers, God heard their own voice and saved them (Kehilas Moshe).

אֶת בְּרִיתוֹ אֶת אַבְרָהָם, אֶת יִצְחָק, וְאֶת יַעֲקֹב.¹

» Yaakov. ‹ and with ‹ Yitzchak, ‹ with ‹ Avraham, ‹ with ‹ His covenant

וַיַּרְא אֶת עָנְיֵנוּ – זוּ פְּרִישׁוּת דֶּרֶךְ אֶרֶץ,²

« of family life, ‹ the ‹ – that « our affliction ‹ **And He saw**
suspension is

כְּמָה שֶׁנֶּאֱמַר, וַיַּרְא אֱלֹהִים אֶת בְּנֵי יִשְׂרָאֵל,

‹ of Israel ‹ the Children ‹ God saw « it says: ‹ as

וַיֵּדַע אֱלֹהִים.³

« and God knew.

וְאֶת עֲמָלֵנוּ – אֵלּוּ הַבָּנִים, כְּמָה שֶׁנֶּאֱמַר,

« it says: ‹ as « the children, ‹ – these are « **Our travail**

כָּל הַבֵּן הַיִּלּוֹד הַיְאֹרָה תַּשְׁלִיכֻהוּ, וְכָל הַבַּת

‹ daughter ‹ but « shall you ‹ – into « that is ‹ son ‹ Every
every cast him, the river born

תְּחַיּוּן.⁴

« you shall keep alive.

וְאֶת לַחֲצֵנוּ – זוּ הַדֹּחַק, כְּמָה שֶׁנֶּאֱמַר,

« it says: ‹ as « the ‹ – this « **And our oppression**
pressure, [refers to]

וְגַם רָאִיתִי אֶת הַלַּחַץ אֲשֶׁר מִצְרַיִם לֹחֲצִים

‹ are ‹ the ‹ with ‹ the oppression ‹ I have also seen
oppressing Egyptians which

אֹתָם.⁵

« them.

וַיּוֹצִאֵנוּ יהוה מִמִּצְרַיִם בְּיָד חֲזָקָה,

‹ that is ‹ with a ‹ of Egypt ‹ HASHEM took us out
mighty, hand

---

(1) Exodus 2:24. (2) Lit. the way of the land. (3) Exodus 2:25. (4) 1:22. (5) 3:9.

וּבְזְרֹעַ נְטוּיָה, וּבְמֹרָא גָּדֹל, וּבְאֹתוֹת
‹ with signs, ‹ that is great, ‹ with fear ‹ that is outstretched, ‹ and with an arm

וּבְמֹפְתִים.[1]
« and with wonders.

וַיּוֹצִאֵנוּ יהוה מִמִּצְרַיִם — לֹא עַל יְדֵי
‹ through ‹ — not « of Egypt ‹ HASHEM took us out

מַלְאָךְ, וְלֹא עַל יְדֵי שָׂרָף, וְלֹא עַל יְדֵי שָׁלִיחַ,
« a messenger, ‹ through ‹ not ‹ a seraph, ‹ through ‹ not ‹ an angel,

אֶלָּא הַקָּדוֹשׁ בָּרוּךְ הוּא בִּכְבוֹדוֹ וּבְעַצְמוֹ.
« He alone, ‹ in His glory, « is He — ‹ — Blessed « the Holy One ‹ but rather

שֶׁנֶּאֱמַר, וְעָבַרְתִּי בְאֶרֶץ מִצְרַיִם בַּלַּיְלָה הַזֶּה,
‹ on this night; ‹ of Egypt ‹ through the land ‹ I will pass « as it says:

וְהִכֵּיתִי כָל בְּכוֹר בְּאֶרֶץ מִצְרַיִם מֵאָדָם וְעַד
‹ to ‹ from man ‹ of Egypt ‹ in the land ‹ the firstborn ‹ all ‹ I will slay

בְּהֵמָה, וּבְכָל אֱלֹהֵי מִצְרַיִם אֶעֱשֶׂה שְׁפָטִים,
« judgments; ‹ I will execute ‹ of Egypt ‹ the gods ‹ and upon all « beast;

אֲנִי יהוה.[2]
« HASHEM. ‹ I am

וְעָבַרְתִּי בְאֶרֶץ מִצְרַיִם בַּלַּיְלָה הַזֶּה — אֲנִי
‹ — I Myself « on this night ‹ of Egypt ‹ through the land ‹ I will pass

וְלֹא מַלְאָךְ. וְהִכֵּיתִי כָל בְּכוֹר בְּאֶרֶץ מִצְרַיִם —
« of Egypt ‹ in the land ‹ the firstborn ‹ all ‹ I will slay ‹ angel; ‹ and no

אֲנִי וְלֹא שָׂרָף. וּבְכָל אֱלֹהֵי מִצְרַיִם אֶעֱשֶׂה
‹ I will execute ‹ of Egypt ‹ the gods ‹ And upon all ‹ seraph; ‹ and no ‹ — I Myself

שְׁפָטִים — אֲנִי וְלֹא הַשָּׁלִיחַ. אֲנִי יהוה — אֲנִי
‹ — I Myself « HASHEM ‹ I am ‹ messenger; ‹ and no ‹ — I Myself « judgments

(1) *Deuteronomy* 26:8. (2) *Exodus* 12:12.

הוּא, וְלֹא אַחֵר.

《 other. 〈 and no 〈 am the One

בְּיָד חֲזָקָה – זוֹ הַדֶּבֶר, כְּמָה שֶׁנֶּאֱמַר, הִנֵּה

《 Behold, 《 it says: 〈 as 《 the 〈 – this 《 that is 〈 With
the epidemic, [refers to] mighty a hand

יַד יהוה הוֹיָה בְּמִקְנְךָ אֲשֶׁר בַּשָּׂדֶה, בַּסּוּסִים

〈 upon the 《 in the 〈 which 〈 your 〈 is upon 〈 of 〈 the
horses, field, are livestock HASHEM hand

בַּחֲמֹרִים בַּגְּמַלִּים בַּבָּקָר וּבַצֹּאן, דֶּבֶר כָּבֵד

〈 that is 〈 – an 《 and upon 〈 upon the 〈 upon the 〈 upon the
severe epidemic the sheep cattle, camels, donkeys,

מְאֹד.[1]

《 to the extreme.

וּבִזְרֹעַ נְטוּיָה – זוֹ הַחֶרֶב, כְּמָה שֶׁנֶּאֱמַר,

《 it says: 〈 as 《 the 〈 – this 《 that is 〈 And with
sword, [refers to] outstretched an arm

וְחַרְבּוֹ שְׁלוּפָה בְּיָדוֹ, נְטוּיָה עַל יְרוּשָׁלָיִם.[2]

《 Jerusalem. 〈 over 〈 stretched out 《 in His hand, 〈 is drawn 〈 His sword

וּבְמֹרָא גָּדֹל – זוֹ גִּלּוּי שְׁכִינָה, כְּמָה

〈 as 《 of the 〈 the 〈 – this 《 that is 〈 With fear
Shechinah, revelation [refers to] great

שֶׁנֶּאֱמַר, אוֹ הֲנִסָּה אֱלֹהִים לָבוֹא לָקַחַת לוֹ

〈 unto 〈 to take 〈 to come 〈 has [any] god ever attempted 〈 Or 《 it says:
himself

גּוֹי מִקֶּרֶב גּוֹי, בְּמַסֹּת, בְּאֹתֹת, וּבְמוֹפְתִים,

〈 and with 〈 with [miraculous] 〈 with 〈 of [another] 〈 from 〈 a
wonders, signs, challenges, nation the midst nation

וּבְמִלְחָמָה, וּבְיָד חֲזָקָה, וּבִזְרֹעַ נְטוּיָה,

〈 that is 〈 and with 〈 that is 〈 and with 〈 with war
outstretched an arm mighty a hand

---

(1) *Exodus* 9:3. (2) *I Chronicles* 21:16.

NIRTZAh hALLeL bAReCh TZAFUN shULChAN OReCh KOReCh MAROR

וּבְמוֹרָאִים גְּדֹלִים, כְּכֹל אֲשֶׁר עָשָׂה לָכֶם יהוה

‹— Hashem ‹‹ for ‹ He did ‹ that ‹ like all ‹‹ that are ‹ and by revelations
you impressive,

אֱלֹהֵיכֶם בְּמִצְרַיִם לְעֵינֶיךָ.[1]

‹‹before your eyes? ‹ in Egypt, ‹‹ your God —

וּבְאֹתוֹת — זֶה הַמַּטֶּה, כְּמָה שֶׁנֶּאֱמַר,

‹‹ it says: ‹ as ‹‹ the staff, ‹ — this [refers to] ‹‹ **With signs**

וְאֶת הַמַּטֶּה הַזֶּה תִּקַּח בְּיָדֶךָ, אֲשֶׁר תַּעֲשֶׂה בּוֹ

‹ with ‹ you may ‹ so that ‹‹ in your ‹ you should ‹ This staff
it perform hand, take

אֶת הָאֹתֹת.[2]

‹‹ the [miraculous] signs.

וּבְמֹפְתִים — זֶה הַדָּם, כְּמָה שֶׁנֶּאֱמַר, וְנָתַתִּי

‹ I will ‹‹ it says: ‹ as ‹‹ the ‹ — this ‹‹ **And with wonders**
show blood, [refers to]

מוֹפְתִים בַּשָּׁמַיִם וּבָאָרֶץ

‹ and on the earth: ‹ in the heavens ‹ wonders

AS EACH OF THE WORDS דָּם, BLOOD, אֵשׁ, FIRE, AND עָשָׁן, SMOKE, IS SAID, A BIT OF WINE
IS REMOVED FROM THE CUP, WITH THE FINGER OR BY POURING.

דָּם וָאֵשׁ וְתִמְרוֹת עָשָׁן.[3]*

‹‹ of smoke.* ‹ and columns ‹ fire, ‹ Blood,

דָּבָר אַחֵר בְּיָד חֲזָקָה, שְׁתַּיִם. וּבִזְרֹעַ נְטוּיָה,

‹‹ that is ‹ and with ‹‹ — two; ‹‹ that is ‹ With a ‹‹ An alternative
outstretched an arm mighty hand explanation:

שְׁתַּיִם. וּבְמֹרָא גָּדֹל, שְׁתַּיִם. וּבְאֹתוֹת, שְׁתַּיִם.

‹‹ — two; ‹‹ **with signs** ‹‹ — two; ‹‹ that is great ‹ with fear ‹‹ — two;

---

(1) *Deuteronomy* 4:34. (2) *Exodus* 4:17. (3) *Joel* 3:3.

עָשָׁן וְתִמְרוֹת וָאֵשׁ דָּם — *Blood, fire, and columns of
smoke.* The *Jerusalem Talmud* (*Pesachim* 10:1)
explains that the four cups of wine at the Seder
represent the four measures of punishment to be
doled out to the enemies of Israel at the time of

the future redemption. The drops of wine that
we spill from the cup are to symbolize that the
punishment of the Egyptians is like a drop in the
ocean compared to those future punishments
(*Beer Miriam*).

וּבְמֹפְתִים, שְׁתָּיִם: אֵלּוּ עֶשֶׂר מַכּוֹת* שֶׁהֵבִיא

‹‹ which He ‹ plagues* ‹ the ten ‹ These ‹‹ — two. ‹‹ And with wonders
brought   are

הַקָּדוֹשׁ בָּרוּךְ הוּא עַל הַמִּצְרִים בְּמִצְרַיִם,

‹‹ in Egypt, ‹ the Egyptians ‹ upon ‹‹ is He — ‹ Blessed ‹ — the Holy One,

וְאֵלּוּ הֵן:

‹ are ‹ and
they: these

AS EACH OF THE PLAGUES IS MENTIONED, A BIT OF WINE IS REMOVED FROM THE CUP.
THE SAME IS DONE AT EACH WORD OF RABBI YEHUDAH'S MNEMONIC.

דָּם. צְפַרְדֵּעַ. כִּנִּים. עָרוֹב. דֶּבֶר. שְׁחִין.

‹ 6. Boils ‹ 5. Epidemic ‹ 4. Wild Beasts ‹ 3. Lice ‹ 2. Frogs ‹ 1. Blood

בָּרָד. אַרְבֶּה. חֹשֶׁךְ. מַכַּת בְּכוֹרוֹת.

‹‹ of the Firstborn. ‹ 10. Plague ‹ 9. Darkness ‹ 8. Locusts ‹ 7. Hail

רַבִּי יְהוּדָה הָיָה נוֹתֵן בָּהֶם סִמָּנִים:

‹ mnemonic acronyms: ‹ to them ‹ apply ‹ would ‹ Yehudah ‹ Rabbi

דְּצַ"ךְ • עֲדַ"שׁ • בְּאַחַ"ב.

‹‹ B'ACHAV. ‹ ADASH, ‹ D'TZACH,

THE CUPS ARE REFILLED. THE WINE THAT WAS REMOVED IS NOT USED.

רַבִּי יוֹסִי* הַגְּלִילִי אוֹמֵר: מִנַּיִן אַתָּה אוֹמֵר

‹ derive ‹ can you ‹ From what ‹‹ says: ‹ the Galilean ‹ Yose* ‹ Rabbi
[passage]

עֶשֶׂר מַכּוֹת — *The ten plagues. Shem MiShmuel* quotes his grandfather, R' Menachem Mendel of Kotzk, that the ten plagues are analogous in reverse order to the ten Divine pronouncements with which the world was created. As a result, each plague revealed to Israel the corresponding divine pronouncement, such that the plague of darkness revealed the pronouncement of יְהִי אוֹר, *let there be light*, as it says explicitly וּלְכָל בְּנֵי יִשְׂרָאֵל הָיָה אוֹר בְּמוֹשְׁבֹתָם, *and to all of Israel there was light in their dwellings*. This conforms to the Midrash that during the darkness the Jews were able to *see* all the hidden treasures of the Egyptians, since the primordial light allowed one to see from one end of the Earth to the other. The final plague, the smiting of the *firstborn* of the Egyptians, corresponds for Israel to the pronouncement בְּרֵאשִׁית, *At the beginning* — the *birth* of the world.

רַבִּי יוֹסֵי — *Rabbi Yose.* Scripture describes each of the ten plagues in detail, but all combined pale in comparison to the blow delivered at the Sea of Reeds.

שֶׁלָּקוּ הַמִּצְרִים בְּמִצְרַיִם עֶשֶׂר מַכּוֹת, וְעַל

‹ but at ‹‹ plagues, ‹ [was with] ‹ in Egypt ‹ of the ‹ that the
ten Egyptians affliction

הַיָּם לָקוּ חֲמִשִּׁים מַכּוֹת? בְּמִצְרַיִם מָה הוּא

‹ it ‹ what ‹ In Egypt ‹‹ plagues? ‹ [with] fifty ‹ they were ‹ the
does afflicted Sea

אוֹמֵר, וַיֹּאמְרוּ הַחַרְטֻמִּם אֶל פַּרְעֹה, אֶצְבַּע

‹ 'The **finger** ‹‹ Pharaoh, ‹ to ‹ The magicians said ‹‹ say?

אֱלֹהִים הוּא.[1] וְעַל הַיָּם מָה הוּא אוֹמֵר,

‹‹ say? ‹ it ‹ what does ‹‹ the Sea, ‹ But at ‹‹ it is.' ‹ of God

וַיַּרְא יִשְׂרָאֵל אֶת הַיָּד הַגְּדֹלָה אֲשֶׁר עָשָׂה יהוה

‹ HASHEM inflicted ‹ that ‹ that is great ‹ the **hand** ‹ Israel saw

בְּמִצְרַיִם, וַיִּירְאוּ הָעָם אֶת יהוה, וַיַּאֲמִינוּ בַּיהוה

‹ in ‹ and they ‹ HASHEM, ‹ did the ‹ and fear ‹‹ upon Egypt,
HASHEM had faith people

וּבְמֹשֶׁה עַבְדּוֹ.[2] כַּמָּה לָקוּ בְּאֶצְבַּע? עֶשֶׂר

‹ Ten ‹‹ with the ‹ [plagues] were ‹ [With] ‹‹ His ‹ and in Moses
finger? they afflicted how many servant.

מַכּוֹת. אֱמוֹר מֵעַתָּה, בְּמִצְרַיִם לָקוּ עֶשֶׂר מַכּוֹת,

‹‹ plagues, ‹ [with] ‹ they were ‹ [if] in Egypt ‹ from this ‹ Conclude ‹‹ plagues!
ten afflicted

וְעַל הַיָּם לָקוּ חֲמִשִּׁים מַכּוֹת.

‹‹ plagues. ‹ [with] fifty ‹ they were ‹ the ‹ [then]
afflicted Sea at

רַבִּי אֱלִיעֶזֶר* אוֹמֵר. מִנַּיִן שֶׁכָּל מַכָּה וּמַכָּה

‹ single plague ‹ that ‹ From what ‹‹ says: ‹ Eliezer* ‹ Rabbi
every [passage can
one derive]

---

(1) *Exodus* 8:15. (2) 14:31.

רַבִּי אֱלִיעֶזֶר — *Rabbi Eliezer*. Even the detailed the collateral damage contributing to its actual
account of each plague reveals but a fraction of severity.

שֶׁהֵבִיא הַקָּדוֹשׁ בָּרוּךְ הוּא עַל הַמִּצְרִים
⟨ the Egyptians ⟨ upon ⟨⟨ is He — ⟨ Blessed ⟨ — the Holy ⟨⟨ which
One, He brought

בְּמִצְרַיִם הָיְתָה שֶׁל אַרְבַּע מַכּוֹת? שֶׁנֶּאֱמַר,
⟨⟨ — As it says: ⟨⟨ plagues? ⟨ four ⟨ of ⟨ consisted ⟨ in Egypt

יְשַׁלַּח בָּם חֲרוֹן אַפּוֹ – עֶבְרָה, וָזַעַם, וְצָרָה,
⟨⟨ and ⟨ wrath, ⟨ fury, ⟨⟨ His fierce anger, ⟨ upon ⟨ He sent
trouble, them

מִשְׁלַחַת מַלְאֲכֵי רָעִים. עֶבְרָה, אַחַת. וָזַעַם,
⟨ wrath, ⟨⟨ [is] one; ⟨ Fury ⟨⟨ of evil. ⟨ of emissaries ⟨ a band

שְׁתַּיִם. וְצָרָה, שָׁלֹשׁ. מִשְׁלַחַת מַלְאֲכֵי רָעִים,
⟨ of evil, ⟨ of emissaries ⟨ and a band ⟨⟨ three; ⟨ trouble, ⟨⟨ two;

אַרְבַּע. אֱמוֹר מֵעַתָּה, בְּמִצְרַיִם לָקוּ אַרְבָּעִים
⟨ [with] forty ⟨ they were ⟨ [if] in Egypt ⟨ from this ⟨ Conclude ⟨⟨ four.
afflicted

מַכּוֹת, וְעַל הַיָּם לָקוּ מָאתַיִם מַכּוֹת.
⟨⟨ plagues! ⟨ [with] two ⟨ they were ⟨ the ⟨ [then] at ⟨⟨ plagues,
hundred afflicted Sea

רַבִּי עֲקִיבָא אוֹמֵר. מִנַּיִן שֶׁכָּל מַכָּה וּמַכָּה
⟨ single plague ⟨ that ⟨ From what ⟨⟨ says: ⟨ Akiva ⟨ Rabbi
every [passage can
one derive]

שֶׁהֵבִיא הַקָּדוֹשׁ בָּרוּךְ הוּא עַל הַמִּצְרִים
⟨ the Egyptians ⟨ upon ⟨⟨ is He — ⟨ Blessed ⟨ — the Holy ⟨⟨ which
One, He brought

בְּמִצְרַיִם הָיְתָה שֶׁל חָמֵשׁ מַכּוֹת? שֶׁנֶּאֱמַר,
⟨⟨ — As it says: ⟨⟨ plagues? ⟨ five ⟨ of ⟨ consisted ⟨⟨ in Egypt,

יְשַׁלַּח בָּם חֲרוֹן אַפּוֹ, עֶבְרָה, וָזַעַם, וְצָרָה,
⟨⟨ and ⟨ wrath, ⟨ fury, ⟨ His fierce anger, ⟨ upon ⟨ He sent
trouble, them

(1) *Psalms* 78:49.

NIRTZAH   hALLEL   BARECH   TZAFUN   shULCHAN ORECH   KORECH   MAROR

מְשַׁלַּחַת מַלְאֲכֵי רָעִים. חֲרוֹן אַפּוֹ, אַחַת.[1]

‹‹ [is] one; ‹ His fierce anger ‹‹ of evil. ‹ of emissaries ‹ a band

עֶבְרָה, שְׁתַּיִם. וָזַעַם, שָׁלֹשׁ. וְצָרָה, אַרְבַּע.

‹‹ four; ‹ trouble, ‹‹ three; ‹ wrath, ‹‹ two; ‹ Fury

מְשַׁלַּחַת מַלְאֲכֵי רָעִים, חָמֵשׁ. אֱמוֹר מֵעַתָּה,

‹ from this ‹ Conclude ‹‹ five. ‹ of evil, ‹ of emissaries ‹ and a band

בְּמִצְרַיִם לָקוּ חֲמִשִּׁים מַכּוֹת, וְעַל הַיָּם לָקוּ

‹ they were ‹ the ‹ [then] ‹‹ plagues, ‹ [with] fifty ‹ they were ‹ [if] in Egypt
afflicted Sea at afflicted

חֲמִשִּׁים וּמָאתַיִם מַכּוֹת.

‹‹ plagues! ‹ and two hundred ‹ [with] fifty

כַּמָּה מַעֲלוֹת* טוֹבוֹת לַמָּקוֹם עָלֵינוּ.

‹‹ that it behooves us ‹ from the ‹ of goodness ‹ [are] the ‹ How
[to praise Him for]! Omnipresent levels* numerous

אִלּוּ הוֹצִיאָנוּ מִמִּצְרַיִם

‹ of Egypt, ‹ He had ‹ If
brought us out

וְלֹא עָשָׂה בָהֶם שְׁפָטִים דַּיֵּנוּ.

‹‹ we would have enough ‹ judgments, ‹ against ‹ executed ‹ but not
[reason to praise Him]. them

אִלּוּ עָשָׂה בָהֶם שְׁפָטִים

‹ judgments, ‹ against ‹ He had ‹ If
them executed

וְלֹא עָשָׂה בֵאלֹהֵיהֶם דַּיֵּנוּ.

‹‹ we would have enough ‹ against their gods, ‹ acted ‹ but not
[reason to praise Him].

---

(1) Psalms 78:49.

כַּמָּה מַעֲלוֹת — *How numerous [are] the levels.* In bringing us forth from slavery, God's actions went through three stages: 1. He brought punishments upon our oppressors the Egyptians, their gods, their eldest and their property; 2. He effected our physical salvation by leading us through the split Sea and catering to our physical needs; 3. and He presented us with spiritual redemption in the form of the Sabbath, the Torah, the Holy Land and the Temple.

אִלוּ עָשָׂה בֵאלֹהֵיהֶם

‹ against their gods, ‹ He had acted ‹ If

וְלֹא הָרַג אֶת בְּכוֹרֵיהֶם

‹ their firstborn, ‹ slain ‹ but not

דַּיֵּנוּ.

« we would have enough [reason to praise Him].

אִלוּ הָרַג אֶת בְּכוֹרֵיהֶם

‹ their firstborn, ‹ He had slain ‹ If

וְלֹא נָתַן לָנוּ אֶת מָמוֹנָם

‹ their wealth, ‹ us ‹ given ‹ but not

דַּיֵּנוּ.

« we would have enough [reason to praise Him].

אִלוּ נָתַן לָנוּ אֶת מָמוֹנָם

‹ their wealth, ‹ us ‹ He had ‹ If
given

וְלֹא קָרַע לָנוּ אֶת הַיָּם

‹ the Sea, ‹ for us ‹ split ‹ but not

דַּיֵּנוּ.

« we would have enough [reason to praise Him].

אִלוּ קָרַע לָנוּ אֶת הַיָּם

‹ the Sea, ‹ for us ‹ He had ‹ If
split

וְלֹא הֶעֱבִירָנוּ בְּתוֹכוֹ בֶּחָרָבָה דַּיֵּנוּ.

« we would have enough ‹ on dry land, ‹ through it ‹ led us ‹ but not
[reason to praise Him].

אִלוּ הֶעֱבִירָנוּ בְּתוֹכוֹ בֶּחָרָבָה

‹ on dry land, ‹ through it ‹ He had led us ‹ If

וְלֹא שִׁקַּע צָרֵינוּ בְּתוֹכוֹ

‹ in it, ‹ our ‹ drowned ‹ but not
oppressors

דַּיֵּנוּ.

« we would have enough [reason to praise Him].

אִלוּ שִׁקַּע צָרֵינוּ בְּתוֹכוֹ

‹ in it, ‹ our ‹ He had ‹ If
oppressors drowned

וְלֹא סִפֵּק צָרְכֵּנוּ בַּמִּדְבָּר

‹ in the desert ‹ for our needs ‹ provided ‹ but not

NIRTZAH · hALLEL · BARECH · TZAFUN · shULCHAN ORECH · KORECH · MAROR

אַרְבָּעִים שָׁנָה
for forty ⟩ years, ⟩

דַּיֵּנוּ.
⟪ we would have enough [reason to praise Him].

אִלּוּ סִפֵּק צָרְכֵּנוּ בַּמִּדְבָּר אַרְבָּעִים שָׁנָה
If ⟩ He had ⟩ for our ⟩ in the ⟩ for forty ⟩ years, ⟩
provided needs desert

וְלֹא הֶאֱכִילָנוּ אֶת הַמָּן
but not ⟩ fed us ⟩ the manna, ⟩

דַּיֵּנוּ.
⟪ we would have enough [reason to praise Him].

אִלּוּ הֶאֱכִילָנוּ אֶת הַמָּן
If ⟩ He had fed us ⟩ the manna, ⟩

וְלֹא נָתַן לָנוּ אֶת הַשַּׁבָּת
but not ⟩ given ⟩ us ⟩ the Shabbos, ⟩

דַּיֵּנוּ.
⟪ we would have enough [reason to praise Him].

אִלּוּ נָתַן לָנוּ אֶת הַשַּׁבָּת
If ⟩ He had ⟩ us ⟩ the Shabbos, ⟩
given

וְלֹא קֵרְבָנוּ לִפְנֵי הַר סִינַי
but not ⟩ brought us ⟩ before ⟩ Mount ⟩ Sinai, ⟩

דַּיֵּנוּ.
⟪ we would have enough [reason to praise Him].

אִלּוּ קֵרְבָנוּ לִפְנֵי הַר סִינַי
If ⟩ He had ⟩ before ⟩ Mount ⟩ Sinai, ⟩
brought us

וְלֹא נָתַן לָנוּ אֶת הַתּוֹרָה
but not ⟩ given ⟩ us ⟩ the Torah, ⟩

דַּיֵּנוּ.
⟪ we would have enough [reason to praise Him].

אִלּוּ נָתַן לָנוּ אֶת הַתּוֹרָה
If ⟩ He had ⟩ us ⟩ the Torah, ⟩
given

וְלֹא הִכְנִיסָנוּ לְאֶרֶץ יִשְׂרָאֵל
but not ⟩ brought us in ⟩ to the Land ⟩ of Israel, ⟩

דַּיֵּנוּ.
⟪ we would have enough [reason to praise Him].

אִלּוּ הִכְנִיסָנוּ לְאֶרֶץ יִשְׂרָאֵל

⟨ of Israel, ⟨ to the Land ⟨ He had ⟨ If
brought us in

וְלֹא בָנָה לָנוּ אֶת בֵּית הַבְּחִירָה דַּיֵּנוּ.

《 we would have enough ⟨ that is ⟨ the Temple ⟨ for us ⟨ built ⟨ but not
[reason to praise Him]. Chosen

עַל אַחַת כַּמָּה וְכַמָּה טוֹבָה כְפוּלָה וּמְכֻפֶּלֶת

⟨ and ⟨ doubled ⟨ goodnesses ⟨ many ⟨ are the 《 for ⟨ Far beyond
redoubled many one [our obligation
[act], to praise Him]

לַמָּקוֹם עָלֵינוּ. שֶׁהוֹצִיאָנוּ מִמִּצְרַיִם, וְעָשָׂה בָהֶם

⟨ against ⟨ executed 《 of Egypt; ⟨ He brought 《 that it behooves ⟨ from the
them us out us [to praise Omnipresent
Him for]:

שְׁפָטִים, וְעָשָׂה בֵאלֹהֵיהֶם, וְהָרַג אֶת בְּכוֹרֵיהֶם,

《 their firstborn; ⟨ slew 《 against their gods; ⟨ acted 《 judgments;

וְנָתַן לָנוּ אֶת מָמוֹנָם, וְקָרַע לָנוּ אֶת הַיָּם,

《 the Sea; ⟨ for us ⟨ split 《 their wealth; ⟨ us ⟨ gave

וְהֶעֱבִירָנוּ בְתוֹכוֹ בֶּחָרָבָה, וְשִׁקַּע צָרֵינוּ בְּתוֹכוֹ,

《 in it; ⟨ our ⟨ drowned 《 on dry land; ⟨ through it ⟨ led us
oppressors

וְסִפֵּק צָרְכֵּנוּ בַּמִּדְבָּר אַרְבָּעִים שָׁנָה, וְהֶאֱכִילָנוּ

⟨ fed us 《 years; ⟨ for forty ⟨ in the desert ⟨ for our needs ⟨ provided

אֶת הַמָּן, וְנָתַן לָנוּ אֶת הַשַּׁבָּת, וְקֵרְבָנוּ לִפְנֵי

⟨ before ⟨ brought us 《 the Shabbos; ⟨ us ⟨ gave 《 the manna;

הַר סִינַי, וְנָתַן לָנוּ אֶת הַתּוֹרָה, וְהִכְנִיסָנוּ לְאֶרֶץ

⟨ to the Land ⟨ brought us in 《 the Torah; ⟨ us ⟨ gave 《 Sinai; ⟨ Mount

יִשְׂרָאֵל, וּבָנָה לָנוּ אֶת בֵּית הַבְּחִירָה, לְכַפֵּר

⟨ to atone 《 that is chosen, ⟨ the Temple ⟨ for us ⟨ and built 《 of Israel;

עַל כָּל עֲוֹנוֹתֵינוּ.

《 our sins. ⟨ all ⟨ for

מָרוֹר כּוֹרֵךְ שֻׁלְחָן עוֹרֵךְ צָפוּן בָּרֵךְ הַלֵּל נִרְצָה

NIRTZAh hALLEL BARECh TZAFUN ShULChAN ORECh kORECh MAROR

רַבָּן גַּמְלִיאֵל הָיָה אוֹמֵר. כָּל שֶׁלֹּא אָמַר*

< explained* < has not < Whoever << to say: < used < Gamliel < Rabban

שְׁלֹשָׁה דְבָרִים אֵלּוּ בַּפֶּסַח, לֹא יָצָא יְדֵי

< fulfilled < has not < on Pesach < that follow < concepts < the three

חוֹבָתוֹ, וְאֵלּוּ הֵן,

< are they: < and these << his duty,

פֶּסַח. מַצָּה. וּמָרוֹר.

<< Maror — the < Matzah — the < Pesach — the
bitter herbs. unleavened bread; pesach offering;

פֶּסַח שֶׁהָיוּ אֲבוֹתֵינוּ אוֹכְלִים בִּזְמַן שֶׁבֵּית

< that the < at the < eat < — that our fathers would << The pesach
Temple time offering

הַמִּקְדָּשׁ הָיָה קַיָּם, עַל שׁוּם מָה? עַל שׁוּם

< the < For << what purpose? < for << in < was < of Holiness
reason existence —

שֶׁפָּסַח הַקָּדוֹשׁ בָּרוּךְ הוּא עַל בָּתֵּי אֲבוֹתֵינוּ

< of our < the < over << is He — < Blessed < — the Holy << that He
fathers houses One, passed

בְּמִצְרַיִם. שֶׁנֶּאֱמַר, וַאֲמַרְתֶּם, זֶבַח פֶּסַח הוּא

< it is < [for] < 'An << You shall say: << as it says: << in Egypt,
pesach offering

לַיהוה, אֲשֶׁר פָּסַח עַל בָּתֵּי בְּנֵי יִשְׂרָאֵל

< of Israel < of the < the < over < passed < Who << to HASHEM,
Children houses

בְּמִצְרַיִם בְּנָגְפּוֹ אֶת מִצְרַיִם, וְאֶת בָּתֵּינוּ הִצִּיל,

<< He saved'; < while our houses < the Egyptians < when He struck < in Egypt

וַיִּקֹּד הָעָם וַיִּשְׁתַּחֲווּ.[1]

<< and prostrated themselves. < and the people bowed down

---

(1) Exodus 12:27.

כָּל שֶׁלֹּא אָמַר — Whoever has not explained.
Even if one has performed the physical act of
eating pesach, matzah, and maror, as long as
he has not explained the reason for these

THE MIDDLE MATZAH IS LIFTED AND DISPLAYED WHILE THE FOLLOWING PARAGRAPH IS RECITED.

מַצָּה זוּ שֶׁאָנוּ אוֹכְלִים, עַל שׁוּם מָה? עַל

‹ For ❯❯ what purpose? ‹ for ❮❮ eat — ‹ — that we ❮❮ This unleavened bread

שׁוּם שֶׁלֹּא הִסְפִּיק בְּצֵקָם שֶׁל אֲבוֹתֵינוּ

‹ our fathers ‹ of ‹ for the dough ‹ sufficient time ‹ that there was not ‹ the reason

לְהַחֲמִיץ, עַד שֶׁנִּגְלָה עֲלֵיהֶם מֶלֶךְ מַלְכֵי

‹ over kings ‹ the King ‹ to them ‹ there was revealed ‹ before ❮❮ to become leavened,

הַמְּלָכִים הַקָּדוֹשׁ בָּרוּךְ הוּא וּגְאָלָם. שֶׁנֶּאֱמַר,

❮❮ as it says: ❮❮ and He ❮❮ is He, ‹ Blessed ‹ the Holy One, redeemed them, of kings,

וַיֹּאפוּ אֶת הַבָּצֵק אֲשֶׁר הוֹצִיאוּ מִמִּצְרַיִם עֻגֹת

‹ into bread ‹ of Egypt ‹ they had taken out ‹ which ‹ the dough ‹ They baked

מַצּוֹת כִּי לֹא חָמֵץ, כִּי גֹרְשׁוּ מִמִּצְרַיִם, וְלֹא

‹ and they were not ‹ of Egypt ‹ they were driven out ‹ because ❮❮ fermented, ‹ it had not ‹ for ❮❮ that was unleavened,

יָכְלוּ לְהִתְמַהְמֵהַּ, וְגַם צֵדָה לֹא עָשׂוּ לָהֶם.¹

❮❮ for themselves. ‹ prepared ‹ they ‹ provisions ‹ in ❮❮ to delay; ‹ able had not [for the way] addition,

THE *MAROR* IS LIFTED AND DISPLAYED WHILE THE FOLLOWING PARAGRAPH IS RECITED.

מָרוֹר זֶה שֶׁאָנוּ אוֹכְלִים, עַל שׁוּם מָה? עַל

‹ For ❮❮ what purpose? ‹ for ❮❮ eat — ‹ — that we ❮❮ These bitter herbs

שׁוּם שֶׁמֵּרְרוּ הַמִּצְרִים אֶת חַיֵּי אֲבוֹתֵינוּ

‹ of our fathers ‹ the lives ‹ that the Egyptians embittered ‹ the reason

בְּמִצְרָיִם. שֶׁנֶּאֱמַר, וַיְמָרְרוּ אֶת חַיֵּיהֶם, בַּעֲבֹדָה

‹ with work ‹ their lives ‹ They embittered ❮❮ as it says: ❮❮ in Egypt,

(1) Exodus 12:39.

mitzvos, he has not met his obligation. The Torah intertwines אֲמִירָה וְהַגָּדָה (Exodus 12:27; 13:8,14; et al.), *saying and retelling,* with the observance of these *mitzvos* (Orchos Chaim).

NIRTZAH hALLEL BARECh TZAFUN shULCHAN ORECh KORECh MAROR

קָשֶׁה, בְּחֹמֶר וּבִלְבֵנִים, וּבְכָל עֲבֹדָה בַּשָּׂדֶה,
‹‹ in the field; ‹ manner of labor ‹ and with every ‹ and with bricks, ‹ with mortar ‹‹ that is hard,

אֵת כָּל עֲבֹדָתָם אֲשֶׁר עָבְדוּ בָהֶם בְּפָרֶךְ.[1]
‹‹ crushing harshness. ‹ with them ‹ they performed ‹ that ‹ their labors ‹ all

בְּכָל דּוֹר וָדוֹר חַיָּב אָדָם לִרְאוֹת אֶת עַצְמוֹ
‹ himself ‹ to regard ‹ it is one's duty ‹ after ‹ generation ‹ In every generation

כְּאִלּוּ הוּא יָצָא מִמִּצְרָיִם. שֶׁנֶּאֱמַר, וְהִגַּדְתָּ
‹ You shall tell ‹‹ of Egypt, ‹ had gone out ‹ he personally ‹ as though ‹‹ as it says:

לְבִנְךָ בַּיּוֹם הַהוּא לֵאמֹר, בַּעֲבוּר זֶה עָשָׂה יהוה
‹ that HASHEM did ‹ this ‹ 'It was because of ‹‹ saying: ‹ on that day, ‹ your son

לִי, בְּצֵאתִי מִמִּצְרָיִם.[2] לֹא אֶת אֲבוֹתֵינוּ בִּלְבָד
‹ alone ‹ our fathers ‹ Not ‹‹ of Egypt.' ‹ when I went out ‹ for 'me'

גָּאַל הַקָּדוֹשׁ בָּרוּךְ הוּא, אֶלָּא אַף אֹתָנוּ גָּאַל
‹ did He redeem ‹ us ‹ also ‹ but ‹‹ is He; ‹ Blessed ‹ — the Holy One, ‹‹ did He redeem

עִמָּהֶם. שֶׁנֶּאֱמַר, וְאוֹתָנוּ הוֹצִיא מִשָּׁם, לְמַעַן
‹ in order ‹ from there ‹ He took out ‹ 'Us' ‹‹ as it says: ‹‹ with them,

הָבִיא אֹתָנוּ לָתֵת לָנוּ אֶת הָאָרֶץ אֲשֶׁר נִשְׁבַּע
‹ He swore ‹ that ‹ the land ‹ to us ‹ to give ‹‹ us, ‹ to bring

לַאֲבוֹתֵינוּ.[3]
‹‹ to our fathers.

(1) Exodus 1:14. (2) 13:8. (3) Deuteronomy 6:23.

ATZAh MOTZI RACHTZAh **MAGGID** YACHATZ KARPAS URECHATZ KADDESH

THE MATZOS ARE COVERED AND THE CUP IS LIFTED AND HELD UNTIL IT IS TO BE DRUNK. ACCORDING TO SOME CUSTOMS, HOWEVER, THE CUP IS PUT DOWN AFTER THE FOLLOWING PARAGRAPH, IN WHICH CASE THE MATZOS SHOULD ONCE MORE BE UNCOVERED.

לְפִיכָךְ אֲנַחְנוּ חַיָּבִים לְהוֹדוֹת, לְהַלֵּל,

‹ to laud, ‹ to thank, ‹ are obligated ‹ we ‹ Therefore

לְשַׁבֵּחַ, לְפָאֵר, לְרוֹמֵם, לְהַדֵּר, לְבָרֵךְ, לְעַלֵּה,

‹ to elevate, ‹ to bless, ‹ to honor, ‹ to exalt, ‹ to glorify, ‹ to praise,

וּלְקַלֵּס, לְמִי שֶׁעָשָׂה לַאֲבוֹתֵינוּ וְלָנוּ אֶת כָּל

‹ all ‹ and for us ‹ for our fathers ‹ Who performed ‹ to the One ‹ and to sing praises

הַנִּסִּים הָאֵלּוּ, הוֹצִיאָנוּ מֵעַבְדוּת לְחֵרוּת,

《 to freedom, ‹ from slavery ‹ He brought us forth 《 these miracles:

מִיָּגוֹן לְשִׂמְחָה, וּמֵאֵבֶל לְיוֹם טוֹב, וּמֵאֲפֵלָה

‹ from darkness ‹ of festivity, 《 to days ‹ from mourning 《 to joy, ‹ from sorrow

לְאוֹר גָּדוֹל, וּמִשִּׁעְבּוּד לִגְאֻלָּה. וְנֹאמַר לְפָנָיו

‹ before Him ‹ Therefore, we shall recite 《 to redemption. ‹ and from bondage 《 to great light,

שִׁירָה חֲדָשָׁה, הַלְלוּיָהּ.

《 Halleluyah! 《 a new song!

——— תהלים קיג / Psalm 113 ———

הַלְלוּיָהּ* הַלְלוּ עַבְדֵי יהוה, הַלְלוּ אֶת שֵׁם

‹ Name ‹ the ‹ praise 《 of ‹ you ‹ Give 《 Halleluyah!*
HASHEM; servants praise,

יהוה. יְהִי שֵׁם יהוה מְבֹרָךְ, מֵעַתָּה וְעַד עוֹלָם.

《 eternity. ‹ until ‹ from this time 《 be blessed, ‹ of HASHEM ‹ the Name ‹ Let 《 of HASHEM!

מִמִּזְרַח שֶׁמֶשׁ עַד מְבוֹאוֹ, מְהֻלָּל שֵׁם יהוה. רָם

‹ High 《 of HASHEM. ‹ is the Name ‹ praised 《 its setting, ‹ to ‹ of the sun ‹ From the rising

הַלְלוּיָה — *Halleluyah!* We are no longer Pharaoh's slaves; our obligations are solely to the One who elevated us from our lowly stature in Egypt and endowed us with nobility.

NIRTZAh   hALLEL   BARECH   TZAFUN   shULCHAN ORECH   KORECH   MARO

עַל כָּל גּוֹיִם יהוה, עַל הַשָּׁמַיִם כְּבוֹדוֹ. מִי

‹ Who ‹‹ is His ‹ the heavens ‹ above ‹‹ is ‹ nations ‹ all ‹ above
glory. HASHEM,

כַּיהוה אֱלֹהֵינוּ, הַמַּגְבִּיהִי לָשָׁבֶת. הַמַּשְׁפִּילִי

‹ — yet deigns ‹‹ is enthroned ‹ Who on high ‹‹ our God, ‹ is like HASHEM,

לִרְאוֹת, בַּשָּׁמַיִם וּבָאָרֶץ. מְקִימִי מֵעָפָר דָּל,

‹‹ the ‹ from the ‹ He raises ‹‹ and the earth? ‹ upon the ‹ to look
needy, dust heavens

מֵאַשְׁפֹּת יָרִים אֶבְיוֹן. לְהוֹשִׁיבִי עִם נְדִיבִים,

‹‹ nobles, ‹ with ‹ to seat them ‹‹ the ‹ He lifts ‹ from the
destitute, trash heaps

עִם נְדִיבֵי עַמּוֹ. מוֹשִׁיבִי עֲקֶרֶת הַבַּיִת, אֵם

‹ into a ‹ of the house ‹ the barren ‹ He transforms ‹‹ of His ‹ the nobles ‹ with
mother woman people.

הַבָּנִים שְׂמֵחָה; הַלְלוּיָהּ.

‹‹ Halleluyah! ‹‹ who is joyous. ‹ of children

——— Psalm 114 / תהלים קיד ———

בְּצֵאת יִשְׂרָאֵל* מִמִּצְרָיִם, בֵּית יַעֲקֹב

‹ of Jacob ‹ the household ‹‹ of Egypt, ‹ When Israel went out*

מֵעַם לֹעֵז. הָיְתָה יְהוּדָה לְקָדְשׁוֹ, יִשְׂרָאֵל

‹ Israel ‹‹ His sanctuary, ‹ Judah became ‹‹ of alien ‹ from a
tongue, people

מַמְשְׁלוֹתָיו. הַיָּם רָאָה וַיָּנֹס, הַיַּרְדֵּן יִסֹּב

‹ turned ‹ the Jordan ‹‹ and fled; ‹ saw ‹ The sea ‹‹ His dominions.

לְאָחוֹר. הֶהָרִים רָקְדוּ כְאֵילִים, גְּבָעוֹת כִּבְנֵי

‹ like young ‹ the hills ‹‹ like rams; ‹ skipped ‹ The mountains ‹‹ backward.

צֹאן. מַה לְּךָ הַיָּם כִּי תָנוּס, הַיַּרְדֵּן תִּסֹּב

‹ that you turn ‹ O Jordan, ‹‹ you flee? ‹ that ‹ O sea, ‹ ails you, ‹ What ‹‹ lambs.

בְּצֵאת יִשְׂרָאֵל — *When Israel went out.* The laws of nature were subverted during the Exodus. Sea and mountain fled to allow God and His nation to pass.

קַדֵּשׁ וּרְחַץ כַּרְפַּס יַחַץ מַגִּיד רָחְצָה מוֹצִיא מַצָּ
ATZAh MOTZI RACHTZAh MAGGID YACHATZ KARPAS URECHATZ KADDESH

לְאָחוֹר. הֶהָרִים תִּרְקְדוּ כְאֵילִים, גְּבָעוֹת כִּבְנֵי

‹ like young ⟨ O hills, ⟪ like rams? ‹ that you skip ⟨ O mountains, ⟪ backward?

צֹאן. מִלִּפְנֵי אָדוֹן חוּלִי אָרֶץ, מִלִּפְנֵי אֱלוֹהַּ

‹ of the God ‹ before the presence ⟪ did the earth, ‹ tremble ‹ of the Lord ‹ Before the Presence ⟪ lambs?

יַעֲקֹב. הַהֹפְכִי הַצּוּר אֲגַם מָיִם, חַלָּמִישׁ

‹ the flint ⟪ of water, ‹ into a pond ‹ the rock ‹ Who turns ⟪ of Jacob,

לְמַעְיְנוֹ מָיִם.

⟪ of water. ‹ into a flowing fountain

ACCORDING TO ALL CUSTOMS THE CUP IS HELD ALOFT AND THE MATZOS COVERED
DURING THE RECITATION OF THIS BLESSING.

בָּרוּךְ אַתָּה יהוה אֱלֹהֵינוּ מֶלֶךְ הָעוֹלָם, אֲשֶׁר

‹ Who ⟪ of the universe, ‹ King ‹ our God, ‹ HASHEM, ‹ are ‹ Blessed You,

גְּאָלָנוּ וְגָאַל אֶת אֲבוֹתֵינוּ מִמִּצְרַיִם, וְהִגִּיעָנוּ

‹ and brought us, ⟪ from Egypt, ‹ our fathers ‹ and redeemed ‹ redeemed us

הַלַּיְלָה הַזֶּה לֶאֱכָל בּוֹ מַצָּה וּמָרוֹר. כֵּן יהוה

‹ HASHEM, ‹ So, [we ⟪ and pray that] *maror.* ‹ matzah ‹ on it ‹ that we may eat ‹ this night,

אֱלֹהֵינוּ וֵאלֹהֵי אֲבוֹתֵינוּ, יַגִּיעֵנוּ* לְמוֹעֲדִים

‹ to the appointed Holidays ‹ will bring us* ⟪ of our fathers, ‹ and the God ‹ our God

וְלִרְגָלִים אֲחֵרִים הַבָּאִים לִקְרָאתֵנוּ לְשָׁלוֹם,

⟪ in peace, ‹ upon us ‹ that come ‹ and other pilgrimage Festivals

שְׂמֵחִים* בְּבִנְיַן עִירֶךְ וְשָׂשִׂים* בַּעֲבוֹדָתֶךָ,

⟪ in Your [Temple] service. ‹ and joyful* ‹ of Your City ‹ in the building ‹ gladdened*

יַגִּיעֵנוּ — *Will bring us.* The Exodus was not an end unto itself, but a prelude to our entry into the Holy Land and the erection of the Temple in Jerusalem. Thus, the formal thanksgiving blessing for the redemption includes a prayer

for a rebuilt Temple and the resumption of our worship there.

שְׂמֵחִים וְשָׂשִׂים — *Gladdened . . . and joyful.* The Vilna Gaon (*Divrei Eliyahu, Job* 3:21) explains the difference between שִׂמְחָה, *gladness,* and

NIRTZAH HALLEL BARECH TZAFUN SHULCHAN ORECH KORECH MAROR

ON SATURDAY NIGHT SOME SUBSTITUTE: | **ON A REGULAR NIGHT:**

וְנֹאכַל שָׁם מִן
‹ from ‹ there ‹ We shall eat

וְנֹאכַל שָׁם מִן
‹ from ‹ there ‹ We shall eat

הַפְּסָחִים וּמִן הַזְּבָחִים*
‹ the [Festival] ‹ and ‹ the *pesach*
offerings* from offerings

הַזְּבָחִים וּמִן הַפְּסָחִים
‹ the *pesach* ‹ and ‹ the [Festival]
offerings from offerings

אֲשֶׁר יַגִּיעַ דָּמָם עַל קִיר מִזְבַּחֲךָ* לְרָצוֹן. וְנוֹדֶה
‹ We shall ‹‹ for gracious ‹ of Your ‹ the ‹ upon ‹ their blood will ‹ that
then sing acceptance. Altar* wall be touched

לְךָ שִׁיר חָדָשׁ עַל גְּאֻלָּתֵנוּ וְעַל פְּדוּת נַפְשֵׁנוּ.
‹‹ of our ‹ the ‹ and for ‹ our ‹ for ‹ a new song ‹ to You
souls. liberation redemption

בָּרוּךְ אַתָּה יהוה, גָּאַל יִשְׂרָאֵל.
‹‹ Israel. ‹ Who redeemed ‹‹ Hashem, ‹ are You, ‹ Blessed

SOME RECITE THE FOLLOWING BEFORE THE SECOND CUP:

הֲרֵינִי מוּכָן וּמְזוּמָּן לְקַיֵּם מִצְוַת כּוֹס שֵׁנִי מֵאַרְבַּע כּוֹסוֹת.
‹‹ Cups. ‹ of the ‹ of the ‹ the ‹ to ‹ and ‹ am ‹ I now
Four second cup mitzvah perform ready prepared

לְשֵׁם יִחוּד קֻדְשָׁא בְּרִיךְ הוּא וּשְׁכִינְתֵּיהּ, עַל יְדֵי הַהוּא טָמִיר
‹ Who is ‹ Him ‹ through ‹‹ and His ‹‹ is He, ‹ Blessed ‹‹ of the Holy ‹ of the ‹ For the
hidden Presence, One, unification sake

וְנֶעְלָם, בְּשֵׁם כָּל יִשְׂרָאֵל. וִיהִי נֹעַם אֲדֹנָי אֱלֹהֵינוּ
‹ our God, ‹ of the ‹ the plea- ‹ May ‹‹ Israel. ‹ of all ‹ [I pray] ‹‹ and Who is
Lord, santness in the name inscrutable

עָלֵינוּ, וּמַעֲשֵׂה יָדֵינוּ כּוֹנְנָה עָלֵינוּ, וּמַעֲשֵׂה יָדֵינוּ כּוֹנְנֵהוּ.¹
‹‹ establish ‹ of our ‹ the work ‹ for us; ‹ establish ‹ of our ‹ the work ‹‹ be
it. hands, hands, upon us;

---

(1) *Psalms* 90:17.

שָׂשׂוֹן, joy, is that שִׂמְחָה relates to the beginning of the event, and שָׂשׂוֹן relates to its completion. Thus we are שְׂמֵחִים, *gladdened, in the building of Your City*, the first phase, and שָׂשִׂים, *joyful in Your [Temple] service*, the culmination of the process with the reestablishment of the Temple service.

מִן הַפְּסָחִים וּמִן הַזְּבָחִים — *From the pesach offerings and from the [Festival] offerings.* R' Yaakov Weil directs that when the *Seder* is on

Motzei Shabbos, we mentioned the *pesach* offering first, since only it was brought on the Sabbath. The Festival offerings were brought on subsequent days of the Festival.

עַל קִיר מִזְבַּחֲךָ — *Upon the wall of your altar.* In contrast to the חַטָּאת וְאָשָׁם, the sin and guilt offerings, whose blood was sprinkled on the corners of the altar, the offerings denoting rejoicing, תּוֹדָה, עוֹלָה, שְׁלָמִים, פֶּסַח, וַחֲגִיגָה, the thanksgiving, elevation, peace, *pesach*, and

KADDESH URECHATZ KARPAS YACHATZ MAGGID RACHTZAH MOTZI MATZAH

בָּרוּךְ אַתָּה יהוה אֱלֹהֵינוּ מֶלֶךְ הָעוֹלָם,
《《 of the universe, 《 King 〈 our God, 〈 HASHEM, 〈 are You, 〈 Blessed

בּוֹרֵא פְּרִי הַגָּפֶן.
《《 of the 〈 the 〈 Who
vine. fruit creates

THE WINE SHOULD BE DRUNK WITHOUT DELAY WHILE RECLINING ON THE LEFT SIDE. IT IS PREFERABLE TO DRINK THE ENTIRE CUP, BUT AT THE VERY LEAST, MOST OF THE CUP SHOULD BE DRAINED.

❊{ RACHTZAH / רחצה }❊

THE HANDS ARE WASHED FOR MATZAH AND THE FOLLOWING BLESSING IS RECITED. IT IS PREFERABLE TO BRING WATER AND A BASIN TO THE HEAD OF THE HOUSEHOLD AT THE SEDER TABLE.

בָּרוּךְ אַתָּה יהוה אֱלֹהֵינוּ מֶלֶךְ הָעוֹלָם, אֲשֶׁר
〈 Who 《《 of the universe, 〈 King 〈 our God, 〈 HASHEM, 〈 are You, 〈 Blessed

קִדְּשָׁנוּ בְּמִצְוֹתָיו, וְצִוָּנוּ עַל נְטִילַת יָדָיִם.
《《 the 〈 washing 〈 regarding 〈 and has com- 〈 with His 〈 has sancti-
hands. manded us commandments fied us

❊{ MOTZI / *מוֹצִיא }❊

SOME RECITE THE FOLLOWING BEFORE THE BLESSING *HAMOTZI*:

הִנְנִי מוּכָן וּמְזוּמָּן לְקַיֵּם מִצְוַת אֲכִילַת מַצָּה. לְשֵׁם יִחוּד
〈 of the 〈 For the 《《 matzah. 〈 of eating 〈 the 〈 to 〈 and 〈 am 〈 I now
unification sake mitzvah perform ready prepared

קֻדְשָׁא בְּרִיךְ הוּא וּשְׁכִינְתֵּיהּ, עַל יְדֵי הַהוּא טָמִיר וְנֶעְלָם,
《《 and Who is 〈 Who is 〈 Him 〈 through 《《 and His 《《 is He, 〈 Blessed 《《 of the
inscrutable hidden Presence, Holy One,

בְּשֵׁם כָּל יִשְׂרָאֵל. וִיהִי נֹעַם אֲדֹנָי אֱלֹהֵינוּ עָלֵינוּ, וּמַעֲשֵׂה
〈 the work 《《 be 〈 our God, 〈 of the 〈 the plea- 〈 May 《《 Israel. 〈 of all 〈 — [I pray] in
upon us; Lord, santness the name

יָדֵינוּ כּוֹנְנָה עָלֵינוּ, וּמַעֲשֵׂה יָדֵינוּ כּוֹנְנֵהוּ.¹
《《 establish it. 〈 of our 〈 the work 《《 for us; 〈 establish 〈 of our
hands, hands,

---

(1) *Psalms* 90:17.

festival offerings all have their blood sprinkled on the wall of the altar. Thus we are requesting that in the rebuilt Temple our offerings be of rejoicing and not sin related (*Be'er Miriam*).

מוֹצִיא — *Motzi.* The blessing over matzah as food, as the more common benediction, is recited first. But the matzah of Pesach is no mere substitute for bread. Its use is in fulfillment of a commandment, and requires a blessing of its own.

THE FOLLOWING TWO BLESSINGS ARE RECITED OVER MATZAH; THE FIRST IS RECITED OVER MATZAH
AS FOOD, AND THE SECOND FOR THE SPECIAL MITZVAH OF EATING MATZAH ON THE NIGHT OF
PESACH. [THE LATTER BLESSING IS TO BE MADE WITH THE INTENTION THAT IT ALSO APPLY TO THE
KORECH, "SANDWICH," AND THE *AFIKOMAN*.]

THE HEAD OF THE HOUSEHOLD RAISES ALL THE MATZOS ON THE SEDER PLATE AND RECITES THE
FOLLOWING BLESSING FOR HIMSELF AND FOR ALL PARTICIPANTS:

בָּרוּךְ אַתָּה יהוה אֱלֹהֵינוּ מֶלֶךְ הָעוֹלָם,
《 of the universe, 〈 King 〈 our God, 〈 Hashem, 〈 are You, 〈 Blessed

הַמּוֹצִיא לֶחֶם מִן הָאָרֶץ.
《 the earth. 〈 from 〈 bread 〈 Who brings forth

❊{ MATZAH / מצה }❊

THE BOTTOM MATZAH IS PUT DOWN AND THE FOLLOWING BLESSING IS RECITED WHILE
THE TOP (WHOLE) MATZAH AND THE MIDDLE (BROKEN) PIECE ARE STILL RAISED.

בָּרוּךְ אַתָּה יהוה אֱלֹהֵינוּ מֶלֶךְ הָעוֹלָם, אֲשֶׁר
〈 Who 《 of the universe, 〈 King 〈 our God, 〈 Hashem, 〈 are You, 〈 Blessed

קִדְּשָׁנוּ בְּמִצְוֺתָיו, וְצִוָּנוּ עַל אֲכִילַת מַצָּה.
《 of matzah. 〈 the eating 〈 regarding 〈 and has com-manded us 〈 with His commandments 〈 has sancti-fied us

⋖§ Laws of Matzah

1. A piece should be broken off from both of the top two matzos at the same time and eaten together. Each piece should be a *k'zayis* (*Orach Chayim* 475:1, *Mishnah Berurah* §3). (Those who do not have three matzos of their own take the required amount from other matzos, but should receive a small piece from each of the top two matzos. Many maintain that those without their own matzos need eat only one *kezayis*.)
2. Although both *k'zeisim* should be put into the mouth and chewed at one time, they do not have to be swallowed at one time (ibid., *Mishnah Berurah* §9).
3. One must eat this amount of matzah within a period of *kedei achilas pras* (about 2-9 minutes) (ibid.).
4. If it is too hard for someone to eat both *k'zeisim* at one time, he should eat the *k'zayis* from the whole matzah first, and then the second from the broken matzah.
5. If for some reason two *k'zeisim* were not eaten, but only one (from either matzah or from both together), the mitzvah has nevertheless been fulfilled (*Mishnah Berurah* §11).
6. If the matzah was eaten without reclining, one *k'zayis* must be eaten again while reclining (472:7; *Be'ur Halachah* ad loc.).
7. One must be sure to eat the matzah before halachic midnight. (If one did not do so, it is doubtful whether he can still fulfill the mitzvah, and he should eat the matzah without the berachah of אֲשֶׁר קִדְּשָׁנוּ בְּמִצְוֺתָיו (477:1, *Mishnah Berurah* §6).
   If, for some reason, the beginning of the Seder was delayed until just before midnight, one should eat the matzah and maror immediately following Kiddush, and afterwards go back and recite the Haggadah and finish his meal (*Mishnah Berurah* ibid.).
8. Most follow the custom not to dip the matzah in salt after *Hamotzi* at the Seder (475:1).

EACH PARTICIPANT IS REQUIRED TO EAT AN AMOUNT OF MATZAH EQUAL IN VOLUME TO AN EGG (THE SIZE OF TWO OLIVES). SINCE IT IS USUALLY IMPOSSIBLE TO PROVIDE A SUFFICIENT AMOUNT OF MATZAH FROM THE TWO MATZOS FOR ALL MEMBERS OF THE HOUSEHOLD, OTHER MATZOS SHOULD BE AVAILABLE AT THE HEAD OF THE TABLE FROM WHICH TO COMPLETE THE REQUIRED AMOUNTS. HOWEVER, EACH PARTICIPANT SHOULD RECEIVE A PIECE FROM EACH OF THE TOP TWO MATZOS. [IN ORDER TO AVOID DELAY, SOME SUGGEST PREPARING THE PORTIONS OF MATZAH FOR EACH PERSON BEFORE THE SEDER; AT THE SEDER, THE SMALL PIECES FROM THE TOP AND MIDDLE MATZOS ARE ADDED (*MOADIM UZMANIM*).]

THE MATZOS ARE TO BE EATEN WHILE RECLINING ON THE LEFT SIDE AND WITHOUT DELAY; MOST HAVE THE CUSTOM NOT TO DIP THEM IN SALT AT THE SEDER.

❧ MAROR / מָרוֹר* ❧

THE HEAD OF THE HOUSEHOLD TAKES AN OLIVE-SIZE VOLUME OF *MAROR*, DIPS IT INTO *CHAROSES*, AND GIVES EACH PARTICIPANT A LIKE AMOUNT.

SOME RECITE THE FOLLOWING BEFORE *MAROR*:

הִנְנִי מוּכָן וּמְזוּמָּן לְקַיֵּם מִצְוַת אֲכִילַת מָרוֹר. לְשֵׁם יִחוּד

⟨ of the ⟨ For the ⟨⟨ *maror*. ⟨ of eating ⟨ the ⟨ to ⟨ and ⟨ am ⟨ I now
unification sake   mitzvah perform ready prepared

קָדְשָׁא בְּרִיךְ הוּא וּשְׁכִינְתֵּיהּ, עַל יְדֵי הַהוּא טָמִיר וְנֶעְלָם,

⟨⟨ and Who is ⟨ Who is ⟨ Him ⟨ through ⟨⟨ and His ⟨⟨ is He, ⟨ Blessed ⟨⟨ of the
inscrutable hidden   Presence,   Holy One,

בְּשֵׁם כָּל יִשְׂרָאֵל. וִיהִי נֹעַם אֲדֹנָי אֱלֹהֵינוּ עָלֵינוּ, וּמַעֲשֵׂה

⟨ the work ⟨⟨ be ⟨ our God, ⟨ of the ⟨ the plea- ⟨ May ⟨⟨ Israel. ⟨ of all ⟨ — [I pray] in
upon us;   Lord,   santness   the name

יָדֵינוּ כּוֹנְנָה עָלֵינוּ, וּמַעֲשֵׂה יָדֵינוּ כּוֹנְנֵהוּ.¹

⟨⟨ establish it. ⟨ of our ⟨ the work ⟨⟨ for us; ⟨ establish ⟨ of our
hands,   hands,

THE FOLLOWING BLESSING IS RECITED WITH THE INTENTION THAT IT ALSO APPLY TO THE *MAROR* OF THE "SANDWICH." THE *MAROR* IS EATEN WITHOUT RECLINING, AND WITHOUT DELAY.

בָּרוּךְ אַתָּה יהוה אֱלֹהֵינוּ מֶלֶךְ הָעוֹלָם, אֲשֶׁר

⟨ Who ⟨⟨ of the ⟨ King ⟨ our God, ⟨ HASHEM, ⟨ are You, ⟨ Blessed
universe,

קִדְּשָׁנוּ בְּמִצְוֹתָיו, וְצִוָּנוּ עַל אֲכִילַת מָרוֹר.

⟨⟨ of *maror*. ⟨ the ⟨ regarding ⟨ and has com- ⟨ with His ⟨ has sancti-
eating   manded us   commandments   fied us

---

(1) *Psalms* 90:17.

מָרוֹר — *Maror*. The maror symbolizes the bitterness inflicted by the Egyptians. Charoses (literally, potter's clay) resembles the mortar with which our ancestors built Egyptian cities. Addi-

tionally, the apples, nuts, cinnamon and other ingredients of the charoses are used in *Song of Songs* as symbols of the qualities of the Jewish people.

NIRTZAh   hALLEL   BARECh   TZAFUN   ShULChAN OREСh   KORECh   MAROR

∗{ KORECH / כּוֹרֵךְ }∗

THE BOTTOM (THUS FAR UNBROKEN) MATZAH IS NOW TAKEN. FROM IT, WITH THE ADDITION OF OTHER MATZOS, EACH PARTICIPANT RECEIVES AN OLIVE-SIZE VOLUME OF MATZAH WITH AN EQUAL VOLUME PORTION OF *MAROR* (DIPPED INTO *CHAROSES* WHICH IS SHAKEN OFF). THE FOLLOWING PARAGRAPH IS RECITED AND THE "SANDWICH" IS EATEN WHILE RECLINING.

זֵכֶר לְמִקְדָּשׁ כְּהִלֵּל. כֵּן עָשָׂה הִלֵּל בִּזְמַן

⟨ at the ⟨   did Hillel do   ⟨ So ⟪ [we do] as ⟨ of the Temple ⟨ In remem-
time   Hillel [did]   brance

שֶׁבֵּית הַמִּקְדָּשׁ הָיָה קַיָּם. הָיָה כּוֹרֵךְ (פֶּסַח)

⟨ (the *pesach* ⟨ combine in ⟨ He ⟪ still ⟨ was ⟨   that the Temple
offering,)   a sandwich would   standing:

מַצָּה וּמָרוֹר וְאוֹכֵל בְּיַחַד. לְקַיֵּם מַה שֶּׁנֶּאֱמַר,

⟪ it says: ⟨ what ⟨ to fulfill ⟪ together, ⟨ and eat them ⟨ and *maror* ⟨ matzah,

עַל מַצּוֹת וּמְרֹרִים יֹאכְלֻהוּ.¹

⟪ they shall eat it. ⟨ and bitter herbs ⟨ matzos ⟨ with

∗{ SHULCHAN ORECH / שֻׁלְחָן עוֹרֵךְ }∗

THE MEAL SHOULD BE EATEN IN A COMBINATION OF JOY AND SOLEMNITY, FOR THE MEAL, TOO, IS A PART OF THE *SEDER* SERVICE. WHILE IT IS DESIRABLE THAT *ZEMIROS* AND DISCUSSION OF THE LAWS AND EVENTS OF PESACH BE PART OF THE MEAL, EXTRANEOUS CONVERSATION SHOULD BE AVOIDED. IT SHOULD BE REMEMBERED THAT THE *AFIKOMAN* MUST BE EATEN WHILE THERE IS STILL SOME APPETITE FOR IT.

IN FACT, IF ONE IS SO SATED THAT HE MUST LITERALLY FORCE HIMSELF TO EAT IT, HE IS NOT CREDITED WITH THE PERFORMANCE OF THE MITZVAH OF *AFIKOMAN*. THEREFORE, IT IS UNWISE TO EAT MORE THAN A MODERATE AMOUNT DURING THE MEAL.

---

(1) *Numbers* 9:11.

◆§ Laws of *Korech*

1. A *k'zayis* of matzah is broken off from the bottom matzah, and a *k'zayis* of *maror* is sandwiched together with the matzah. The sandwich should be dipped into the *charoses*, and then the *charoses* should be shaken off. Some people have the custom not to dip the sandwich into *charoses*. Although the first opinion is preferable, if someone's tradition is the second custom, he may follow it (475:1, *Mishnah Berurah* §19).

2. The entire mixture of matzah and *maror* should be eaten at one time. (That is, it should be put in the mouth and chewed together, but not necessarily swallowed at once.) (*Mishnah Berurah* §22.)

3. The *korech* sandwich should be eaten while reclining. If one forgot to recline, it would appear from the *Be'ur Halachah* that he need not eat it again (475:1, *Be'ur Halachah* 472 s.v. לא).

4. One should not speak at all between the *berachah* of Hamotzi and the *korech* sandwich, but if he did speak he need not make another *berachah* (*Mishnah Berurah* 475:24).

קַדֵּשׁ וּרְחַץ כַּרְפַּס יַחַץ מַגִּיד רָחְצָה מוֹצִיא מַצָּ

ATZAh   MOTZI   RACHTZAh   MAGGID   YACHATZ   KARPAS   URECHATZ   KADDESH

⊰{ TZAFUN / *צָפוּן }⊱

FROM THE *AFIKOMAN* MATZAH (AND FROM ADDITIONAL MATZOS TO MAKE UP THE REQUIRED AMOUNT) AN OLIVE-SIZE PORTION — ACCORDING TO SOME, A PORTION WITH THE VOLUME OF TWO OLIVES — IS GIVEN TO EACH PARTICIPANT. IT SHOULD BE EATEN BEFORE MIDNIGHT, WHILE RECLINING, WITHOUT DELAY, AND UNINTERRUPTEDLY. NOTHING MAY BE EATEN OR DRUNK AFTER THE *AFIKOMAN* (WITH THE EXCEPTION OF WATER AND THE LIKE) EXCEPT FOR THE LAST TWO SEDER CUPS OF WINE.

צָפוּן — *Tzafun*. We allow the taste of the afikoman ("desert") to linger in our mouths; for the afikoman — a piece of bland matzah — signifies that it is not the sweetness of the food which whets our palate, but the observance of mitzvos which is "sweeter than honey dripping from the combs (*Psalms* 19:11)."

⊷§ Laws of the Seder Meal and the Afikoman

1. A person should not eat so much during the meal that he has no appetite whatsoever for the *afikoman*. If a person is so full that he has to force himself to eat the *afikoman* (אֲכִילָה גַּסָּה), it is considered as if he has not eaten the *afikoman* at all (476:1, *Mishnah Berurah* §6).

2. It is preferable to recline while eating the entire meal (472:6).

3. Concerning the custom of eating eggs at the *Seder* meal, see above: p. [Section on preparing for the seder].

4. It is the custom to refrain from eating any roasted meat or poultry on the Seder night, even a pot roast cooked in its own juices (without water). Roasted meat which was subsequently boiled is permitted (but not vice versa) (476:1, *Mishnah Berurah* ad loc.).

5. It is preferable to finish the meal in time to recite the entire Hallel before midnight. At the very least, the eating of the *afikoman* must not be delayed until after midnight (477:1).

6. The *afikoman* should be eaten while reclining. If someone forgot to recline while eating it, he should eat another piece of matzah for *afikoman* while reclining. If this is difficult, it may be forgone (*Mishnah Berurah* 477:4).

7. If someone forgot to eat the *afikoman* altogether and remembered only after having recited *Bircas HaMazon*, he must wash and recite *Hamotzi* and eat the *afikoman*, and then say *Bircas HaMazon* again. (The second *Bircas HaMazon* should not be said over a cup of wine, as this would constitute an addition to the requisite number of four cups. If the fourth cup of wine has not yet been drunk, however, he may say *Bircas HaMazon* over a cup of wine but not drink it until after Hallel.) If he remembered before *Bircas HaMazon*, but after having washed his hands for מַיִם אַחֲרוֹנִים, he should eat the *afikoman* at that point (without a *berachah*) (477:2).

8. A person should not eat the matzah of *afikoman* in two different places. Even two different tables in the same room are considered two different "places" (478:1, *Mishnah Berurah* §4).

9. It is forbidden to eat anything after the *afikoman*. If one did eat something, he should eat another *k'zayis* of matzah afterwards, which then becomes his *afikoman*. One should also not drink wine (except for the third and fourth cups of the *Seder*). Water, however, is permitted. Concerning other soft drinks — such as fruit juice, tea, etc. — strong-tasting drinks should be avoided, but those with a light taste may be drunk. In cases of need, the opinion of the *Gra*, who holds that only intoxicating beverages are forbidden, may be relied upon, especially at the second *Seder* (478:1, *Mishnah Berurah* 481:1).

10. Some have the custom of saving a piece of the *afikoman* on the second *Seder* (some take from both *Sederim*) until the following year, when they burn it with the *chometz* on *Erev Pesach*. The reason is given as a way of remembering the Exodus all year long (*Shaarei Teshuvah* 477:2) or, based on the *Zohar* (*Pinchas* 251b), as an extension of the לֵיל שִׁימוּרִים, *Night of Protection* from harmful spirits (*Pesachim* 109b).

SOME RECITE THE FOLLOWING BEFORE EATING THE *AFIKOMAN*:

הִנְנִי מוּכָן וּמְזוּמָן לְקַיֵּם מִצְוַת אֲכִילַת אֲפִיקוֹמָן. לְשֵׁם יִחוּד

⟨ of the ⟨ For the ⟪ the ⟨ of eating ⟨ the ⟨ to ⟨ and ⟨ am ⟨ I now
unification sake *afikoman*. mitzvah perform ready prepared

קֻדְשָׁא בְּרִיךְ הוּא וּשְׁכִינְתֵּיהּ, עַל יְדֵי הַהוּא טָמִיר וְנֶעְלָם,

⟪ and Who is ⟨ Who is ⟨ Him ⟨ through ⟪ and His ⟪ is He, ⟨ Blessed ⟪ of the
inscrutable hidden Presence, Holy One,

בְּשֵׁם כָּל יִשְׂרָאֵל. וִיהִי נֹעַם אֲדֹנָי אֱלֹהֵינוּ עָלֵינוּ, וּמַעֲשֵׂה

⟨ the work ⟪ be ⟨ our God, ⟨ of the ⟨ the plea- ⟨ May ⟪ Israel. ⟨ of all ⟨—[I pray] in
upon us; Lord, santness the name

יָדֵינוּ כּוֹנְנָה עָלֵינוּ, וּמַעֲשֵׂה יָדֵינוּ כּוֹנְנֵהוּ.¹

⟪ establish it. ⟨ of our ⟨ the work ⟨ for us; ⟨ establish ⟨ of our
hands, hands,

⚜ BARECH / ברך ⚜

THE THIRD CUP IS RINSED INSIDE AND OUT AND THEN FILLED; *BIRCAS HAMAZON* (*BLESSING AFTER MEALS*) IS RECITED. ACCORDING TO SOME CUSTOMS, THE CUP OF ELIYAHU IS POURED AT THIS POINT.

—————— Psalm 126 / תהלים קכו ——————

שִׁיר הַמַּעֲלוֹת; בְּשׁוּב יהוה אֶת שִׁיבַת צִיּוֹן, הָיִינוּ

⟨ we ⟪ of ⟨ captivity ⟨ the ⟨ When Hashem ⟪ of ascents. ⟨ A song
will be Zion, will return

כְּחֹלְמִים. אָז יִמָּלֵא שְׂחוֹק פִּינוּ, וּלְשׁוֹנֵנוּ רִנָּה; אָז

⟨ Then ⟪ with ⟨ and our ⟪ our ⟨ with ⟨ filled ⟨ Then ⟪ like dreamers.
glad song. tongue mouth laughter will be

יֹאמְרוּ בַגּוֹיִם: הִגְדִּיל יהוה לַעֲשׂוֹת עִם אֵלֶּה. הִגְדִּיל

⟨ Greatly ⟪ these. ⟨ with ⟨ done ⟨ has Hashem ⟨ Greatly ⟪ among the ⟨ will they
nations, declare

יהוה לַעֲשׂוֹת עִמָּנוּ, הָיִינוּ שְׂמֵחִים. שׁוּבָה יהוה

⟨ O Hashem, ⟨ Return, ⟪ gladdened. ⟨ we were ⟪ with us, ⟨ done ⟨ has Hashem

אֶת שְׁבִיתֵנוּ, כַּאֲפִיקִים בַּנֶּגֶב. הַזֹּרְעִים בְּדִמְעָה, בְּרִנָּה

⟨ with ⟪ tearfully, ⟨ Those ⟪ in the ⟨ like springs ⟪ our captivity,
glad song who sow desert.

יִקְצֹרוּ. הָלוֹךְ יֵלֵךְ וּבָכֹה נֹשֵׂא מֶשֶׁךְ הַזָּרַע; בֹּא יָבֹא

⟨ he will ⟨ but ⟪ of ⟨ the ⟨ does he ⟪ weeping, ⟨ he ⟨ Walk on, ⟪ will reap.
return return seeds, measure who carries walks

בְּרִנָּה, נֹשֵׂא אֲלֻמֹּתָיו.

⟪ of his sheaves. ⟨ a bearer ⟪ in exultation,

---

(1) *Psalms* 90:17.

קַדֵּשׁ וּרְחַץ כַּרְפַּס יַחַץ מַגִּיד רָחְצָה מוֹצִיא מַצָּ
ATZAh MOTZI RACHTZAh MAGGIĎ YACHTZ KARPAS URECHATZ KADDESH

SOME ADD THE FOLLOWING VERSES:

תְּהִלַּת יהוה יְדַבֶּר פִּי, וִיבָרֵךְ כָּל בָּשָׂר שֵׁם קָדְשׁוֹ

‹ of His ‹ the ‹ flesh ‹ may ‹ and bless ‹‹ may my ‹ of ‹ The praise
Holiness Name all mouth declare, HASHEM

לְעוֹלָם וָעֶד.¹ וַאֲנַחְנוּ נְבָרֵךְ יָהּ, מֵעַתָּה וְעַד עוֹלָם,

‹ eternity, ‹ until ‹ from this time ‹ God ‹ will bless ‹ But we ‹‹ and ever. ‹ for ever

הַלְלוּיָהּ.² הוֹדוּ לַיהוה כִּי טוֹב, כִּי לְעוֹלָם חַסְדּוֹ.³ מִי

‹ Who ‹‹ is His ‹ enduring ‹ for ‹‹ He is ‹ for ‹ to HASHEM ‹ Give ‹‹ Halleluyah!
kindness! forever good; thanks

יְמַלֵּל גְּבוּרוֹת יהוה, יַשְׁמִיעַ כָּל תְּהִלָּתוֹ.⁴

‹‹ of His praise? ‹ all ‹ [who] can ‹‹ of HASHEM, ‹ the mighty ‹ can
make heard acts express

SOME RECITE THE FOLLOWING BEFORE *BIRCAS HAMAZON*:

הִנְנִי מוּכָן וּמְזוּמָּן לְקַיֵּם מִצְוַת עֲשֵׂה שֶׁל בִּרְכַּת

‹ Blessing ‹ of ‹ the positive ‹ to perform ‹ and ready ‹ am ‹ I now
After commandment prepared

הַמָּזוֹן, שֶׁנֶּאֱמַר: וְאָכַלְתָּ וְשָׂבָעְתָּ, וּבֵרַכְתָּ אֶת יהוה

‹ HASHEM, ‹ and you ‹ and you shall ‹ And you ‹ for it is said: ‹‹ Meals,
shall bless be satisfied shall eat

אֱלֹהֶיךָ, עַל הָאָרֶץ הַטֹּבָה אֲשֶׁר נָתַן לָךְ.⁵

‹‹ you. ‹ He gave ‹ which ‹ that is good ‹ the land ‹ for ‹‹ your God,

ZIMUN/INVITATION / זימון

IF THREE OR MORE MALES, AGED THIRTEEN OR OLDER, PARTICIPATED IN THE MEAL, THE LEADER FORMALLY INVITES THE OTHERS TO JOIN HIM IN THE RECITATION OF *BIRCAS HAMAZON*. IT IS CUSTOMARY FOR THE HEAD OF THE HOUSEHOLD TO LEAD THE *ZIMUN* AT THE *SEDER*. THE LEADER RAISES THE THIRD CUP AND THE *ZIMUN*, OR FORMAL INVITATION, IS RECITED.

Leader — רַבּוֹתַי מִיר וֶועלֶען בֶּענְטְשֶׁען [רַבּוֹתַי נְבָרֵךְ].

‹‹[let us bless. ‹ Gentlemen,] ‹‹ bless. ‹ let us ‹ Gentlemen,

Others — יְהִי שֵׁם יהוה מְבֹרָךְ מֵעַתָּה וְעַד עוֹלָם.⁶

‹‹ eternity. ‹ until ‹ from this time ‹ be blessed ‹ of HASHEM ‹ the Name ‹ Let

Leader — יְהִי שֵׁם יהוה מְבֹרָךְ* מֵעַתָּה וְעַד עוֹלָם.⁶

‹‹ eternity. ‹ until ‹ from this time ‹ be blessed* ‹ of HASHEM ‹ the Name ‹ Let

---

(1) *Psalms* 145:21. (2) 115:18. (3) 118:1. (4) 106:2. (5) *Deuteronomy* 8:10. (6) *Psalms* 113:2.

זימון / *Zimun* (Invitation)

The word *zimun* connotes both *invitation* and *presentation*. When three or more people eat together, one *invites* the others to respond to his praise of God; and all of them jointly

are required to *present themselves* as a group to come together in praise of God (based on *Berachos* 49b).

יְהִי שֵׁם ה׳ מְבֹרָךְ — *Let the Name of HASHEM be blessed*. The leader, too, repeats the blessings

NIRTZAh hALLEL BARECh TZAFUN shULChAN OREch kORECh MAROR

IF TEN MEN JOIN IN THE *ZIMUN*, AMONG WHOM AT LEAST SEVEN ATE MATZAH, ADD GOD'S NAME (IN PARENTHESES).

בִּרְשׁוּת מָרָנָן וְרַבָּנָן וְרַבּוֹתַי, נְבָרֵךְ* (אֱלֹהֵינוּ)

⟨ (our God,) ⟨ let us bless* ⟨ and ⟨ and ⟨ of the distin- ⟨ With the
[Him,] gentlemen, rabbis guished people permission

שֶׁאָכַלְנוּ מִשֶּׁלוֹ.

⟪ of what is His. ⟨ for we have eaten.

בָּרוּךְ (אֱלֹהֵינוּ) שֶׁאָכַלְנוּ מִשֶּׁלוֹ וּבְטוּבוֹ חָיִינוּ. — Others

⟪ we ⟨ and through ⟨ of what ⟨ for we ⟨ (our God,) ⟨ Blessed
live. His goodness is His have eaten is [He,]

THOSE WHO HAVE NOT EATEN RESPOND:

בָּרוּךְ (אֱלֹהֵינוּ) וּמְבֹרָךְ שְׁמוֹ תָּמִיד לְעוֹלָם וָעֶד.

⟪ and ⟨ for ever ⟨ continuously, ⟨ is His ⟨ and ⟨ (our God,) ⟨ Blessed
ever. Name blessed is [He,]

בָּרוּךְ (אֱלֹהֵינוּ) שֶׁאָכַלְנוּ מִשֶּׁלוֹ וּבְטוּבוֹ חָיִינוּ. — Leader

⟪ we ⟨ and through ⟨ of what ⟨ for we ⟨ (our God,) ⟨ Blessed
live. His goodness is His have eaten is [He,]

(בָּרוּךְ הוּא וּבָרוּךְ שְׁמוֹ.)

⟪ is His Name.) ⟨ and Blessed ⟨ is He ⟨ (Blessed

THE *ZIMUN* LEADER RECITES ALOUD THE BLESSING AFTER MEALS (AT LEAST THE FIRST BLESSING AND THE CONCLUSION OF THE OTHERS). ASIDE FROM RESPONDING AMEN AT THE CONCLUSION OF EACH BLESSING, IT IS FORBIDDEN TO INTERRUPT THE BLESSING AFTER MEALS FOR ANY RESPONSE OTHER THAN THOSE PERMITTED DURING THE *SHEMA*.

FIRST BLESSING: FOR THE NOURISHMENT / הַבְּרָכָה הָרִאשׁוֹנָה – בִּרְכַּת הַזָּן

בָּרוּךְ אַתָּה יהוה אֱלֹהֵינוּ מֶלֶךְ הָעוֹלָם,

⟪ of the universe, ⟨ King ⟨ our God, ⟨ HASHEM, ⟨ are You, ⟨ Blessed

הַזָּן אֶת הָעוֹלָם כֻּלּוֹ, בְּטוּבוֹ, בְּחֵן בְּחֶסֶד

⟨ with ⟨ — with ⟪ in His ⟨ all of it, ⟨ the world, ⟨ Who
kindness, grace, goodness nourishes

---

because it would be improper and even sacrilegious for him to ask others to bless God while he, being part of the group, refrains from joining them (*Rashba*).

נְבָרֵךְ — *Let us bless.* A commandment done by an individual cannot be compared to one performed by a group. When many people unite to do God's will, each individual in the group attains a far higher level than he would have had he acted alone, no matter how meritori-

ously he had acted (*Chofetz Chaim*).

⦿ הַבְּרָכָה הָרִאשׁוֹנָה – בִּרְכַּת הַזָּן /
First Blessing: For the Nourishment

Bircas HaMazon comprises four blessings, of which the first three are Scripturally ordained and the fourth was instituted by the Sages. The first to compose a text for Blessing After Meals was Moses, whose text is still recited as the first blessing. Although Moses' blessing was composed in gratitude for the *manna* in the

וּבְרַחֲמִים, הוּא נֹתֵן לֶחֶם לְכָל בָּשָׂר, כִּי
‹ for ‹‹ flesh, ‹ to all ‹ food ‹ gives ‹ He ‹‹ and with compassion.

לְעוֹלָם חַסְדּוֹ.[1] וּבְטוּבוֹ הַגָּדוֹל, תָּמִיד לֹא
‹ never ‹ that is great, ‹ And through ‹‹ is His ‹ forever
His goodness kindness.

חָסַר לָנוּ, וְאַל יֶחְסַר לָנוּ מָזוֹן לְעוֹלָם וָעֶד.
‹‹ and ever. ‹ for ever ‹ nourishment, ‹ may we lack, ‹ and never ‹ have we lacked,

בַּעֲבוּר שְׁמוֹ הַגָּדוֹל, כִּי הוּא אֵל זָן וּמְפַרְנֵס
‹ and ‹ Who ‹ is ‹ He ‹ because ‹‹ that is ‹ of His ‹ For the sake
sustains nourishes God great, Name

לַכֹּל, וּמֵטִיב לַכֹּל, וּמֵכִין מָזוֹן לְכָל בְּרִיּוֹתָיו
‹ of His ‹ for all ‹ nourishment ‹ and He ‹‹ all, ‹ and benefits ‹ all,
creatures prepares

אֲשֶׁר בָּרָא. (כָּאָמוּר: פּוֹתֵחַ אֶת יָדֶךָ, וּמַשְׂבִּיעַ
‹ and satisfy ‹‹ Your hand, ‹ You open ‹‹ (As it is said, ‹‹ He has created. ‹ which

לְכָל חַי רָצוֹן.[2] ‹› בָּרוּךְ אַתָּה יהוה, הַזָּן
‹ Who ‹‹ HASHEM, ‹ are You, ‹ Blessed ‹‹ [with its] ‹ living ‹ every
nourishes desire.) thing

אֶת הַכֹּל.
‹‹ all.

(אָמֵן. – Others)
‹‹ (Amen.)

SECOND BLESSING: FOR THE LAND / הַבְּרָכָה הַשְּׁנִיָּה – בִּרְכַּת הָאָרֶץ

נוֹדֶה לְךָ יהוה אֱלֹהֵינוּ, עַל שֶׁהִנְחַלְתָּ
‹ You have given ‹ because ‹‹ our God, ‹ HASHEM, ‹ You, ‹ We thank
as a heritage

---

(1) *Psalms* 136:25. (2) 145:16.

Wilderness, it makes no mention of the *manna*. It is equally noteworthy that the commandment of Blessing After Meals was given in the context of a general exhortation to Israel that it remember the heavenly food with which God nourished them in the Wilderness. The message seems obvious: When we thank God for giving us food, we are recognizing that there is no intrinsic difference between the *manna* and the

livelihood one wrests from the earth through sweat and hard toil; both are gifts from heaven.

הַבְּרָכָה הַשְּׁנִיָּה – בִּרְכַּת הָאָרֶץ / ❧
Second Blessing: For the Land

The second blessing was also ordained by the Torah [*Deut.* 8:10, see *Overview* to ArtScroll *Bircas HaMazon*] and formulated by Joshua (*Berachos* 48a). He saw how deeply Moses desired to enter *Eretz Yisrael*, and how eager the

לַאֲבוֹתֵינוּ אֶרֶץ חֶמְדָּה טוֹבָה וּרְחָבָה.* וְעַל

‹ because ‹‹ and spacious;* ‹ good, ‹ desirable, ‹ a land, ‹ to our forefathers

שֶׁהוֹצֵאתָנוּ יהוה אֱלֹהֵינוּ מֵאֶרֶץ מִצְרַיִם,

‹‹ of Egypt ‹ from the land ‹‹ our God, ‹ HASHEM, ‹‹ You brought us out,

וּפְדִיתָנוּ מִבֵּית עֲבָדִים, וְעַל בְּרִיתְךָ שֶׁחָתַמְתָּ

‹ which ‹ Your ‹ for ‹‹ of bondage; ‹ from the ‹ and You
You sealed covenant house redeemed us

בִּבְשָׂרֵנוּ, וְעַל תּוֹרָתְךָ שֶׁלִּמַּדְתָּנוּ, וְעַל חֻקֶּיךָ

‹ Your ‹ and for ‹‹ which You ‹ Your Torah ‹ for ‹‹ in our flesh;
statutes taught us

שֶׁהוֹדַעְתָּנוּ, וְעַל חַיִּים חֵן וָחֶסֶד שֶׁחוֹנַנְתָּנוּ,

‹‹ which You ‹ and ‹ grace, ‹ life, ‹ for ‹‹ which You made
granted us; lovingkindness known to us;

וְעַל אֲכִילַת מָזוֹן שָׁאַתָּה זָן וּמְפַרְנֵס אוֹתָנוּ

‹ us ‹ and sustain ‹ nourish ‹ with which ‹ of the ‹ [our] eating ‹ and for
You food

תָּמִיד, בְּכָל יוֹם וּבְכָל עֵת וּבְכָל שָׁעָה.

‹‹ hour. ‹ and in every ‹ time, ‹ in every ‹ day, ‹ in every ‹‹ constantly,

וְעַל הַכֹּל, יהוה אֱלֹהֵינוּ, אֲנַחְנוּ מוֹדִים לָךְ

‹ You ‹ thank ‹ we ‹‹ our God, ‹ HASHEM, ‹‹ everything, ‹ For

וּמְבָרְכִים אוֹתָךְ, יִתְבָּרַךְ שִׁמְךָ בְּפִי כָּל חַי

‹‹ the ‹ of all ‹ by the ‹ may Your ‹ Blessed ‹‹ You. ‹ and bless
living, mouth Name be

תָּמִיד לְעוֹלָם וָעֶד. כַּכָּתוּב, וְאָכַלְתָּ וְשָׂבָעְתָּ,

‹ and you shall ‹ And you ‹‹ As it is ‹‹ and ever. ‹ for ever ‹ continuously
be satisfied shall eat written:

Patriarchs were to be buried there. When Joshua was privileged to enter *Eretz Yisrael*, he composed this blessing in honor of the Land (*Shibbolei HaLeket*).

The blessing begins and ends with thanks. The expression of gratitude refers to each of the enumerated items: the Land, the Exodus, the covenant, the Torah, the statutes, life, grace, kindness, and food.

חֶמְדָּה טוֹבָה וּרְחָבָה — *Desirable, good and spacious*. Whoever does not say that the Land is *desirable, good and spacious* has not properly fulfilled his obligation [of *Bircas HaMazon*] (*Berachos* 48b), because once the Torah re-

---

וּבֵרַכְתָּ אֶת יהוה אֱלֹהֶיךָ, עַל הָאָרֶץ הַטֹּבָה
⟨ that is good ⟨ the land ⟨ for ⟨ your God, ⟨ HASHEM, ⟨ and you shall bless

אֲשֶׁר נָתַן לָךְ.[1] ❖ בָּרוּךְ אַתָּה יהוה, עַל הָאָרֶץ
⟨ the land ⟨ for ⟪ HASHEM, ⟨ are You, ⟨ Blessed ⟪ you. ⟨ He gave ⟨ which

וְעַל הַמָּזוֹן.
(אָמֵן. – Others)
⟪ (Amen.)
⟪ the nourishment. ⟨ and for

THIRD BLESSING: FOR JERUSALEM / הברכה השלישית – בונה ירושלים

רַחֵם (נָא) יהוה אֱלֹהֵינוּ עַל יִשְׂרָאֵל עַמֶּךָ,
⟪ Your people; ⟨ Israel ⟨ on ⟪ our God, ⟨ HASHEM, ⟨ (we beg You) ⟨ Have mercy,

וְעַל יְרוּשָׁלַיִם עִירֶךָ, וְעַל צִיּוֹן מִשְׁכַּן כְּבוֹדֶךָ,
⟪ of Your ⟨ the resting ⟨ Zion, ⟨ on ⟪ Your City; ⟨ Jerusalem, ⟨ on
Glory; place

וְעַל מַלְכוּת בֵּית דָּוִד מְשִׁיחֶךָ,* וְעַל הַבַּיִת
⟨ the ⟨ and on ⟪ Your anointed;* ⟨ of David, ⟨ of the ⟨ on the monarchy
House, house

הַגָּדוֹל וְהַקָּדוֹשׁ שֶׁנִּקְרָא שִׁמְךָ עָלָיו. אֱלֹהֵינוּ
⟨ Our God, ⟪ upon which Your Name is called. ⟨ and holy, ⟨ great

אָבִינוּ, רְעֵנוּ זוּנֵנוּ פַּרְנְסֵנוּ וְכַלְכְּלֵנוּ וְהַרְוִיחֵנוּ,
⟨ relieve us, ⟨ support us, ⟨ sustain us, ⟨ nourish ⟨ – tend ⟪ our Father
us, us,

---

(1) *Deuteronomy* 8:10.

quired that the Land be mentioned, the Sages decreed that its praises should likewise be enumerated (*Talmidei R' Yonah*).

הַבְּרָכָה הַשְּׁלִישִׁית – בּוֹנֵה יְרוּשָׁלַיִם /
Third Blessing: For Jerusalem

This blessing is the final one required by the Torah. It was composed by David and Solomon. David, who conquered Jerusalem, referred to *Israel, Your people,* and *Jerusalem, Your City.* After the Temple was built, Solomon added, *the House, great and holy* (*Berachos* 48b).

As composed by David and Solomon, the blessing was a prayer that God maintain the tranquility of the Land. Following the destruc-

tion and exile, the blessing was changed to embody a prayer for the return of the Land, the Temple, and the Davidic dynasty. Before David's conquest of Jerusalem, the blessing had yet another form (*Tur*), a request for God's mercy upon the nation (*Aruch HaShulchan*).

וְעַל מַלְכוּת בֵּית דָּוִד מְשִׁיחֶךְ — *On the monarchy of the house of David, Your anointed.* It is mandatory that the monarchy of David's dynasty be mentioned in this blessing. Whoever has not mentioned it has not fulfilled his obligation (*Berachos* 49a), because it was David who sanctified Jerusalem (*Rashi*), and because the consolation for the exile will not be complete until David's kingdom is restored (*Rambam*).

מרור כורך שלחן עורך צפון בָּרֵךְ הלל נרצה
NIRTZAh hALLeL BAReCh TZAFUN shULChAN OReCh KOReCh MAROR

וְהָרְוַח לָנוּ יהוה אֱלֹהֵינוּ מְהֵרָה מִכָּל
‹ from all ‹ speedily, ‹ our God, ‹ HASHEM, ‹ to us, ‹ and grant relief

צָרוֹתֵינוּ. וְנָא אַל תַּצְרִיכֵנוּ, יהוה אֱלֹהֵינוּ,
« our God— ‹— HASHEM, « make us dependent ‹ do not ‹ Please, « our troubles.

לֹא לִידֵי מַתְּנַת בָּשָׂר וָדָם, וְלֹא לִידֵי
‹ upon ‹ nor ‹ and blood ‹ of flesh ‹ the gifts ‹ upon ‹ neither

הַלְוָאָתָם, כִּי אִם לְיָדְךָ הַמְּלֵאָה הַפְּתוּחָה
‹ open, ‹ that is full, ‹ upon Your Hand ‹ but only « their loans,

הַקְּדוֹשָׁה וְהָרְחָבָה, שֶׁלֹּא נֵבוֹשׁ וְלֹא נִכָּלֵם
‹ be humiliated ‹ nor ‹ be ashamed ‹ that we not « and generous, ‹ holy,

לְעוֹלָם וָעֶד.
« and ever. ‹ for ever

ON THE SABBATH ADD THE FOLLOWING. [IF FORGOTTEN, SEE BOX ON PAGE 77.]

רְצֵה וְהַחֲלִיצֵנוּ יהוה אֱלֹהֵינוּ בְּמִצְוֹתֶיךָ, וּבְמִצְוַת
‹ and through the ‹ through Your ‹ our God, ‹ HASHEM, ‹ to give us rest, ‹ May it be
commandment commandments pleasing to You

יוֹם הַשְּׁבִיעִי הַשַּׁבָּת הַגָּדוֹל וְהַקָּדוֹשׁ הַזֶּה, כִּי יוֹם זֶה
‹ this day, ‹ For «— this « and holy ‹ that is great ‹ the ‹ of the
one. Sabbath Seventh Day,

גָּדוֹל וְקָדוֹשׁ הוּא לְפָנֶיךָ, לִשְׁבָּת בּוֹ וְלָנוּחַ בּוֹ בְּאַהֲבָה
« in love, ‹ on it, ‹ and to ‹ on it ‹ to cease « before ‹ it is ‹ and holy ‹ great
rest work You,

כְּמִצְוַת רְצוֹנֶךָ, וּבִרְצוֹנְךָ הָנִיחַ לָנוּ יהוה אֱלֹהֵינוּ,
« our God, ‹ HASHEM, « to us, ‹ grant rest ‹ And through « by Your will. ‹ as ordained
Your will,

שֶׁלֹּא תְהֵא צָרָה וְיָגוֹן וַאֲנָחָה בְּיוֹם מְנוּחָתֵנוּ, וְהַרְאֵנוּ
‹ And « of our rest. ‹ on this ‹ or lament ‹ grief, ‹ any ‹ be ‹ that there
show us, day distress, should not

יהוה אֱלֹהֵינוּ בְּנֶחָמַת צִיּוֹן עִירֶךָ, וּבְבִנְיַן יְרוּשָׁלַיִם
‹ of Jerusalem, ‹ and the « Your City, ‹ of Zion, ‹ the ‹ our God, ‹ HASHEM,
rebuilding consolation

עִיר קָדְשֶׁךָ, כִּי אַתָּה הוּא בַּעַל הַיְשׁוּעוֹת וּבַעַל הַנֶּחָמוֹת.
« of ‹ and ‹ of salvations ‹ Master ‹ Who ‹ it is ‹ for « of Your ‹ City
consolations. Master are You holiness,

קַדֵּשׁ וּרְחַץ כַּרְפַּס יַחַץ מַגִּיד רָחְצָה מוֹצִיא מַצָּה
ATZAH MOTZI RACHTZAH MAGGID YACHATZ KARPAS URECHATZ KADDESH

אֱלֹהֵינוּ וֵאלֹהֵי אֲבוֹתֵינוּ, יַעֲלֶה, וְיָבֹא, וְיַגִּיעַ,

‹ reach, ‹ come, ‹ may there rise, «‹ of our forefathers, ‹ and the God ‹ Our God

וְיֵרָאֶה, וְיֵרָצֶה, וְיִשָּׁמַע, וְיִפָּקֵד, וְיִזָּכֵר זִכְרוֹנֵנוּ

‹— the remembrance of us «‹ and be remembered ‹ be considered, ‹ be heard, ‹ be favored, ‹ be noted,

וּפִקְדוֹנֵנוּ, וְזִכְרוֹן אֲבוֹתֵינוּ, וְזִכְרוֹן מָשִׁיחַ בֶּן דָּוִד

‹ of David, ‹ son ‹ of Messiah, «‹ remembrance of our forefathers; ‹ the remembrance «‹ and consideration of us;

עַבְדֶּךָ, וְזִכְרוֹן יְרוּשָׁלַיִם עִיר קָדְשֶׁךָ, וְזִכְרוֹן

‹ and the remembrance «‹ of Your holiness; ‹ the City ‹ of Jerusalem, ‹ the remembrance «‹ Your servant;

כָּל עַמְּךָ בֵּית יִשְׂרָאֵל לְפָנֶיךָ, לִפְלֵיטָה לְטוֹבָה

‹ for goodness, ‹ for deliverance, ‹ before You «‹ of Israel — ‹ the Family ‹ of Your entire people

לְחֵן וּלְחֶסֶד וּלְרַחֲמִים, לְחַיִּים וּלְשָׁלוֹם,

«‹ and for peace, ‹ for life, ‹ and for compassion, ‹ for kindness, ‹ for grace,

בְּיוֹם חַג הַמַּצּוֹת הַזֶּה. זָכְרֵנוּ יְהֹוָה אֱלֹהֵינוּ בּוֹ

‹ on it ‹ our God, ‹ HASHEM, ‹ Remember us «‹ of this Festival of Matzos. ‹ on the day

לְטוֹבָה, וּפָקְדֵנוּ בוֹ לִבְרָכָה, וְהוֹשִׁיעֵנוּ בּוֹ

‹ on it ‹ and save us «‹ for blessing; ‹ on it ‹ consider us «‹ for goodness;

⋖§ If One Omitted יַעֲלֶה וְיָבֹא or רְצֵה

1. If he realizes his omission after having recited the blessing of בּוֹנֵה, *Who rebuilds,* he makes up for the omission by reciting the appropriate Compensatory Blessing (pp. 126-127).

2. If he realizes his omission after having recited the first six words of the fourth blessing, he may still switch immediately into the Compensatory Blessing since the words . . . בָּרוּךְ אַתָּה הָעוֹלָם are identical in both blessings. (However, the Compensatory Blessing need not be recited after the third Sabbath meal if *Bircas HaMazon* is recited after sunset.)

3. If the omission is discovered after having recited the word הָאֵל, *the Almighty,* of the fourth blessing, it is too late for the Compensatory Blessing to be recited. In that case:
   (i) On the Sabbath and on a Festival day, at the first two meals *Bircas HaMazon* must be repeated in its entirety; at the third meal, nothing need be done.
   (ii) On Chol HaMoed, nothing need be done except if the day fell on the Sabbath and רְצֵה, *Retzei,* was omitted. In that case, at the first two meals *Bircas HaMazon* must be repeated. But if רְצֵה was recited and יַעֲלֶה וְיָבֹא was omitted, nothing need be done.

מָרוֹר כּוֹרֵךְ שֻׁלְחָן עוֹרֵךְ צָפוּן בָּרֵךְ הַלֵּל נִרְצָה

NIRTZAH hALLEL BARECH TZAFUN shULCHAN ORECH koRECH MAROR

לְחַיִּים. וּבִדְבַר יְשׁוּעָה וְרַחֲמִים, חוּס

‹ have pity, ‹‹ and compassion, ‹ of salvation ‹ In the matter ‹‹ for life.

וְחָנֵּנוּ וְרַחֵם עָלֵינוּ וְהוֹשִׁיעֵנוּ, כִּי אֵלֶיךָ עֵינֵינוּ,

‹‹ are our ‹ to You ‹ for ‹‹ and save us, ‹ with us, ‹ and be com- ‹ be
eyes [turned], passionate gracious,

כִּי אֵל (מֶלֶךְ) חַנּוּן וְרַחוּם אָתָּה.[1]

‹‹ are You. ‹ and ‹ gracious ‹ (a King,) ‹ O ‹ because,
compassionate God,

❖ וּבְנֵה יְרוּשָׁלַיִם* עִיר הַקֹּדֶשׁ בִּמְהֵרָה

‹ soon ‹ of holiness, ‹ the City ‹ Jerusalem,* ‹ Rebuild

בְיָמֵינוּ. בָּרוּךְ אַתָּה יהוה, בּוֹנֵה (בְּרַחֲמָיו)

‹ (in His mercy) ‹ Who rebuilds ‹‹ Hashem, ‹ are You, ‹ Blessed ‹‹ in our days.

יְרוּשָׁלָיִם. אָמֵן. אָמֵן.*) – Others)

‹‹ Amen. ‹‹ Jerusalem. ‹‹ Amen.*

[WHEN REQUIRED, THE COMPENSATORY BLESSING (PP. 126-127) IS RECITED HERE.]

FOURTH BLESSING: GOD'S GOODNESS / הַבְּרָכָה הָרְבִיעִית – הַטּוֹב וְהַמֵּטִיב

בָּרוּךְ אַתָּה יהוה אֱלֹהֵינוּ מֶלֶךְ הָעוֹלָם,

‹‹ of the universe, ‹ King ‹ our God, ‹ Hashem, ‹ are You, ‹ Blessed

הָאֵל אָבִינוּ מַלְכֵּנוּ אַדִּירֵנוּ בּוֹרְאֵנוּ גּוֹאֲלֵנוּ

‹ our ‹ our Creator, ‹ our ‹ our King, ‹ our ‹ the
Redeemer, Sovereign, Father, Almighty,

יוֹצְרֵנוּ קְדוֹשֵׁנוּ קְדוֹשׁ יַעֲקֹב, רוֹעֵנוּ רוֹעֵה

‹ the ‹ our ‹ of Jacob, ‹ Holy One ‹ our Holy One, ‹ our Maker,
Shepherd Shepherd,

יִשְׂרָאֵל, הַמֶּלֶךְ הַטּוֹב וְהַמֵּטִיב לַכֹּל, שֶׁבְּכָל

‹ For, every ‹‹ for all. ‹ and Who does ‹ Who is ‹ the King ‹‹ of Israel,
good good

(1) Cf. *Nehemiah* 9:31.

וּבְנֵה יְרוּשָׁלַיִם — *Rebuild Jerusalem.* This concludes the third blessing, and returns to the
theme with which the blessing began — a plea
for God's mercy on Jerusalem (*Pesachim* 104a).

ATZAH MOTZI RACHTZAH MAGGID YACHATZ KARPAS URECHATZ KADDESH

יוֹם וָיוֹם הוּא הֵטִיב, הוּא מֵטִיב, הוּא יֵיטִיב

‹ will do good ‹ and He ‹ does good, ‹ He ‹ did good, ‹ He ‹ after day ‹ day

לָנוּ. הוּא גְמָלָנוּ הוּא גוֹמְלֵנוּ הוּא יִגְמְלֵנוּ

‹ will be boun- ‹ and He ‹ is bountiful ‹ He ‹ was bountiful ‹ He ‹‹ to us.
tiful with us   with us,   with us,

לָעַד, לְחֵן וּלְחֶסֶד וּלְרַחֲמִים וּלְרֶוַח הַצָּלָה

‹ rescue, ‹ with relief, ‹‹ and with ‹ and with ‹ — with ‹‹ forever
                          compassion,   kindness   grace

וְהַצְלָחָה, בְּרָכָה וִישׁוּעָה נֶחָמָה פַּרְנָסָה

‹ sustenance, ‹ consolation, ‹ salvation, ‹ blessing, ‹ success,

וְכַלְכָּלָה ❖ וְרַחֲמִים וְחַיִּים וְשָׁלוֹם וְכָל טוֹב,

‹‹ good; ‹ and all ‹ peace, ‹ life, ‹ compassion, ‹ support,

וּמִכָּל טוּב לְעוֹלָם אַל יְחַסְּרֵנוּ.* (אָמֵן. – Others)

‹‹ (Amen.) ‹‹ deprive us.* ‹ not ‹ may He forever ‹ good things ‹ and of all

THE CUP OF WINE MAY BE PUT DOWN AT THIS POINT.

הָרַחֲמָן הוּא יִמְלוֹךְ עָלֵינוּ לְעוֹלָם וָעֶד.

‹‹ and ever. ‹ for ever ‹ over us ‹ reign ‹ May He ‹ The compassionate One!

הָרַחֲמָן הוּא יִתְבָּרַךְ בַּשָּׁמַיִם וּבָאָרֶץ. הָרַחֲמָן

‹ The compas- ‹‹ and on earth. ‹ in heaven ‹ be blessed ‹ May He ‹ The compassionate One!   sionate One!

הוּא יִשְׁתַּבַּח לְדוֹר דּוֹרִים, וְיִתְפָּאַר בָּנוּ

‹ through ‹ may He be ‹‹ after ‹ generation ‹ be praised ‹ May He
us   glorified   generation;

לָעַד וּלְנֵצַח נְצָחִים, וְיִתְהַדַּר בָּנוּ לָעַד

‹ forever ‹ through us ‹ and be honored ‹‹ and to the ultimate time, ‹ forever

וּלְעוֹלְמֵי עוֹלָמִים. הָרַחֲמָן הוּא יְפַרְנְסֵנוּ

‹ sustain us ‹ May He ‹ The compassionate One! ‹‹ and for all eternity.

❖ הַבְּרָכָה הָרְבִיעִית – הַטּוֹב וְהַמֵּטִיב /
Fourth Blessing: For God's Goodness

The essence of this blessing is the phrase הַטּוֹב
וְהַמֵּטִיב, Who is good and Who does good. The
court of Rabban Gamliel the Elder in Yavneh
composed this blessing in gratitude to God for
preserving the bodies of the victims of the
Roman massacre at Beitar, and for allowing for
their eventual burial (Berachos 48b).

אַל יְחַסְּרֵנוּ — May He ... not deprive us. This

MAROR   korech   shulchan orech   TZAFUN   BAREch   hALLEL   NIRTZAh

בְּכָבוֹד. הָרַחֲמָן הוּא יִשְׁבּוֹר עֻלֵּנוּ מֵעַל צַוָּארֵנוּ,

‹‹ our necks ‹ from ‹ our yoke ‹ break ‹ May He ‹ The compas- ‹‹ in honor.
[of oppression] sionate One!

וְהוּא יוֹלִיכֵנוּ קוֹמְמִיּוּת לְאַרְצֵנוּ. הָרַחֲמָן הוּא

‹ May ‹ The compas- ‹‹ to our Land. ‹ erect ‹ guide us ‹ and may
He sionate One! He

יִשְׁלַח לָנוּ בְּרָכָה מְרֻבָּה בַּבַּיִת הַזֶּה, וְעַל

‹ and upon ‹‹ to this house ‹ that is abundant ‹ blessing ‹ us ‹ send

שֻׁלְחָן זֶה שֶׁאָכַלְנוּ עָלָיו. הָרַחֲמָן הוּא יִשְׁלַח

‹ send ‹ May He ‹ The compas- ‹‹ on it. ‹ that we ‹ this table
sionate One! have eaten

לָנוּ אֶת אֵלִיָּהוּ הַנָּבִיא זָכוּר לַטּוֹב, וִיבַשֶּׂר

‹ to ‹‹ for good — ‹ — who is ‹‹ the Prophet ‹ Elijah ‹ us
proclaim remembered

לָנוּ בְּשׂוֹרוֹת טוֹבוֹת יְשׁוּעוֹת וְנֶחָמוֹת.

‹‹ and consolations. ‹ salvations, ‹‹ that are good, ‹ tidings ‹ to us

THE FOLLOWING IS A BLESSING THAT A GUEST RECITES FOR HIS HOST.

יְהִי רָצוֹן שֶׁלֹּא יֵבוֹשׁ וְלֹא יִכָּלֵם בַּעַל הַבַּיִת הַזֶּה,

‹‹ of this house — ‹ — the ‹‹ be ‹ nor ‹ be ‹ that ‹ [God's] ‹ May
master humiliated ashamed he not will it be

לֹא בָעוֹלָם הַזֶּה וְלֹא בָעוֹלָם הַבָּא, וְיַצְלִיחַ בְּכָל

‹ in all ‹ May he be ‹‹ to Come. ‹ in the World ‹ nor ‹ in This World ‹ not
successful

נְכָסָיו, וְיִהְיוּ נְכָסָיו מֻצְלָחִים וּקְרוֹבִים לָעִיר, וְאַל

‹ May ‹‹ at ‹ and [conveniently] ‹ successful ‹ May his dealings ‹‹ his
there not hand. close be dealings.

יִשְׁלוֹט שָׂטָן בְּמַעֲשֵׂה יָדָיו, וְאַל יִזְדַּקֵּק לְפָנָיו שׁוּם

‹ any ‹ to him ‹ attach ‹ and may ‹‹ of his ‹ over ‹ any evil ‹ be in
itself there not hands, the work impediment control

דְּבַר חֵטְא וְהִרְהוּר עָוֹן, מֵעַתָּה וְעַד עוֹלָם.

‹‹ eternity. ‹ until ‹ from this ‹‹ of sin ‹ or thought ‹ of ‹ matter
time transgression

concludes the fourth blessing. Unlike the other blessings of *Bircas HaMazon*, this one does not conclude with a brief blessing summing up the theme of the section. It is similar to the short blessings recited before performing a commandment or partaking of food. The addition

קַדֵּשׁ וּרְחַץ כַּרְפַּס יַחַץ מַגִּיד רָחְצָה מוֹצִיא מַצָּה

MATZAh MOTZI RACHTZAh MAGGID YACHATZ KARPAS URECHATZ KADDESH

**GUESTS RECITE THE FOLLOWING (CHILDREN AT THEIR PARENTS'
TABLE INCLUDE THE APPLICABLE WORDS IN PARENTHESES):**

הָרַחֲמָן הוּא יְבָרֵךְ

‹ bless ‹ May He ‹ The compassionate One!

אֶת (אָבִי מוֹרִי) בַּעַל הַבַּיִת הַזֶּה,

‹ of this house, ‹ the master (‹ my teacher ‹ my father,)

וְאֶת (אִמִּי מוֹרָתִי) בַּעֲלַת הַבַּיִת הַזֶּה,

‹‹ of this house ‹ the lady (‹ my teacher ‹ my mother,) ‹ and

אוֹתָם וְאֶת בֵּיתָם וְאֶת זַרְעָם וְאֶת כָּל אֲשֶׁר לָהֶם.

‹‹ is theirs. ‹ that ‹ all ‹ and ‹ their family, ‹ their house, ‹ — them,

AT ONE'S OWN TABLE (INCLUDE THE APPLICABLE WORDS IN PARENTHESES):

הָרַחֲמָן הוּא יְבָרֵךְ אוֹתִי

‹ me ‹ bless ‹ May He ‹ The compassionate One!

(וְאֶת אִשְׁתִּי / וְאֶת בַּעְלִי. וְאֶת זַרְעִי)

(‹ and my children ‹ my husband ‹ and / ‹ my wife ‹ and)

וְאֶת כָּל אֲשֶׁר לִי.

‹‹ is mine. ‹ that ‹ all ‹ and

ALL CONTINUE:

אוֹתָנוּ וְאֶת כָּל אֲשֶׁר לָנוּ, כְּמוֹ שֶׁנִּתְבָּרְכוּ

‹ blessed were ‹ — just as ‹‹ is ours ‹ that ‹ all ‹ and ‹ Us

אֲבוֹתֵינוּ אַבְרָהָם יִצְחָק וְיַעֲקֹב בַּכֹּל מִכֹּל

‹ from ‹ in ‹‹ and ‹ Isaac, ‹ Abraham, ‹ our forefathers,
everything, everything, Jacob —

כֹּל,[1] כֵּן יְבָרֵךְ אוֹתָנוּ כֻּלָּנוּ יַחַד בִּבְרָכָה

‹ with a ‹ together, ‹ all of us, ‹ us, ‹ may He ‹ So ‹‹ with
blessing bless everything.

שְׁלֵמָה, וְנֹאמַר, אָמֵן.

‹‹ Amen! ‹ And let us say: ‹‹ that is perfect.

---

(1) Cf. *Genesis* 24:1; 27:33; 33:11.

---

to the text of considerable outpourings of gratitude does not alter the fact that the brief text

does not require a double blessing (*Rashi* to
Berachos 49a).

מָרוֹר כּוֹרֵךְ שֻׁלְחָן עוֹרֵךְ צָפוּן בָּרֵךְ הַלֵּל נִרְצָה

NIRTZAh hALLEL BAREch TZAFUN shULCHAN ORECh koRECh MAROR

בַּמָּרוֹם יְלַמְּדוּ עֲלֵיהֶם וְעָלֵינוּ זְכוּת,

< merit << and upon us, < upon them << may there be pleaded < On high,

שֶׁתְּהֵא לְמִשְׁמֶרֶת שָׁלוֹם. וְנִשָּׂא בְרָכָה

< a blessing < May we receive << of peace. < for a safeguard < that may serve

מֵאֵת יהוה, וּצְדָקָה מֵאֱלֹהֵי יִשְׁעֵנוּ, וְנִמְצָא

< and may << of our < from the God < and kindness << from Hashem
we find salvation, that is just

חֵן וְשֵׂכֶל טוֹב בְּעֵינֵי אֱלֹהִים וְאָדָם.

<< and man. < of God < in the eyes < and good understanding < favor

---

ON THE SABBATH ADD:

הָרַחֲמָן הוּא יַנְחִילֵנוּ יוֹם שֶׁכֻּלּוֹ שַׁבָּת

< a Sabbath < which will < the < cause us < May He < The compas-
be completely day to inherit sionate One!

וּמְנוּחָה לְחַיֵּי הָעוֹלָמִים.

<< that is eternal. < for life < and a rest day

THE WORDS IN PARENTHESES ARE ADDED ON THE TWO *SEDER* NIGHTS IN SOME COMMUNITIES.

הָרַחֲמָן הוּא יַנְחִילֵנוּ יוֹם שֶׁכֻּלּוֹ טוֹב (יוֹם

< (that << good; < which is < that < cause us < May He < The compas-
day completely day to inherit sionate One!

שֶׁכֻּלּוֹ אָרוּךְ, יוֹם שֶׁצַּדִּיקִים יוֹשְׁבִים

< will sit < when the righteous < that day << everlasting; < which is completely

וְעַטְרוֹתֵיהֶם בְּרָאשֵׁיהֶם וְנֶהֱנִים מִזִּיו הַשְּׁכִינָה,

<< of [God's] < the < enjoying << on their heads, < with their crowns
Presence radiance

וִיהִי חֶלְקֵנוּ עִמָּהֶם).

<< be with them!). < our portion < — and may

הָרַחֲמָן הוּא יְזַכֵּנוּ לִימוֹת הַמָּשִׁיחַ וּלְחַיֵּי

< and of << of Messiah < of the days < make us < May He < The compas-
the life worthy sionate One!

הָעוֹלָם הַבָּא. מִגְדּוֹל יְשׁוּעוֹת מַלְכּוֹ וְעֹשֶׂה

< and does < to His < of salvations < He Who is << to Come. < of the
king a tower World

קַדֵּשׁ וּרְחַץ כַּרְפַּס יַחַץ מַגִּיד רָחְצָה מוֹצִיא מַצָּה

MATZAH MOTZI RACHTZAH MAGGID YACHATZ KARPAS URECHATZ KADDESH

חֶסֶד לִמְשִׁיחוֹ לְדָוִד וּלְזַרְעוֹ עַד עוֹלָם.[1]

《 forever. 〈 and to his offspring 〈 to David 〈 to His anointed, 〈 kindness

עֹשֶׂה שָׁלוֹם בִּמְרוֹמָיו, הוּא יַעֲשֶׂה שָׁלוֹם עָלֵינוּ

《《 upon us 〈 peace 〈 make 〈 may He 《《 in His heights, 〈 peace 〈 He Who makes

וְעַל כָּל יִשְׂרָאֵל. וְאִמְרוּ, אָמֵן.

《 Amen! 〈 Now respond: 《《 Israel. 〈 all 〈 and upon

יְראוּ אֶת יהוה קְדֹשָׁיו, כִּי אֵין מַחְסוֹר

〈 deprivation 〈 there is no 〈 for 《 O [you] 〈 HASHEM, 〈 Fear
His holy ones,

לִירֵאָיו. כְּפִירִים רָשׁוּ וְרָעֵבוּ, וְדֹרְשֵׁי יהוה

〈 HASHEM 〈 but those who seek 〈 and hunger, 〈 may want 〈 Young lions 《《 for His reverent ones.

לֹא יַחְסְרוּ כָל טוֹב.[2] הוֹדוּ לַיהוה כִּי טוֹב,

〈 He is good, 〈 for 〈 to HASHEM 〈 Give thanks 《《 good. 〈 any 〈 lack 〈 will not

כִּי לְעוֹלָם חַסְדּוֹ.[3] פּוֹתֵחַ אֶת יָדֶךָ, וּמַשְׂבִּיעַ

〈 and satisfy 《《 Your hand, 〈 You open 《《 is His kindness. 〈 enduring forever 〈 for

לְכָל חַי רָצוֹן.[4] בָּרוּךְ הַגֶּבֶר אֲשֶׁר יִבְטַח

〈 trusts 〈 who 〈 is the man 〈 Blessed 《《 [with its] desire. 〈 living thing 〈 every

בַּיהוה, וְהָיָה יהוה מִבְטַחוֹ.[5] נַעַר הָיִיתִי גַּם

〈 and also 〈 I have been 〈 A youth 《《 his security. 〈 then HASHEM will be 《《 in HASHEM;

זָקַנְתִּי, וְלֹא רָאִיתִי צַדִּיק נֶעֱזָב, וְזַרְעוֹ

〈 nor his children 《《 forsaken, 〈 a righteous man 〈 but I have not seen 《《 I have aged;

מְבַקֶּשׁ לָחֶם.[6] יהוה עֹז לְעַמּוֹ יִתֵּן, יהוה

〈 HASHEM 《《 will give; 〈 to His people 〈 strength 〈 HASHEM 《《 for bread. 〈 begging

יְבָרֵךְ אֶת עַמּוֹ בַשָּׁלוֹם.[7]

《《 with peace. 〈 His people 〈 will bless

---

(1) *II Samuel* 22:51. (2) *Psalms* 34:10-11. (3) 136:1 et al.
(4) 145:16. (5) *Jeremiah* 17:7. (6) *Psalms* 37:25. (7) 29:11.

NIRTZAH   hALLEL   BARECH   TZAFUN   shulchan orech   korech   MAROR

UPON COMPLETION OF *BIRCAS HAMAZON* THE BLESSING OVER WINE IS RECITED AND THE THIRD CUP IS DRUNK WHILE RECLINING ON THE LEFT SIDE. IT IS PREFERABLE TO DRINK THE ENTIRE CUP, BUT AT THE VERY LEAST, MOST OF THE CUP SHOULD BE DRAINED.

SOME RECITE THE FOLLOWING BEFORE THE THIRD CUP:

הִנְנִי מוּכָן וּמְזוּמָּן לְקַיֵּם מִצְוַת כּוֹס שְׁלִישִׁי שֶׁל אַרְבַּע כּוֹסוֹת.

》 Cup. 〈 the Four 〈 of 〈 of the 〈 the 〈 to 〈 and 〈 am 〈 I now
third cup mitzvah perform ready prepared

לְשֵׁם יִחוּד קֻדְשָׁא בְּרִיךְ הוּא וּשְׁכִינְתֵּיהּ, עַל יְדֵי הַהוּא טָמִיר

〈 Who is 〈 Him 〈 through 》 and His 》 is He, 〈 Blessed 》of the Holy 〈 of the 〈 For the
hidden Presence, One, unification sake

וְנֶעְלָם, בְּשֵׁם כָּל יִשְׂרָאֵל. וִיהִי נְעַם אֲדֹנָי אֱלֹהֵינוּ

〈 our God, 〈 of the 〈 the plea- 〈 May 》 Israel. 〈 of all 〈 — [I pray] 》 and Who is
Lord, santness in the name inscrutable

עָלֵינוּ, וּמַעֲשֵׂה יָדֵינוּ כּוֹנְנָה עָלֵינוּ, וּמַעֲשֵׂה יָדֵינוּ כּוֹנְנֵהוּ.[1]

》 establish 〈 of our 〈 the work 》 for us; 〈 establish 〈 of our 〈 the work 》 be
it. hands, hands, upon us;

בָּרוּךְ אַתָּה יהוה אֱלֹהֵינוּ מֶלֶךְ הָעוֹלָם,

》 of the universe, 〈 King 〈 our God, 〈 HASHEM, 〈 are You, 〈 Blessed

בּוֹרֵא פְּרִי הַגָּפֶן.

》 of the vine. 〈 the fruit 〈 Who creates

THE FOURTH CUP IS POURED. ACCORDING TO MOST CUSTOMS, THE CUP OF ELIYAHU IS POURED AT THIS POINT, AFTER WHICH THE DOOR IS OPENED IN ACCORDANCE WITH THE VERSE, "IT IS A GUARDED NIGHT." THEN THE FOLLOWING PARAGRAPH IS RECITED.

שְׁפֹךְ* חֲמָתְךָ אֶל הַגּוֹיִם אֲשֶׁר לֹא יְדָעוּךְ

》 recognize 〈 do 〈 that 〈 the nations 〈 upon 〈 Your wrath 〈 Pour*
You, not

וְעַל מַמְלָכוֹת אֲשֶׁר בְּשִׁמְךָ לֹא קָרָאוּ.[2] כִּי אָכַל

〈 they have 〈 For 》 call. 〈 do 〈 upon Your 〈 that 〈 the kingdoms 〈 and
devoured not Name upon

אֶת יַעֲקֹב וְאֶת נָוֵהוּ הֵשַׁמּוּ. שְׁפֹךְ עֲלֵיהֶם

〈 upon them 〈 Pour 》 they have destroyed. 〈 and His habitation 》 Jacob,

---

(1) *Psalms* 90:17. (2) 79:6-7.

שְׁפֹךְ — *Pour.* Past redemption from Egypt was the theme of the part of the Haggadah recited before the meal. Now, the tense switches and the future Messianic redemption is brought to the fore. We open the door, indi-cating our readiness to recieve the Prophet Elijah, herald of the Messiah, as we beseech God to pour His wrath upon those who would play Pharaoh's spiritual successors in oppressing the Jews.

תַּרְדֹּף בְּאַף‎ יַשִּׂיגֵם.‎¹ אַפְּךָ וַחֲרוֹן זַעְמֶךָ

‹ in anger ‹ Pursue them « overtake them. ‹ of Your anger ‹ and let the fierceness « Your fury,

וְתַשְׁמִידֵם מִתַּחַת שְׁמֵי יהוה.‎²

« of HASHEM. ‹ the heavens ‹ from beneath ‹ and destroy them

THE DOOR IS CLOSED AND THE RECITATION OF THE *HAGGADAH* CONTINUES WITH *HALLEL*.

❧ הלל / HALLEL ❧

—— Psalm 115:1-11 / תהלים קטו:א-יא ——

תֵּן לְשִׁמְךָ כִּי לָנוּ; לֹא יהוה, **לֹא לָנוּ***

‹ give ‹ for Your Name's sake ‹ but « for our sake, ‹ not ‹ HASHEM, ‹ for our sake,* ‹ Not

יֹאמְרוּ לָמָה אֲמִתֶּךָ. עַל חַסְדְּךָ עַל כָּבוֹד,

« should they say ‹ Why « Your truth! ‹ [and] for ‹ Your kindness ‹ for « glory,

בַשָּׁמָיִם, וֵאלֹהֵינוּ אֱלֹהֵיהֶם. נָא אַיֵּה הַגּוֹיִם,

« is in the heavens; ‹ Our God « is their God? ‹ now ‹ Where «— the nations,

וְזָהָב, כֶּסֶף עֲצַבֵּיהֶם עָשָׂה. חָפֵץ אֲשֶׁר כֹּל

« and gold, ‹ are silver ‹ Their idols « He does! ‹ He pleases ‹ whatever

יְדַבֵּרוּ, וְלֹא לָהֶם פֶּה אָדָם. יְדֵי מַעֲשֵׂה

« speak; ‹ but cannot ‹ they have, ‹ A mouth « of man. ‹ of the hands ‹ the work

וְלֹא לָהֶם אָזְנַיִם יִרְאוּ. וְלֹא לָהֶם עֵינַיִם

‹ but cannot ‹ they have, ‹ ears « see; ‹ but cannot ‹ they have, ‹ eyes

יְדֵיהֶם יְרִיחוּן. וְלֹא לָהֶם אַף יִשְׁמָעוּ,

« Their hands « smell. ‹ but cannot ‹ they have, ‹ a nose « hear;

יֶהְגּוּ לֹא יְהַלֵּכוּ, וְלֹא רַגְלֵיהֶם יְמִישׁוּן, וְלֹא

‹ they cannot utter [a sound] «— they cannot walk; « their feet «— they cannot feel;

---

(1) *Psalms* 69:25. (2) *Lamentations* 3:66.

❧ **לֹא לָנוּ** — *Not for our sake.* The preceding psalm (recited before the meal) depicts the awe inspired by God's miracles. Here the Psalmist describes the aftermath of that inspiration. Although Israel remained imbued with faith, our oppressors soon began to scoff, "Where is our

NIRTZAh   hALLEL   BARECh   TZAFUN   ShULChAN OREch   KORECh   MAROR

בִּגְרוֹנָם. כְּמוֹהֶם יִהְיוּ עֹשֵׂיהֶם, כֹּל אֲשֶׁר בֹּטֵחַ

‹ trust ‹ who ‹ all ‹‹ those who make them, ‹ should become ‹ Like them ‹‹ from their throat.

בָּהֶם. יִשְׂרָאֵל בְּטַח בַּיהוה,* עֶזְרָם וּמָגִנָּם הוּא.*

‹‹ is He!* ‹ and their shield ‹ their help ‹‹ in HASHEM;* ‹ trust ‹ O Israel, ‹‹ in them!

בֵּית אַהֲרֹן בִּטְחוּ בַיהוה, עֶזְרָם וּמָגִנָּם הוּא.*

‹‹ is He!* ‹ and their shield ‹ their help ‹‹ in HASHEM; ‹ trust ‹ of Aaron, ‹ House

יִרְאֵי יהוה בִּטְחוּ בַיהוה, עֶזְרָם וּמָגִנָּם הוּא.*

‹‹ is He!* ‹ and their shield ‹ their help ‹‹ in HASHEM; ‹ trust ‹ HASHEM, ‹ You who fear

———— תהלים קטו:יב-יח / Psalm 115:12-18 ————

יהוה זְכָרָנוּ יְבָרֵךְ;* יְבָרֵךְ אֶת בֵּית יִשְׂרָאֵל,

‹‹ of Israel, ‹ the House ‹ He will bless ‹‹ will bless:* ‹ Who has remembered us ‹ HASHEM

יְבָרֵךְ אֶת בֵּית אַהֲרֹן. יְבָרֵךְ יִרְאֵי יהוה,

‹‹ HASHEM, ‹ those who fear ‹ He will bless ‹‹ of Aaron. ‹ the House ‹ He will bless

הַקְּטַנִּים עִם הַגְּדֹלִים. יֹסֵף יהוה עֲלֵיכֶם,

‹‹ upon you, ‹ May HASHEM increase ‹‹ the great. ‹ as well as ‹ the small

עֲלֵיכֶם וְעַל בְּנֵיכֶם. בְּרוּכִים אַתֶּם לַיהוה,

‹‹ by HASHEM, ‹ are you ‹ Blessed ‹‹ your children! ‹ and upon ‹ upon you

God?" We pray that God will intervene again in the affairs of man, not for our sake, but for His.

יִשְׂרָאֵל בְּטַח בַּה' — *O Israel, trust in HASHEM*. The psalm now contrasts the Children of Israel, who trust in God alone, with those described in the previous verse, who trust in the lifeless and helpless idols (*Ibn Ezra*).

The Psalmist speaks of three kinds of Jews, each with a different motive for serving God. Some cling to God simply because they feel that He is their Father, and they are His devoted sons. These are called יִשְׂרָאֵל, *Israel*, God's chosen, beloved nation. The second group serves God out of love. They resemble the *House of* Aaron, the *Kohanim*-priests who never betrayed God and were therefore designated to stand in His presence, in the Temple, for all time. Finally, *you who fear HASHEM* refers to a third group of Jews, who serve God out of fear and awe (*Maharal*).

עֶזְרָם וּמָגִנָּם הוּא — *Their help and their shield is He!* This is thrice repeated. Since each successive group possesses a different level of faith, it deserves a totally different degree of Divine protection. Thus God's response to each group is mentioned separately.

ה' זְכָרָנוּ יְבָרֵךְ — *HASHEM Who has remembered us will bless*. The Psalmist expresses con-

קַדֵּשׁ וּרְחַץ כַּרְפַּס יַחַץ מַגִּיד רָחְצָה מוֹצִיא מַצָּה

MATZAH MOTZI RACHTZAH MAGGID YACHATZ KARPAS URECHATZ KADDESH

עֹשֶׂה שָׁמַיִם וָאָרֶץ. הַשָּׁמַיִם שָׁמַיִם לַיהוה,

‹‹ are for ‹ the heavens ‹ As for ‹‹ and earth. ‹ of heaven ‹ Maker
HASHEM;   the heavens,

וְהָאָרֶץ נָתַן לִבְנֵי אָדָם. לֹא הַמֵּתִים

‹ the dead ‹ Neither ‹‹ to mankind. ‹ He has given ‹ but the earth

יְהַלְלוּ יָהּ,* וְלֹא כָּל יֹרְדֵי דוּמָה. וַאֲנַחְנוּ

‹ But we ‹‹ silence. ‹ who descend into ‹ any ‹ nor ‹‹ God,* ‹ can praise

נְבָרֵךְ יָהּ, מֵעַתָּה וְעַד עוֹלָם; הַלְלוּיָהּ.

‹‹ Halleluyah! ‹‹ eternity. ‹ until ‹ from this time ‹‹ God ‹ will bless

——— Psalm 116:1-11 / תהלים קטז:א-יא ———

אָהַבְתִּי* כִּי יִשְׁמַע יהוה, אֶת קוֹלִי תַּחֲנוּנָי.

‹‹ my ‹ my voice, ‹ HASHEM hears ‹ for ‹ I love [Him],*
supplications.

כִּי הִטָּה אָזְנוֹ לִי, וּבְיָמַי אֶקְרָא. אֲפָפוּנִי חֶבְלֵי

‹ have the ‹ Encircled ‹‹ shall I call. ‹ so in ‹‹ to me, ‹ His ear ‹ He has ‹ As
pains   me   my days   inclined

מָוֶת, וּמְצָרֵי שְׁאוֹל מְצָאוּנִי; צָרָה וְיָגוֹן אֶמְצָא.

‹‹ I would ‹ and grief ‹ distress ‹‹ have found ‹ of the grave ‹ and the ‹‹ of
find.   me;   confines   death;

וּבְשֵׁם יהוה אֶקְרָא: אָנָּה יהוה מַלְּטָה נַפְשִׁי.

‹‹ my soul. ‹ save ‹ HASHEM, ‹ Please, ‹‹ I would ‹ of HASHEM ‹ [Then]
invoke,   the Name

חַנּוּן יהוה וְצַדִּיק, וֵאלֹהֵינוּ מְרַחֵם. שֹׁמֵר

‹ Protector ‹‹ is merciful. ‹ our God ‹‹ and righteous, ‹ is HASHEM ‹ Gracious

---

fidence that just as God has blessed His people in the past, so will He bless them in the future. לֹא הַמֵּתִים יְהַלְלוּ יָהּ — *Neither the dead can praise God.* The people who fail to recognize God's omnipresence and influence over the world resemble the dead, who are insensitive to all external stimuli and who are oblivious to reality (*R' Azariah Figo*). However, the souls of the righteous continue to praise God even after they depart from their bodies (*Ibn Ezra*).

אָהַבְתִּי — *I love [Him].* The Psalmist foresaw

that Israel would feel completely alone in exile. The nations would taunt them, "Your prayers and pleas are worthless, because God has turned a deaf ear to you." Therefore, he composed this psalm to encourage the downcast exiles with the assurance that indeed: *HASHEM hears my voice, my supplications.*

The Talmud (*Rosh Hashanah* 16b-17a) explains that this psalm describes the day of Final Judgment at the time of תְּחִיַּת הַמֵּתִים, *the Revivification of the Dead.* The average person, who

NIRTZAh   hALLEL   BARECh   TZAFUN   shULChAN ORECh   KORECh   MAROR

פְּתָאיִם יְהוָה, דַּלּוֹתִי וְלִי יְהוֹשִׁיעַ. שׁוּבִי נַפְשִׁי

‹ my soul, ‹ Return, « He saved. ‹ but me ‹ I was « is ‹ of the simple
brought low, HASHEM;

לִמְנוּחָיְכִי, כִּי יְהוָה גָּמַל עָלָיְכִי. כִּי חִלַּצְתָּ

‹ You have ‹ For « you. ‹ has ‹ HASHEM ‹ for « to your rest;
delivered rewarded

נַפְשִׁי מִמָּוֶת; אֶת עֵינִי מִן דִּמְעָה, אֶת רַגְלִי

‹ my feet « tears, ‹ from ‹ my eyes « from death, ‹ my soul

מִדֶּחִי. אֶתְהַלֵּךְ לִפְנֵי יְהוָה, בְּאַרְצוֹת הַחַיִּים.*

« of the living.* ‹ in the lands ‹ HASHEM ‹ before ‹ I shall walk « from stumbling.

הֶאֱמַנְתִּי כִּי אֲדַבֵּר, אֲנִי עָנִיתִי מְאֹד. אֲנִי

‹ I « exceedingly. ‹ suffer ‹ I « I say, ‹ although ‹ I have kept faith

אָמַרְתִּי בְחָפְזִי, כָּל הָאָדָם כֹּזֵב.*

« is deceitful.* ‹ mankind ‹ All « in my haste, ‹ said

——— תהלים קטז:יב-יט / Psalm 116:12-19 ———

מָה אָשִׁיב לַיהוָה,* כָּל תַּגְמוּלוֹהִי עָלָי.

« on me? ‹ the kindnesses he ‹ for all « HASHEM* ‹ can I repay ‹ How
has bestowed

כּוֹס יְשׁוּעוֹת אֶשָּׂא, וּבְשֵׁם יְהוָה אֶקְרָא.

« I will ‹ of ‹ and the « I will raise ‹ of salvations ‹ The cup
invoke. HASHEM Name

is neither completely righteous nor completely wicked, will be saved from *Gehinnom* because God will hear his cries, and He will forgive him. In gratitude, he will sing, "*I love Him, for HASHEM hears my voice, my supplications.*"

אֶתְהַלֵּךְ לִפְנֵי ה' בְּאַרְצוֹת הַחַיִּים — *I shall walk before HASHEM in the lands of the living.* How I yearn to return to *Eretz Yisrael* where the very air makes men healthy and robust and the holy atmosphere grants the mind renewed vitality and alertness! (*Radak*). *Eretz Yisrael* is identified as the *land of the living* because the dead are destined to be resurrected there.

אֲנִי אָמַרְתִּי בְחָפְזִי כָּל הָאָדָם כֹּזֵב — *I said in my haste, "All mankind is deceitful."* This bitter

comment was originally uttered by David when the people of Zif betrayed his hiding place to King Saul [see *I Samuel* 23:19-29] (*Rashi*). It is also a reference to the bleak, dismal exile [for the exile discourages the Jews and leads them to the hasty, premature conclusion that all the prophets' promises concerning redemption were *deceitful*] (*Abarbanel*).

מָה אָשִׁיב לַה' — *How can I repay HASHEM?* What gift can I give to the King Who owns everything? (*Ibn Ezra*). How can I possibly repay His acts of kindness, for they are too numerous to recount? (*Radak*). How can I even approach Him? He is eternal and I am finite; He is the highest, and I am the lowest! (*Ibn Yachya*).

נְדָרַי לַיהוה אֲשַׁלֵּם, נֶגְדָה נָּא לְכָל עַמּוֹ.

« people. ‹ of His entire ‹ now, ‹ in the presence, « I will pay, ‹ to HASHEM ‹ My vows

יָקָר בְּעֵינֵי יהוה, הַמָּוְתָה לַחֲסִידָיו. אָנָּה יהוה

‹ HASHEM, ‹ Please, « of His devout ones. ‹ is the death ‹ of HASHEM ‹ in the eyes ‹ Difficult

כִּי אֲנִי עַבְדֶּךָ; אֲנִי עַבְדְּךָ בֶּן אֲמָתֶךָ, פִּתַּחְתָּ

‹ You have released « of Your handmaiden; ‹ son ‹ Your servant, ‹ I am « Your servant, ‹ I am ‹ for

לְמוֹסֵרָי. לְךָ אֶזְבַּח זֶבַח תּוֹדָה, וּבְשֵׁם יהוה

‹ of HASHEM ‹ and the Name « of thanksgiving, ‹ an offering ‹ I will sacrifice ‹ To You « my bonds.

אֶקְרָא. נְדָרַי לַיהוה אֲשַׁלֵּם, נֶגְדָה נָּא לְכָל

‹ of His entire ‹ now, ‹ in the presence, « I will pay, ‹ to HASHEM ‹ My vows « I will invoke.

עַמּוֹ. בְּחַצְרוֹת בֵּית יהוה, בְּתוֹכֵכִי יְרוּשָׁלָיִם;

« O Jerusalem. ‹ in your midst, « of HASHEM, ‹ of the House ‹ in the courtyards « people,

הַלְלוּיָהּ.

« Halleluyah!

——————— תהלים קיז / Psalm 117 ———————

הַלְלוּ אֶת יהוה,* כָּל גּוֹיִם; שַׁבְּחוּהוּ כָּל

‹ all ‹ extol Him, « nations; ‹ all ‹ HASHEM,* ‹ Praise

הָאֻמִּים. כִּי גָבַר עָלֵינוּ חַסְדּוֹ,* וֶאֱמֶת יהוה

‹ of HASHEM ‹ and the truth « has His kindness,* ‹ us ‹ overwhelmed ‹ For « the states!

לְעוֹלָם; הַלְלוּיָהּ.

« Halleluyah! ‹ is eternal.

◄§ הַלְלוּ אֶת ה' — *Praise HASHEM.* This psalm, containing only two verses, is the shortest chapter in all of Scripture. *Radak* explains that its brevity symbolizes the simplicity of the world order which will prevail after the advent of the Messiah.

כִּי גָבַר עָלֵינוּ חַסְדּוֹ — *For overwhelmed us has His kindness.* Why should non-Jewish peoples and nations praise God for overwhelming Israel with Divine kindness? Israel will merit God's kindness because of the extraordinary service they rendered to Him. Recognizing Israel's dis-

Psalm 118 / תהלים קיח

WHEN AT LEAST THREE PEOPLE ARE PRESENT, EACH OF THE FOLLOWING FOUR VERSES IS RECITED ALOUD BY THE LEADER. ALL PRESENT RESPOND WITH THE FIRST VERSE, הוֹדוּ לַיהוה כִּי טוֹב, AND THEN QUIETLY RECITE THE NEXT VERSE THAT THE LEADER WILL RECITE ALOUD.

הוֹדוּ לַיהוה כִּי טוֹב,* כִּי לְעוֹלָם חַסְדּוֹ.

Give thanks ‹ to HASHEM ‹ for ‹ He is good;* ‹‹ for ‹ enduring forever ‹ is His kindness! ‹‹

יֹאמַר נָא יִשְׂרָאֵל, כִּי לְעוֹלָם חַסְדּוֹ.

Let Israel say now, ‹‹ For ‹ enduring forever ‹ is His kindness! ‹‹

יֹאמְרוּ נָא בֵית אַהֲרֹן, כִּי לְעוֹלָם חַסְדּוֹ.

Let them say ‹ now ‹‹ the ‹ — House of Aaron — ‹‹ For ‹ enduring forever ‹ is His kindness! ‹‹

יֹאמְרוּ נָא יִרְאֵי יהוה, כִּי לְעוֹלָם חַסְדּוֹ.

Let them say ‹ now ‹‹ those who fear ‹ — HASHEM — ‹‹ For ‹ enduring forever ‹ is His kindness! ‹‹

מִן הַמֵּצַר קָרָאתִי יָּהּ, עָנָנִי בַמֶּרְחָב יָהּ.

From ‹ the straits ‹ did I call ‹ upon ‹‹ God; ‹ answer me ‹ with expansiveness ‹ did ‹‹ God.

יהוה לִי לֹא אִירָא, מַה יַּעֲשֶׂה לִי אָדָם.

HASHEM ‹ is with me, ‹ I have no fear; ‹‹ how ‹ can man affect me? ‹‹

יהוה לִי בְּעֹזְרָי, וַאֲנִי אֶרְאֶה בְשֹׂנְאָי.

HASHEM ‹ is with me ‹ through my helpers; ‹‹ therefore I ‹ can face ‹ my foes. ‹‹

טוֹב לַחֲסוֹת בַּיהוה, מִבְּטֹחַ בָּאָדָם. טוֹב

It is better ‹ to take refuge ‹ in HASHEM ‹‹ than to rely ‹ on man. ‹‹ It is better ‹

---

tinction, the nations will consider it a privilege to become subservient to God's chosen ones, and will praise Him for His kindness to the Jews (Yaavetz HaDoresh).

הוֹדוּ לַה׳ כִּי טוֹב — Give thanks to HASHEM for He is good. This is a general expression of thanksgiving to God. No matter what occurs, God is always good and everything He does is for the best, even though this may not be readily apparent to man (Abarbanel).

טוֹב לַחֲסוֹת בַּה׳ מִבְּטֹחַ בָּאָדָם — It is better to take refuge in HASHEM than to rely on man. חִסָּיוֹן, taking refuge, denotes absolute confidence even though no guarantees have been given; בְּטָחוֹן, reliance, however, presupposes a promise of protection. The Psalmist says that it is far better to put one's trust in God's protection, even without a pledge from Him, than to rely on the most profuse assurances of human beings (R' Bachya; Vilna Gaon).

לַחֲסוֹת בַּיהוה, מִבְּטֹחַ בִּנְדִיבִים. כָּל גּוֹיִם
‹ the nations ‹ All ‹‹ on nobles. ‹ than to rely ‹‹ in Hashem ‹ to take refuge

סְבָבוּנִי, בְּשֵׁם יהוה כִּי אֲמִילַם. סַבּוּנִי גַם
‹ also ‹ They ‹‹ I cut them ‹ that ‹ of Hashem ‹ it is in ‹‹ surround me;
encircle me, down! the Name

סְבָבוּנִי, בְּשֵׁם יהוה כִּי אֲמִילַם. סַבּוּנִי כִדְבֹרִים,
‹‹ like bees, ‹ They ‹‹ I cut them ‹ that ‹ of ‹ it is in ‹‹ they surround
encircle me down! Hashem, the Name me;

דֹּעֲכוּ כְּאֵשׁ קוֹצִים; בְּשֵׁם יהוה כִּי אֲמִילַם.
‹‹ I cut them ‹ that ‹ of ‹ it is in ‹‹ of thorns; ‹ as a fire ‹ but they are
down! Hashem, the Name extinguished

דָּחֹה דְחִיתַנִי לִנְפֹּל, וַיהוה עֲזָרָנִי. עָזִּי וְזִמְרָת
‹ and my ‹ My ‹‹ assisted ‹ but Hashem ‹‹ that I ‹ You pushed me hard
praise might me. might fall,

יָהּ, וַיְהִי לִי לִישׁוּעָה. קוֹל רִנָּה וִישׁוּעָה
‹ and salvation ‹ of rejoicing ‹ The sound ‹‹ a salvation. ‹ for me ‹ and He was ‹‹ is God,

בְּאָהֳלֵי צַדִּיקִים, יְמִין יהוה עֹשָׂה חָיִל.
‹‹ [deeds of] valor. ‹ does ‹ of Hashem ‹ The right hand ‹‹ of the righteous, ‹ is in the tents

יְמִין יהוה רוֹמֵמָה, יְמִין יהוה עֹשָׂה חָיִל.
‹‹ [deeds of] ‹ does ‹ of Hashem ‹ the ‹‹ is raised ‹ of Hashem ‹ The right
valor. right hand triumphantly; hand

לֹא אָמוּת כִּי אֶחְיֶה, וַאֲסַפֵּר מַעֲשֵׂי יָהּ.
‹‹ of God. ‹ the deeds ‹ and relate ‹‹ I shall live ‹ But ‹ I shall not die!

יַסֹּר יִסְּרַנִי יָּהּ, וְלַמָּוֶת לֹא נְתָנָנִי.* פִּתְחוּ לִי
‹ for ‹ Open ‹‹ He did not ‹ but to death ‹‹ has ‹ Chastened me
me give me over.* God, exceedingly

שַׁעֲרֵי צֶדֶק, אָבֹא בָם אוֹדֶה יָּהּ. זֶה הַשַּׁעַר
‹ the gate ‹ This is ‹‹ God. ‹ and ‹ them ‹ I will ‹‹ of ‹ the gates
thank enter righteousness;

יַסֹּר יִסְּרַנִי יָּהּ וְלַמָּוֶת לֹא נְתָנָנִי — *Chastened me
exceedingly has God, but to death He did not
give me over.* Throughout the duration of the

exile, I survived because whatever suffering
God decreed was only to atone for my sins
(Rashi).

לַיהוה, צַדִּיקִים יָבֹאוּ בוֹ. אוֹדְךָ* כִּי עֲנִיתָנִי,
<< You have < for < I thank << through < shall < the righteous << of HASHEM;
answered me You* it. enter

וַתְּהִי לִי לִישׁוּעָה. אוֹדְךָ כִּי עֲנִיתָנִי, וַתְּהִי
< and << You have < for < I thank << a salvation. < for < and
[You have] answered me You me [You have]
become become

לִי לִישׁוּעָה. אֶבֶן מָאֲסוּ הַבּוֹנִים, הָיְתָה
< has become < by the builders < despised < The stone << a salvation. < for me

לְרֹאשׁ פִּנָּה.* אֶבֶן מָאֲסוּ הַבּוֹנִים, הָיְתָה
< has become < by the builders < despised < The stone << the cornerstone.*

לְרֹאשׁ פִּנָּה. מֵאֵת יהוה הָיְתָה זֹּאת, הִיא
< it << this; < emanated < HASHEM < From << the cornerstone.

נִפְלָאת בְּעֵינֵינוּ. מֵאֵת יהוה הָיְתָה זֹּאת, הִיא
< it << this; < emanated < HASHEM < From << in our eyes. < is wondrous

נִפְלָאת בְּעֵינֵינוּ. זֶה הַיּוֹם עָשָׂה יהוה, נָגִילָה
< let us rejoice << HASHEM has made; < is the day < This << in our eyes. < is wondrous

וְנִשְׂמְחָה בוֹ. זֶה הַיּוֹם עָשָׂה יהוה, נָגִילָה
< let us rejoice << HASHEM has made; < is the day < This << on it. < and be glad

וְנִשְׂמְחָה בוֹ.
<< on it. < and be glad

⋄§ Repetition of Verses

אוֹדְךָ — *I thank You.* From this point until the end of the Scriptural part of *Hallel* — the nine verses until יְהַלְלוּךָ — each verse is recited twice.

Up until this point, this entire psalm, which begins with הוֹדוּ לַה', *Give thanks to HASHEM*, follows a pattern, namely, that each new theme is repeated in the next verse or two in the same or slightly different words. Therefore the custom was introduced to follow through on this repetition by repeating the rest of the verses as well (*Rashi* to *Succah* 38a).

אֶבֶן מָאֲסוּ הַבּוֹנִים הָיְתָה לְרֹאשׁ פִּנָּה — *The stone despised by the builders has become the corner-*

stone. This verse refers to David, who was rejected by his own father and brothers (*Targum*). When the prophet Samuel announced that one of Jesse's sons was to be anointed king, no one even thought of summoning David, who was tending the sheep [see *I Samuel* 16:4-13].

Israel too is called אֶבֶן, *stone* (*Genesis* 49:24), for Israel is the cornerstone of God's design for the world. The world endures only by virtue of Israel's observance of God's laws, a fact that has influenced all nations to appreciate and accept certain aspects of God's commands. If not for the order and meaning that Israel has brought

קַדֵּשׁ וּרְחַץ כַּרְפַּס יַחַץ מַגִּיד רָחְצָה מוֹצִיא מַצָּה
[ATZAh MOTZI RACHTZAh MAGGID YACHATZ KARPAS URECHATZ KADDESH

WHEN AT LEAST THREE PEOPLE ARE PRESENT, EACH OF THE FOLLOWING FOUR LINES IS RECITED RESPONSIVELY, THE LEADER FOLLOWED BY ALL PRESENT.

אָנָּא יהוה, הוֹשִׁיעָה נָּא.

‹‹ now! ‹ save ‹ Hashem, ‹ Please,

אָנָּא יהוה, הוֹשִׁיעָה נָּא.

‹‹ now! ‹ save ‹ Hashem, ‹ Please,

אָנָּא יהוה, הַצְלִיחָה נָא.

‹‹ now! ‹ bring success ‹ Hashem, ‹ Please,

אָנָּא יהוה, הַצְלִיחָה נָא.

‹‹ now! ‹ bring success ‹ Hashem, ‹ Please,

בָּרוּךְ הַבָּא בְּשֵׁם יהוה, בֵּרַכְנוּכֶם מִבֵּית

‹ from the ‹ we bless you ‹‹ of Hashem; ‹ in the ‹ is he who ‹ Blessed
House   Name   comes

יהוה. בָּרוּךְ הַבָּא בְּשֵׁם יהוה, בֵּרַכְנוּכֶם מִבֵּית

‹ from the ‹ we bless you ‹‹ of Hashem; ‹ in the ‹ is he who ‹ Blessed ‹‹ of
House   Name   comes   Hashem.

יהוה. אֵל יהוה וַיָּאֶר לָנוּ, אִסְרוּ חַג בַּעֲבֹתִים

‹ with cords ‹ the festival ‹ bind ‹ for us; ‹ He ‹‹ is ‹ The ‹‹ of
[offering]   illuminated Hashem. Almighty Hashem.

עַד קַרְנוֹת הַמִּזְבֵּחַ. אֵל יהוה וַיָּאֶר לָנוּ, אִסְרוּ

‹ bind ‹‹ for us; ‹ He ‹‹ is ‹ The ‹‹ of the Altar. ‹ the corners ‹ until
illuminated Hashem. Almighty

חַג בַּעֲבֹתִים עַד קַרְנוֹת הַמִּזְבֵּחַ. אֵלִי אַתָּה

‹ You are, ‹ My God ‹‹ of the Altar. ‹ the corners ‹ until ‹ with cords ‹ the festival
[offering]

וְאוֹדֶךָּ, אֱלֹהַי אֲרוֹמְמֶךָּ. אֵלִי אַתָּה וְאוֹדֶךָּ,

‹‹ and I will ‹ You are, ‹ My God ‹‹ I will exalt You. ‹ my God, ‹‹ and I will
thank You;   thank You;

---

to the world, it would long ago have sunk into chaos. But the builders, the rulers of the nations, despised the Jews, claiming that they were parasites who made no contribution to the common good. When the dawn of redemption arrives, however, all nations will realize that Israel is indeed the cornerstone of the world (*Radak*).

NIRTZAh   hALLeL   BAReCh   TZAFUN   ShULChAN OReCh   KOReCh   MAROR

אֱלֹהַי אֲרוֹמְמֶךָּ. הוֹדוּ לַיהוה כִּי טוֹב, כִּי לְעוֹלָם

‹ enduring forever ‹ for ‹‹ He is good; ‹ for ‹ to HASHEM, ‹ Give thanks ‹‹ I will exalt You. ‹ my God,

חַסְדּוֹ. הוֹדוּ לַיהוה כִּי טוֹב, כִּי לְעוֹלָם חַסְדּוֹ.

‹‹ is His kindness. ‹ enduring forever ‹ for ‹‹ He is good; ‹ for ‹ to HASHEM, ‹ Give thanks ‹‹ is His kindness.

ACCORDING TO THE *ASHKENAZIC* CUSTOM, THE FOLLOWING PASSAGE IS RECITED HERE. THE *NUSACH SEFARD* CUSTOM IS TO RECITE IT AFTER יִשְׁתַּבַּח, *PRAISED*, (PAGE 104).

יְהַלְלוּךָ* יהוה אֱלֹהֵינוּ כָּל מַעֲשֶׂיךָ,*

‹‹ of Your works.* ‹ — all ‹‹ our God ‹ HASHEM, ‹‹ They shall praise You,*

וַחֲסִידֶיךָ צַדִּיקִים עוֹשֵׂי רְצוֹנֶךָ, וְכָל עַמְּךָ בֵית

‹ the House ‹ of Your people, ‹ and all ‹‹ Your will, ‹ who do ‹ the righteous, ‹ And Your devout ones,

יִשְׂרָאֵל בְּרִנָּה יוֹדוּ וִיבָרְכוּ וִישַׁבְּחוּ וִיפָאֲרוּ

‹ glorify, ‹ praise, ‹ bless, ‹ will thank, ‹ with glad song ‹‹ of Israel,

וִירוֹמְמוּ וְיַעֲרִיצוּ וְיַקְדִּישׁוּ וְיַמְלִיכוּ אֶת שִׁמְךָ

‹ Your Name, ‹ and proclaim the sovereignty of ‹ sanctify, ‹ extol, ‹ exalt,

מַלְכֵּנוּ. כִּי לְךָ טוֹב לְהוֹדוֹת וּלְשִׁמְךָ נָאֶה

‹ it is proper ‹ and unto Your Name ‹‹ to give thanks, ‹ it is good ‹ to You ‹ For ‹‹ our King.

לְזַמֵּר, כִּי מֵעוֹלָם וְעַד עוֹלָם אַתָּה אֵל.

‹‹ are God. ‹ You ‹ the World [to Come] ‹ to ‹ from [This] World ‹ for ‹‹ to sing praises,

---

⧫§ יְהַלְלוּךָ ... כָּל מַעֲשֶׂיךָ — *They shall praise You ... all of Your works.* This means that in the perfect world of the future, the entire universe, including the broad variety of human beings, will function harmoniously according to God's will. This is the highest form of praise, for without it all the beautiful spoken and sung words and songs of praise are insincere and meaningless.

עוֹשֵׂי רְצוֹנֶךָ — *Who do Your will.* In an inspiring homiletical interpretation, Yismach Yisrael interprets that the good deeds of the righteous can remake God's will, as it were. In other words, when Jews serve Him properly, God responds by lavishing kindness and a sense of fulfillment upon the world. *Hallel* is then not only a song of thanksgiving for past miracles, but also a song of praise for the longed-for redemption.

—— Psalm 136 / תהלים קלו ——

הוֹדוּ לַיהוה כִּי טוֹב,* כִּי לְעוֹלָם חַסְדּוֹ.*

≫ is His ‹ enduring ‹ for ‹ ≫ He is ‹ for ‹ to Hashem ‹ Give
kindness.* forever good,* thanks

הוֹדוּ לֵאלֹהֵי הָאֱלֹהִים, כִּי לְעוֹלָם חַסְדּוֹ.

≫ is His ‹ enduring ‹ for ≫ of the heavenly ‹ to the God ‹ Give
kindness. forever powers, thanks

הוֹדוּ לַאֲדֹנֵי הָאֲדֹנִים, כִּי לְעוֹלָם חַסְדּוֹ.

≫ is His ‹ enduring ‹ for ≫ of the lords, ‹ to the Lord ‹ Give
kindness. forever thanks

לְעֹשֵׂה נִפְלָאוֹת גְּדֹלוֹת לְבַדּוֹ, כִּי לְעוֹלָם חַסְדּוֹ.

≫ is His ‹ enduring ‹ for ≫ by ≫ that are great, ≫ wonders, ‹ To Him Who
kindness. forever Himself, performs

לְעֹשֵׂה הַשָּׁמַיִם בִּתְבוּנָה, כִּי לְעוֹלָם חַסְדּוֹ.

≫ is His ‹ enduring ‹ for ≫ with ‹ the heavens ‹ To Him Who
kindness. forever understanding, made

לְרֹקַע הָאָרֶץ עַל הַמָּיִם, כִּי לְעוֹלָם חַסְדּוֹ.

≫ is His ‹ enduring ‹ for ≫ the waters, ‹ upon ‹ the earth ‹ To Him Who
kindness. forever spread out

לְעֹשֵׂה אוֹרִים גְּדֹלִים, כִּי לְעוֹלָם חַסְדּוֹ.

≫ is His ‹ enduring ‹ for ≫ that are great, ‹ luminaries ‹ To Him
kindness; forever Who made

אֶת הַשֶּׁמֶשׁ לְמֶמְשֶׁלֶת בַּיּוֹם, כִּי לְעוֹלָם חַסְדּוֹ.

≫ is His ‹ enduring ‹ for ≫ of the day, ‹ for the reign ‹ the sun
kindness; forever

هوֹדוּ לַה׳ / Psalm 136

The Talmud (*Pesachim* 118a) calls this psalm הַלֵּל הַגָּדוֹל, *the Great Song of Praise*, because it lauds God for giving sustenance to every living being. Thus, although it speaks of a multitude of mighty miracles, including the Creation of the universe and the Exodus from Egypt, the psalm concludes by saying נֹתֵן לֶחֶם לְכָל בָּשָׂר, *He gives nourishment* [lit., *bread*] *to all flesh*, because God's mercy upon every creature is equal to all the "great" miracles. The twenty-six

verses of the psalm are another allusion to God's mercy, for all twenty-six generations before the Torah was given, God provided for all living things out of His mercy. Once the Torah was given, man can *earn* his keep by performing the commandments. The praises are in present tense because God renews Creation constantly.

כִּי לְעוֹלָם חַסְדּוֹ — *For enduring forever is His kindness.* Homiletically, this can be rendered: His kindness is for the *world*. Man's kindnesses

אֶת הַיָּרֵחַ וְכוֹכָבִים לְמֶמְשְׁלוֹת בַּלָּיְלָה, כִּי לְעוֹלָם

the moon ⟨ and the stars ⟨ for the reign ⟨ of the night, ⟨⟨ for ⟨ enduring forever

חַסְדּוֹ. לְמַכֵּה מִצְרַיִם בִּבְכוֹרֵיהֶם,* כִּי לְעוֹלָם

is His kindness. ⟨⟨ To Him Who smote ⟨ Egypt ⟨ through their firstborn,* ⟨⟨ for ⟨ enduring forever

חַסְדּוֹ. וַיּוֹצֵא יִשְׂרָאֵל מִתּוֹכָם, כִּי לְעוֹלָם חַסְדּוֹ.

is His kindness; ⟨⟨ and Who brought forth ⟨ Israel ⟨ from their midst, ⟨⟨ for ⟨ enduring forever ⟨ is His kindness;

בְּיָד חֲזָקָה וּבִזְרוֹעַ נְטוּיָה, כִּי לְעוֹלָם חַסְדּוֹ.

with hand ⟨ that is strong ⟨ and arm ⟨ outstretched, ⟨⟨ for ⟨ enduring forever ⟨ is His kindness.

לְגֹזֵר יַם סוּף לִגְזָרִים,* כִּי לְעוֹלָם חַסְדּוֹ.

To Him Who divided ⟨ the Sea ⟨ of Reeds ⟨ into parts,* ⟨⟨ for ⟨ enduring forever ⟨ is His kindness;

וְהֶעֱבִיר יִשְׂרָאֵל בְּתוֹכוֹ, כִּי לְעוֹלָם חַסְדּוֹ.

and Who passed ⟨ Israel ⟨ through it, ⟨⟨ for ⟨ enduring forever ⟨ is His kindness;

וְנִעֵר פַּרְעֹה וְחֵילוֹ בְיַם סוּף, כִּי לְעוֹלָם חַסְדּוֹ.

and Who threw ⟨ Pharaoh ⟨ and his army ⟨ into the Sea ⟨ of Reeds, ⟨⟨ for ⟨ enduring forever ⟨ is His kindness.

לְמוֹלִיךְ עַמּוֹ בַּמִּדְבָּר, כִּי לְעוֹלָם חַסְדּוֹ.

To Him Who led ⟨ His people ⟨ through the Wilderness, ⟨⟨ for ⟨ enduring forever ⟨ is His kindness.

לְמַכֵּה מְלָכִים גְּדֹלִים, כִּי לְעוֹלָם חַסְדּוֹ.

To Him Who smote ⟨ kings ⟨ who are great, ⟨⟨ for ⟨ enduring forever ⟨ is His kindness;

can be prompted by selfish motives, but God acts for the sake of the *world*, not Himself (*Alshich*).

לְמַכֵּה מִצְרַיִם בִּבְכוֹרֵיהֶם — *To Him Who smote Egypt through their firstborn.* Upon hearing that they would soon die, the firstborn Egyptians insisted that the Jews be set free. When their countrymen refused, the firstborn at-

tacked and killed many of their fellow Egyptians. Thus, the plague of the firstborn was a double blow (*Midrash*).

יַם סוּף לִגְזָרִים — *The Sea of Reeds into parts.* The Midrash teaches that the sea was divided into twelve parts, one for each tribe. This shows that each tribe has its own mission and merited the miracle for its own sake (*Sfas Emes*).

וַיַּהֲרֹג מְלָכִים אַדִּירִים, כִּי לְעוֹלָם חַסְדּוֹ.

‹‹ is His kindness; ‹ enduring forever ‹ for ‹‹ who are mighty, ‹ kings ‹ and Who slew

לְסִיחוֹן מֶלֶךְ הָאֱמֹרִי, כִּי לְעוֹלָם חַסְדּוֹ.

‹‹ is His kindness; ‹ enduring forever ‹ for ‹ of the Amorite, ‹ King ‹ Sihon,

וּלְעוֹג מֶלֶךְ הַבָּשָׁן, כִּי לְעוֹלָם חַסְדּוֹ.

‹‹ is His kindness; ‹ enduring forever ‹ for ‹‹ of Bashan, ‹ King ‹ and Og,

וְנָתַן אַרְצָם לְנַחֲלָה, כִּי לְעוֹלָם חַסְדּוֹ.

‹‹ is His kindness; ‹ enduring forever ‹ for ‹‹ as a heritage, ‹ their land ‹ and Who presented

נַחֲלָה לְיִשְׂרָאֵל עַבְדּוֹ, כִּי לְעוֹלָם חַסְדּוֹ.

‹‹ is His kindness. ‹ enduring forever ‹ for ‹‹ His servant, ‹ for Israel, ‹ a heritage

שֶׁבְּשִׁפְלֵנוּ זָכַר לָנוּ, כִּי לְעוֹלָם חַסְדּוֹ.

‹‹ is His kindness; ‹ enduring forever ‹ for ‹‹ us, ‹ He remembered ‹ Who in our lowliness

וַיִּפְרְקֵנוּ מִצָּרֵינוּ, כִּי לְעוֹלָם חַסְדּוֹ.

‹‹ is His kindness. ‹ enduring forever ‹ for ‹‹ from our tormentors, ‹ and He released us

נֹתֵן לֶחֶם לְכָל בָּשָׂר, כִּי לְעוֹלָם חַסְדּוֹ.

‹‹ is His kindness. ‹ enduring forever ‹ for ‹‹ flesh, ‹ to all ‹ nourishment ‹ He gives

הוֹדוּ לְאֵל הַשָּׁמָיִם, כִּי לְעוֹלָם חַסְדּוֹ.

‹‹ is His kindness. ‹ enduring forever ‹ for ‹‹ of the heavens, ‹ to God ‹ Give thanks

נִשְׁמַת* כָּל חַי תְּבָרֵךְ אֶת שִׁמְךָ יהוה

‹ HASHEM, ‹ Your Name, ‹ shall bless ‹ living being ‹ of every ‹ The soul*

נִשְׁמַת / Nishmas ◆§

This beautiful and moving prayer is an outpouring of praise and gratitude to God. Lyrically, it depicts our utter dependence on God's mercy, our total inadequacy to laud Him properly, and our enthusiastic resolve to dedicate ourselves to His service. It is especially appropriate for recitation on the Sabbath and Festivals —

NIRTZAH hALLEL BARECH TZAFUN shulchan orech korech MAROR

אֱלֹהֵינוּ, וְרוּחַ כָּל בָּשָׂר תְּפָאֵר וּתְרוֹמֵם זִכְרְךָ

‹‹ Your re-membrance, ‹ and exalt ‹ shall glorify ‹ flesh ‹ of all ‹ and the spirit ‹‹ our God;

מַלְכֵּנוּ תָּמִיד. מִן הָעוֹלָם וְעַד הָעוֹלָם אַתָּה

‹ You are ‹ the most distant future ‹ and to ‹ the remotest past ‹ From ‹‹ always. ‹‹ our King,

אֵל, וּמִבַּלְעָדֶיךָ אֵין לָנוּ מֶלֶךְ גּוֹאֵל וּמוֹשִׁיעַ.

‹‹ or savior. ‹ redeemer, ‹ king, ‹ we have no ‹ and other than You ‹‹ God,

פּוֹדֶה וּמַצִּיל וּמְפַרְנֵס וּמְרַחֵם, בְּכָל עֵת צָרָה

‹ of distress ‹ time ‹ in every ‹ and Merciful One ‹ Sustainer, ‹ Rescuer, ‹ Liberator,

וְצוּקָה,* אֵין לָנוּ מֶלֶךְ אֶלָּא אָתָּה. אֱלֹהֵי

‹ God ‹‹ You! ‹ but ‹ king ‹ we have no ‹‹ and woe;*

הָרִאשׁוֹנִים וְהָאַחֲרוֹנִים, אֱלוֹהַּ כָּל בְּרִיּוֹת,

‹‹ creatures, ‹ of all ‹ God ‹‹ and of the last, ‹ of the first

אֲדוֹן כָּל תּוֹלָדוֹת, הַמְהֻלָּל בְּרֹב הַתִּשְׁבָּחוֹת,

‹‹ of praises, ‹ through a multitude ‹ Who is extolled ‹‹ generations, ‹ of all ‹ Master

הַמְּנַהֵג עוֹלָמוֹ בְּחֶסֶד וּבְרִיּוֹתָיו בְּרַחֲמִים. וַיהוה

‹ Hashem ‹‹ with mercy. ‹ and His creatures ‹‹ with kindness ‹ His world ‹ Who guides

לֹא יָנוּם וְלֹא יִישָׁן. הַמְעוֹרֵר יְשֵׁנִים, וְהַמֵּקִיץ

‹ and awakens ‹‹ sleepers ‹ He Who rouses ‹‹ sleeps. ‹ nor ‹ slumbers ‹ neither

---

although it contains no mention of the day — because the additional holiness of the Sabbath and Festivals and the time they afford for extra contemplation make man better able to understand and express the message of the *Nishmas* prayer.

The Talmud (*Pesachim* 118a) calls this prayer בִּרְכַּת הַשִּׁיר, *the Blessing of the Song*, because it concludes the psalms and songs of *Pesukei D'Zimrah*, and because it continues the theme of the Song of the Sea. In the Sabbath and Festival service, as in the Passover *Haggadah*, Nish-

mas introduces the series of praises that culminate with יִשְׁתַּבַּח, *Yishtabach*. There, too, it climaxes the grateful narrative of the Exodus with an outpouring of dedication to the service of Hashem.

בְּכָל עֵת צָרָה וְצוּקָה — *In every time of distress and woe.* Commonly, people express gratitude in happy times and pray for salvation in hard times. We go further, however — even when we suffer distress and anguish, we express our gratitude to God for allowing us to survive the attacks of our enemies.

נִרְדָּמִים, וְהַמֵּשִׂיחַ אִלְּמִים, וְהַמַּתִּיר אֲסוּרִים,

slumberers; / Who gives speech / [to] the mute, / and Who releases / the bound,

וְהַסּוֹמֵךְ נוֹפְלִים, וְהַזּוֹקֵף כְּפוּפִים. לְךָ לְבַדְּךָ

and Who supports / the fallen, / and Who straightens / the bent / – to You / alone

אֲנַחְנוּ מוֹדִים. אִלּוּ פִינוּ* מָלֵא שִׁירָה כַּיָּם,

do we / give thanks. / Were / our mouth* / as full / of song / as the sea,

וּלְשׁוֹנֵנוּ רִנָּה כַּהֲמוֹן גַּלָּיו, וְשִׂפְתוֹתֵינוּ שֶׁבַח

and our tongue / [as full of] joyous song / as the roar / of its waves, / and our lips / [as full of] praise

כְּמֶרְחֲבֵי רָקִיעַ, וְעֵינֵינוּ מְאִירוֹת כַּשֶּׁמֶשׁ וְכַיָּרֵחַ,

as the breadth / of the heavens, / and our eyes / as brilliant / as the sun / and the moon,

וְיָדֵינוּ פְרוּשׂוֹת כְּנִשְׁרֵי שָׁמָיִם, וְרַגְלֵינוּ קַלּוֹת

and our hands / as outspread / as eagles / of the sky, / and our feet / as swift

כָּאַיָּלוֹת, אֵין אֲנַחְנוּ מַסְפִּיקִים לְהוֹדוֹת לָךְ,

as deer / — we would not / suffice / to thank / You,

יהוה אֱלֹהֵינוּ וֵאלֹהֵי אֲבוֹתֵינוּ, וּלְבָרֵךְ אֶת שְׁמֶךְ

Hashem, / our God / and God / of our forefathers, / and to bless / Your Name

עַל אַחַת מֵאֶלֶף אֶלֶף אַלְפֵי אֲלָפִים וְרִבֵּי רְבָבוֹת

for / [even] one / thousand / of the thousand / thousands / thousand / of / and / of myriads / myriads

פְּעָמִים הַטּוֹבוֹת שֶׁעָשִׂיתָ עִם אֲבוֹתֵינוּ וְעִמָּנוּ.

of instances / of favors / that You performed / for / our ancestors / and for us:

מִמִּצְרַיִם גְּאַלְתָּנוּ יהוה אֱלֹהֵינוּ, וּמִבֵּית עֲבָדִים

From Egypt / You / Hashem, / our God, / and from the house / of bondage / redeemed us,

---

אִלּוּ פִינוּ — *Were our mouth.* Having stated that God is All-powerful and All-merciful, and thus worthy of our expressions of gratitude, the litur-gist now begins to explain that no creature could do justice to this task — even if he were endowed with superhuman qualities.

נִרְצָה הַלֵּל בָּרֵךְ צָפוּן שֻׁלְחָן עוֹרֵךְ כּוֹרֵךְ מָרוֹר

NIRTZAh   hALLEL   BARECh   TZAFUN   shULChAN ORECh   KORECh   MAROR

פְּדִיתָנוּ. בְּרָעָב זַנְתָּנוּ, וּבְשָׂבָע כִּלְכַּלְתָּנוּ, מֵחֶרֶב

You liberated us. In famine You nourished us, and in plenty You sustained us. From the sword

הִצַּלְתָּנוּ, וּמִדֶּבֶר מִלַּטְתָּנוּ, וּמֵחֳלָיִם רָעִים

You saved us, and from plague You gave us escape, and from diseases that are severe

וְנֶאֱמָנִים דִּלִּיתָנוּ. עַד הֵנָּה עֲזָרוּנוּ רַחֲמֶיךָ, וְלֹא

and enduring You spared us. Until now, has Your mercy, helped us and not

עֲזָבוּנוּ חֲסָדֶיךָ. וְאַל תִּטְּשֵׁנוּ יהוה אֱלֹהֵינוּ

forsaken us has Your kindness. Do not abandon us, HASHEM, our God,

לָנֶצַח. עַל כֵּן אֵבָרִים שֶׁפִּלַּגְתָּ בָּנוּ, וְרוּחַ וּנְשָׁמָה

for eternity. Therefore, the organs that You separated within us, and the spirit and soul

שֶׁנָּפַחְתָּ בְּאַפֵּינוּ, וְלָשׁוֹן אֲשֶׁר שַׂמְתָּ בְּפִינוּ, הֵן

that You blew into our nostrils, and the tongue that You placed in our mouth — indeed,

הֵם יוֹדוּ וִיבָרְכוּ וִישַׁבְּחוּ וִיפָאֲרוּ וִירוֹמְמוּ

they shall thank and bless and praise and glorify and exalt

וְיַעֲרִיצוּ וְיַקְדִּישׁוּ וְיַמְלִיכוּ אֶת שִׁמְךָ מַלְכֵּנוּ.

and revere and sanctify and declare the sovereignty of Your Name, our King.

כִּי כָל פֶּה לְךָ יוֹדֶה, וְכָל לָשׁוֹן לְךָ תִשָּׁבַע, וְכָל

For every mouth shall offer thanks, to You and every tongue shall swear [allegiance], to You and every

בֶּרֶךְ לְךָ תִכְרַע, וְכָל קוֹמָה לְפָנֶיךָ תִשְׁתַּחֲוֶה,

knee to You shall kneel, and every upright spine before You shall prostrate itself,

וְכָל לְבָבוֹת יִירָאוּךָ, וְכָל קֶרֶב וּכְלָיוֹת יְזַמֵּרוּ

and all hearts shall fear You, and all innermost feelings and thoughts shall sing praises

קַדֵּשׁ יְרַחַץ כַּרְפַּס יַחַץ מַגִּיד רָחְצָה מוֹצִיא מַצָּ

KATZAH MOTZI RACHTZAH MAGGID YACHATZ KARPAS URECHATZ KADDESH

לִשְׁמֶךָ, כַּדָּבָר שֶׁכָּתוּב: כָּל עַצְמֹתַי תֹּאמַרְנָה,*

‹‹ will say:* ‹ my limbs ‹ All ‹‹ that is written: ‹ as the word‹‹ to Your Name,

יהוה מִי כָמוֹךָ, מַצִּיל עָנִי מֵחָזָק מִמֶּנּוּ, וְעָנִי

‹ the poor ‹‹ than he, ‹ from one mightier ‹ of the poor ‹ Deliverer ‹‹ is like You? ‹ who ‹ HASHEM,

וְאֶבְיוֹן מִגֹּזְלוֹ. מִי יִדְמֶה לָּךְ, וּמִי יִשְׁוֶה לָּךְ,

‹‹ to You? ‹ is equal ‹ Who ‹‹ to You? ‹ is comparable ‹ Who ‹‹ from one who robs him. ‹ and the destitute

וּמִי יַעֲרָךְ לָךְ. הָאֵל הַגָּדוֹל הַגִּבּוֹר וְהַנּוֹרָא,

‹‹ and Who is awesome, ‹ Who is mighty, ‹ Who is great, ‹ The God ‹‹ to You? ‹ can be compared ‹ Who

אֵל עֶלְיוֹן, קֹנֵה שָׁמַיִם וָאָרֶץ. נְהַלֶּלְךָ וּנְשַׁבֵּחֲךָ

‹ and praise You, ‹ We shall laud You ‹‹ and earth. ‹ of heaven ‹ Creator ‹‹ the Most High, ‹ God

וּנְפָאֶרְךָ וּנְבָרֵךְ אֶת שֵׁם קָדְשֶׁךָ, כָּאָמוּר: לְדָוִד,

‹ By David: ‹‹ as it is said, ‹‹ of Your holiness, ‹ the Name ‹ and bless ‹ and glorify You

בָּרְכִי נַפְשִׁי אֶת יהוה, וְכָל קְרָבַי אֶת שֵׁם קָדְשׁוֹ.

‹‹ of His holiness. ‹ [bless] the Name ‹ that is within me ‹ and all ‹ HASHEM; ‹ O my soul, ‹ bless,

הָאֵל בְּתַעֲצֻמוֹת עֻזֶּךָ,* הַגָּדוֹל בִּכְבוֹד שְׁמֶךָ,

‹‹ of Your Name; ‹ – in the glory ‹‹ Who is great ‹‹ of Your strength;* ‹ – in the omnipotence ‹‹ The God

---

כָּל עַצְמֹתַי תֹּאמַרְנָה — *All my limbs will say.* Having just described how each limb and organ will offer praise to God, we cite the Scriptural source for this obligation. The verse concludes with the inspiring praise that God's greatness is manifested in His rescue of the powerless from their oppressors. This is meant both literally and figuratively, for as *Radak* explains, God rescues the seemingly overmatched good inclination from the seductions of the evil inclination.

הָאֵל בְּתַעֲצֻמוֹת עֻזֶּךָ — *The God — in the omnipotence of Your strength.* This and the

following verses elaborate upon the themes of *Nishmas.* The last sentence of *Nishmas* contained the four terms הָאֵל הַגָּדוֹל הַגִּבּוֹר וְהַנּוֹרָא, *The God, Who is great, Who is mighty, and Who is awesome.* Now, each of those terms is used and elaborated upon in a phrase lauding God:

1. הָאֵל — *The God.* This Name refers to God as the All-Powerful. Thus, God's power is expressed by the idea that He does not depend on servants, armies, or the consent of His subjects. He is omnipotent in His strength without reliance on anything else.

2. הַגָּדוֹל — *Who is great.* His greatness is

הַגִּבּוֹר לָנֶצַח וְהַנּוֹרָא בְּנוֹרְאוֹתֶיךָ. הַמֶּלֶךְ

‹ The King ‹‹ — in Your awesome ‹‹ and Who is ‹‹ — for ‹‹ Who is
deeds. awesome eternity; Mighty

הַיּוֹשֵׁב עַל כִּסֵּא רָם וְנִשָּׂא.

‹‹ and lofty! ‹ high ‹ a throne ‹ upon ‹ Who is
enthroned

שׁוֹכֵן עַד* מָרוֹם וְקָדוֹשׁ שְׁמוֹ. וְכָתוּב: רַנְּנוּ

‹ Sing ‹ And it is ‹‹ is His ‹ and holy ‹ exalted ‹‹ forever,* ‹ He Who
joyfully, written: Name. dwells

צַדִּיקִים בַּיהוה לַיְשָׁרִים נָאוָה תְהִלָּה.

‹‹ is praise. ‹ fitting ‹ for the upright, ‹‹ because of HASHEM; ‹ O righteous,

בְּפִי יְשָׁרִים* תִּתְהַלָּל.

‹‹ shall You be lauded; ‹ of the upright* ‹ By the mouth

וּבְדִבְרֵי צַדִּיקִים תִּתְבָּרַךְ.

‹‹ shall You be blessed; ‹ of the righteous ‹ by the words

וּבִלְשׁוֹן חֲסִידִים תִּתְרוֹמָם.

‹‹ shall You be exalted; ‹ of the devout ‹ by the tongue

וּבְקֶרֶב קְדוֹשִׁים תִּתְקַדָּשׁ.

‹‹ shall You be sanctified. ‹ the holy ones ‹ and amid

---

signified by the fact that all creatures give honor to His Name.

3. הַגִּבּוֹר — *Who is mighty.* Unlike mighty human rulers, whose powers ebb as they grow old, God's majesty and strength are eternal and undiminished.

4. וְהַנּוֹרָא — *And Who is awesome.* Unlike human kings who are held in awe only because they have the power to punish their detractors, God's awesomeness is obvious because the entire universe testifies to His greatness.

שׁוֹכֵן עַד §⊷ — *He Who dwells forever.* Although God is *exalted and holy,* He nevertheless makes His abode on earth, for it is only here — through the deeds of the righteous — that His commandments can be carried out. Therefore, this paragraph goes on to say that the primary praise of

God comes from such righteous people. The key, however, is not in their rhetoric but in the "song" of their good deeds.

בְּפִי יְשָׁרִים — *By the mouth of the upright.* Four categories of people are listed as praising God: יְשָׁרִים,צַדִּיקִים,חֲסִידִים,קְדוֹשִׁים, *upright, righteous, devout,* and *holy.* The initials of these four words spell יִצְחָק, leading some to speculate that it is the signature of the unknown author of *Nishmas.*

Rabbi Shraga Feivel Mendlowitz noted that these four categories seem to be listed in ascending order of their spiritual accomplishment, the lowest being the upright, fair-minded people and the highest being the holy ones. The higher the level of the person, the more meaningful the manner in which he praises God. While the *upright* praises God with his *mouth,* the *righteous*

וּבְמַקְהֵלוֹת רִבְבוֹת עַמְּךָ בֵּית יִשְׂרָאֵל,

‹ of Israel, ‹ the House ‹ of Your people, ‹ of the myriads ‹ And in the assemblies

בְּרִנָּה יִתְפָּאַר שִׁמְךָ מַלְכֵּנוּ בְּכָל דּוֹר וָדוֹר.

« generation ‹ throughout ‹ our King, ‹ Your Name, ‹ shall be ‹ with joyous
after generation. every glorified song

שֶׁכֵּן חוֹבַת כָּל הַיְצוּרִים, לְפָנֶיךָ יהוה

‹ Hashem, ‹ — before You, « creatures ‹ of all ‹ is the duty ‹ For such

אֱלֹהֵינוּ וֵאלֹהֵי אֲבוֹתֵינוּ, לְהוֹדוֹת לְהַלֵּל לְשַׁבֵּחַ

‹ to praise, ‹ to laud, ‹ to thank, « of our forefathers, ‹ and the God ‹ our God

לְפָאֵר לְרוֹמֵם לְהַדֵּר לְבָרֵךְ לְעַלֵּה וּלְקַלֵּס, עַל

‹ [even] « and to sing ‹ to elevate, ‹ to bless, ‹ to honor, ‹ to exalt, ‹ to glorify,
beyond praises,

כָּל דִּבְרֵי שִׁירוֹת וְתִשְׁבְּחוֹת דָּוִד בֶּן יִשַׁי עַבְדְּךָ

‹ Your ‹ of ‹ the ‹ of ‹ and praises ‹ of the ‹ the ‹ all
servant, Jesse, son David songs expressions

מְשִׁיחֶךָ.

« Your anointed one.

יִשְׁתַּבַּח שִׁמְךָ לָעַד, מַלְכֵּנוּ, הָאֵל הַמֶּלֶךְ

‹ the King ‹ the God, « our King, « forever, ‹ may Your ‹ Praised
Name be

הַגָּדוֹל וְהַקָּדוֹשׁ, בַּשָּׁמַיִם וּבָאָרֶץ. כִּי לְךָ נָאֶה,

« are ‹ to ‹ Because « and on earth. ‹ in heaven « and Who is holy, ‹ Who is
fitting, You great

יהוה אֱלֹהֵינוּ וֵאלֹהֵי אֲבוֹתֵינוּ, שִׁיר וּשְׁבָחָה,

‹ and praise, ‹ song « of our forefathers, ‹ and the God ‹ our God ‹ Hashem,

הַלֵּל וְזִמְרָה, עֹז וּמֶמְשָׁלָה, נֶצַח גְּדֻלָּה וּגְבוּרָה,

‹ and strength, ‹ greatness, ‹ triumph, ‹ and dominion, ‹ power ‹ and hymns, ‹ lauding

---

uses articulated *words*. The *devout* uses his *tongue*, implying that the praise comes from deeper within himself. The *holy* person, however, praises God with his very *essence* [קֶרֶב, literally, *inner being*].

עַל כָּל דִּבְרֵי...דָּוִד — *[Even] beyond all the expressions...of David.* Although David, the נְעִים זְמִירוֹת יִשְׂרָאֵל, *sweet singer of Israel* (II Samuel 23:1), is the quintessential composer of God's praises, even he could not do justice to God's

תְּהִלָּה וְתִפְאֶרֶת, קְדֻשָׁה וּמַלְכוּת, בְּרָכוֹת
⟨ blessings ⟨ and sovereignty, ⟨ holiness ⟨ and glory, ⟨ praise

וְהוֹדָאוֹת מֵעַתָּה וְעַד עוֹלָם.
⟪ eternity. ⟨ until ⟨ from this time ⟪ and thanksgivings,

THE *ASHKENAZIC* CUSTOM CONTINUES WITH THE FOLLOWING BLESSING.
THE *NUSACH SEFARD* CUSTOM CONTINUES INSTEAD WITH יְהַלְלוּךָ, BELOW.

בָּרוּךְ אַתָּה יהוה, אֵל מֶלֶךְ גָּדוֹל בַּתִּשְׁבָּחוֹת,*
⟪ through praises,* ⟨ King ⟨ God, ⟪ HASHEM, ⟨ are You, ⟨ Blessed
exalted [Who is]

אֵל הַהוֹדָאוֹת, אֲדוֹן הַנִּפְלָאוֹת, הַבּוֹחֵר בְּשִׁירֵי
⟨ songs ⟨ Who ⟪ of wonders, ⟨ Master ⟪ of thanksgivings, ⟨ God
[of praise] chooses

זִמְרָה, מֶלֶךְ אֵל חֵי הָעוֹלָמִים.
⟪ of the worlds. ⟨ Life-giver ⟨ God, ⟨ – King, ⟪ that are
melodious,

THOSE FOLLOWING THE *SEFARDIC* CUSTOM —
WHO DID NOT RECITE יְהַלְלוּךָ AFTER *HALLEL* — RECITE IT HERE.

יְהַלְלוּךָ יהוה אֱלֹהֵינוּ כָּל מַעֲשֶׂיךָ,
⟪ of Your works. ⟨ – all ⟪ our God ⟨ HASHEM, ⟪ They shall praise You,

וַחֲסִידֶיךָ צַדִּיקִים עוֹשֵׂי רְצוֹנֶךָ, וְכָל עַמְּךָ בֵּית
⟨ the ⟨ of Your ⟨ and ⟪ Your will, ⟨ who do ⟨ the righteous, ⟨ And Your
House people, all devout ones,

יִשְׂרָאֵל בְּרִנָּה יוֹדוּ וִיבָרְכוּ וִישַׁבְּחוּ וִיפָאֲרוּ
⟨ glorify, ⟨ praise, ⟨ bless, ⟨ will thank, ⟨ with glad song ⟪ of Israel,

וִירוֹמְמוּ וְיַעֲרִיצוּ וְיַקְדִּישׁוּ וְיַמְלִיכוּ אֶת שִׁמְךָ
⟨ Your Name, ⟨ and proclaim the ⟨ sanctify, ⟨ extol, ⟨ exalt,
sovereignty of

---

greatness. Therefore we now say that we are obligated to praise Him limitlessly — even beyond the songs of David.

גָּדוֹל בַּתִּשְׁבָּחוֹת — *Exalted through praises.* Not that God requires our praises in order to become exalted, for His infinite greatness is beyond our capacity to comprehend, much less express. Rather, it is His will that we have the privilege of exalting Him, despite our inability to do so adequately. This is the implication of *Who chooses songs [of praise] that are melodious*; we praise Him because He wishes us to do so.

מַלְכֵּנוּ. כִּי לְךָ טוֹב לְהוֹדוֹת וּלְשִׁמְךָ נָאֶה
〈 it is 〈 and unto 《 to give thanks, 〈 it is 〈 to You 〈 For 《 our King.
proper Your Name good

לְזַמֵּר, כִּי מֵעוֹלָם וְעַד עוֹלָם אַתָּה אֵל.
《 are 〈 You 〈 the World 〈 to 〈 from [This] 〈 for 《 to sing
God. [to Come] World praises,

**MOST WHO FOLLOW THE *SEFARDIC* CUSTOM CONCLUDE WITH THE FOLLOWING BLESSING.
HOWEVER, SOME CONCLUDE IN ACCORDANCE WITH THE *ASHKENAZIC* CUSTOM ABOVE, (PAGE 104).**

בָּרוּךְ אַתָּה יהוה, מֶלֶךְ מְהֻלָּל בַּתִּשְׁבָּחוֹת.
《 with praises. 〈 Who is lauded 〈 the King 《 HASHEM, 〈 are You, 〈 Blessed

---

ACCORDING TO MOST CUSTOMS, THE FOURTH CUP IS DRUNK AT THIS POINT.

**THE BLESSING OVER WINE IS RECITED AND THE FOURTH CUP IS DRUNK WHILE RECLINING
TO THE LEFT SIDE. IT IS PREFERABLE THAT THE ENTIRE CUP BE DRUNK.**

SOME HAVE THE CUSTOM TO DELAY THE FOURTH CUP UNTIL LATER, PAGE 116.

SOME RECITE THE FOLLOWING BEFORE THE FOURTH CUP:

הִנְנִי מוּכָן וּמְזוּמָּן לְקַיֵּם מִצְוַת כּוֹס רְבִיעִי שֶׁל אַרְבַּע כּוֹסוֹת.
《 Cups. 〈 the Four 〈 of 〈 of the 〈 the 〈 to 〈 and 〈 am 〈 I now
fourth cup mitzvah perform ready prepared

לְשֵׁם יִחוּד קֻדְשָׁא בְּרִיךְ הוּא וּשְׁכִינְתֵּיה, עַל יְדֵי הַהוּא טָמִיר
〈 Who is 〈 Him 〈 through 《 and His 《 is He, 〈 Blessed 《 of the Holy 〈 of the 〈 For the
hidden Presence, One, unification sake

וְנֶעְלָם, בְּשֵׁם כָּל יִשְׂרָאֵל. וִיהִי נְעַם אֲדֹנָי אֱלֹהֵינוּ
〈 our God, 〈 of the 〈 the plea- 〈 May 《 Israel. 〈 of all 〈 — [I pray] 《 and Who is
Lord, santness in the name inscrutable

עָלֵינוּ, וּמַעֲשֵׂה יָדֵינוּ כּוֹנְנָה עָלֵינוּ, וּמַעֲשֵׂה יָדֵינוּ כּוֹנְנֵהוּ.[1]
《 establish 〈 of our 〈 the work 《 for us; 〈 establish 〈 of our 〈 the work 《 be
it. hands, hands, upon us;

בָּרוּךְ אַתָּה יהוה אֱלֹהֵינוּ מֶלֶךְ הָעוֹלָם,
《 of the universe, 〈 King 〈 our God, 〈 HASHEM, 〈 are You, 〈 Blessed

בּוֹרֵא פְּרִי הַגָּפֶן.
《 of the vine. 〈 the fruit 〈 Who creates

---

(1) *Psalms* 90:17.

NIRTZAh · hALLEL · BARECh · TZAFUN · shULChAN OREch · KORECh · MAROR

AFTER DRINKING THE FOURTH CUP, THE CONCLUDING BLESSING IS RECITED:

בָּרוּךְ אַתָּה יהוה אֱלֹהֵינוּ מֶלֶךְ הָעוֹלָם, עַל

‹ for ‹‹ of the universe, ‹ King ‹ our God, ‹ Hashem, ‹ are You, ‹ Blessed

הַגֶּפֶן וְעַל פְּרִי הַגֶּפֶן, וְעַל תְּנוּבַת הַשָּׂדֶה, וְעַל

‹ for ‹‹ of the field; ‹ the produce ‹ and for ‹ of the vine ‹ the fruit ‹ and for ‹ the vine

אֶרֶץ חֶמְדָּה טוֹבָה וּרְחָבָה, שֶׁרָצִיתָ וְהִנְחַלְתָּ

‹ to give as ‹ that You ‹‹ and spacious — ‹ good, ‹ — desirable, ‹‹ the Land
a heritage   desired

לַאֲבוֹתֵינוּ, לֶאֱכוֹל מִפִּרְיָהּ וְלִשְׂבּוֹעַ מִטּוּבָהּ.

‹‹ with its ‹ and to ‹ of its fruit ‹ to eat ‹‹ to our forefathers,
goodness.   be satisfied

רַחֶם (נָא) יהוה אֱלֹהֵינוּ עַל יִשְׂרָאֵל עַמֶּךָ,

‹ Your ‹ Israel ‹ on ‹‹ our God, ‹ Hashem, ‹ (we beg ‹ Have
people;   You,)   mercy,

וְעַל יְרוּשָׁלַיִם עִירֶךָ, וְעַל צִיּוֹן מִשְׁכַּן כְּבוֹדֶךָ,

‹‹ of Your ‹ the resting ‹ Zion, ‹ on ‹ Your City; ‹ Jerusalem, ‹ on
glory;   place

וְעַל מִזְבְּחֶךָ וְעַל הֵיכָלֶךָ. וּבְנֵה יְרוּשָׁלַיִם עִיר

‹ the City ‹ Jerusalem, ‹ Rebuild ‹‹ Your Temple. ‹ and on ‹ Your Altar, ‹ on

הַקֹּדֶשׁ בִּמְהֵרָה בְיָמֵינוּ, וְהַעֲלֵנוּ לְתוֹכָהּ,

‹ into it ‹ Bring us up ‹‹ in our days. ‹ speedily ‹ of holiness,

וְשַׂמְּחֵנוּ בְּבִנְיָנָהּ, וְנֹאכַל מִפִּרְיָהּ, וְנִשְׂבַּע

‹ and let us ‹ from its fruit ‹ let us eat ‹‹ in its rebuilding; ‹ and gladden us
be satisfied

מִטּוּבָהּ, וּנְבָרֶכְךָ עָלֶיהָ בִּקְדֻשָּׁה וּבְטָהֳרָה.

‹‹ and purity. ‹ in holiness ‹ upon it ‹ and let us bless You ‹‹ with its goodness,

ON THE SABBATH:

וּרְצֵה וְהַחֲלִיצֵנוּ בְּיוֹם הַשַּׁבָּת הַזֶּה.

‹‹ on this Sabbath day. ‹ to give ‹ And may it be
us rest   pleasing to You

וְשַׂמְּחֵנוּ בְּיוֹם חַג הַמַּצּוֹת הַזֶּה. כִּי אַתָּה יהוה

‹ Hashem, ‹ You, ‹ For ‹‹ of this Festival of Matzos. ‹ on the day ‹ And gladden us

קַדֵּשׁ וּרְחַץ כַּרְפַּס יַחַץ מַגִּיד רָחְצָה מוֹצִיא מַצָּ

ATZAh   MOTZI   RAChTZAh MAGGID YAChATZ KARPAS URECHATZ KADDESH

טוֹב וּמֵטִיב לַכֹּל, וְנוֹדֶה לְךָ עַל הָאָרֶץ וְעַל

⟨ and for ⟨ the Land ⟨ for ⟨ You ⟨ and we thank ⟪ to all, ⟨ and do good ⟨ are good

פְּרִי הַגָּפֶן.° בָּרוּךְ אַתָּה יהוה, עַל הָאָרֶץ וְעַל

⟨ and for ⟨ the Land ⟨ for ⟪ HASHEM, ⟨ are You, ⟨ Blessed ⟪ of the vine. ⟨ the fruit

פְּרִי הַגָּפֶן.°

⟪ of the vine. ⟨ the fruit

°ON WINE FROM *ERETZ YISRAEL,* SUBSTITUTE גַּפְנָהּ, *OF ITS VINE,* FOR הַגֶּפֶן, *OF THE VINE.*

⚜ נרצה / NIRTZAH ⚜

חֲסַל* סְדוּר פֶּסַח כְּהִלְכָתוֹ, כְּכָל מִשְׁפָּטוֹ

⟨ its rules ⟨ according to all ⟪ in accordance with its laws, ⟨ of Pesach ⟨ is the *Seder* ⟨ Concluded [now]*

וְחֻקָּתוֹ. כַּאֲשֶׁר זָכִינוּ לְסַדֵּר אוֹתוֹ, כֵּן נִזְכֶּה

⟨ may we merit ⟨ so ⟪ it, ⟨ to arrange ⟨ we merited ⟨ Just as ⟪ and its statutes.

לַעֲשׂוֹתוֹ. זָךְ שׁוֹכֵן מְעוֹנָה, קוֹמֵם קְהַל עֲדַת

⟨ of the assembly ⟨ the congregation ⟨ raise up ⟪ in His abode [on high], ⟨ Who dwells ⟨ O Pure One, ⟪ to perform it.

מִי מָנָה.¹ בְּקָרוֹב נַהֵל נִטְעֵי כַנָּה,² פְּדוּיִם

⟨ redeemed, ⟪ *foundation,* ⟨ [Israel,] *the* firmly planted ⟨ lead ⟨ Soon ⟪ *can count* [them]? ⟨ of [whom it was said,] *Who*

לְצִיּוֹן בְּרִנָּה.

⟪ with glad song. ⟨ to Zion

לְשָׁנָה הַבָּאָה בִּירוּשָׁלָיִם.

⟪ in Jerusalem. ⟨ Next year

(1) *Numbers* 23:10. (2) Cf. *Psalms* 80:16.

חֲסַל — *Concluded [now].* In accordance with the verse, *Let my tongue adhere to my palate ... if I fail to elevate Jerusalem above my foremost joy!* we pray that our reenactment of the past redemption set the stage for the future redemption, that we may celebrate next year's *Seder* in the Holy City.

NIRTZAH · hALLEL · bARECh · TZAFUN · shulchAN ORECh · kORECh · MAROR

ON THE FIRST NIGHT RECITE THE FOLLOWING.
ON THE SECOND NIGHT CONTINUE ON PAGE 111.

וּבְכֵן וַיְהִי בַּחֲצִי הַלַּיְלָה.

≪ of the night. ⟨ in the middle ⟨ — it happened⟨≪ And so

אָז רוֹב נִסִּים הִפְלֵאתָ בַּלַּיְלָה,

≪ on this night, ⟨ You have wond- ⟨ miracles ⟨ many ⟨ Of old,
rously performed

בְּרֹאשׁ אַשְׁמוֹרֶת זֶה הַלַּיְלָה,

≪ night. ⟨ of this ⟨ of the [third] watch ⟨ at the beginning

גֵּר צֶדֶק נִצַּחְתּוֹ כְּנֶחֱלַק לוֹ לַיְלָה,[1]

≪ was the ⟨ for ⟨ when ⟨ You granted ⟨ To the righteous
night. him divided victory convert [Abraham]

וַיְהִי בַּחֲצִי הַלַּיְלָה.

≪ of the night. ⟨ in the middle ⟨ It happened

דַּנְתָּ מֶלֶךְ גְּרָר בַּחֲלוֹם הַלַּיְלָה,[2]

≪ at night. ⟨ in a dream ⟨ of Gerar ⟨ the ⟨ You
[Abimelech] king judged

הִפְחַדְתָּ אֲרַמִּי בְּאֶמֶשׁ לַיְלָה,[3]

≪ of night. ⟨ in the dark ⟨ the Aramean, ⟨ You
[Laban,] frightened

וְיִשְׂרָאֵל יָשַׂר לְמַלְאָךְ וַיּוּכַל לוֹ לַיְלָה,[4]

≪ at night. ⟨ him ⟨ and overcame ⟨ with an angel ⟨ struggled ⟨ Israel

וַיְהִי בַּחֲצִי הַלַּיְלָה.

≪ of the night. ⟨ in the middle ⟨ It happened

זֶרַע בְּכוֹרֵי פַתְרוֹס מָחַצְתָּ בַּחֲצִי הַלַּיְלָה,

≪ of the night. ⟨ in the middle ⟨ You crushed ⟨ of Pathros [Egypt] ⟨ The firstborn offspring

חֵילָם לֹא מָצְאוּ בְּקוּמָם בַּלַּיְלָה,[5]

≪ at night. ⟨ when they arose ⟨ find ⟨ they ⟨ Their wealth
could not

(1) Cf. *Genesis* 14:15. (2) 20:3. (3) Cf. 31:24,29.
(4) 32:23-26; cf. *Hosea* 12:5. (5) Cf. *Deuteronomy* 8:17, *Exodus* 12:36.

ATZAh MOTZI RAChTZAh MAGGID YAChATZ KARPAS URECHATZ KADDESH

טִישַׁת נְגִיד חֲרוֹשֶׁת¹ סִלִּיתָ² בְּכוֹכְבֵי לַיְלָה,³

》 of night. 〈 with the 〈 You 〈 of Harosheth 〈 of the 〈 The swift
stars trampled [Sisera] prince army

וַיְהִי בַּחֲצִי הַלַּיְלָה.

》 of the night. 〈 in the middle 〈 It happened

יָעַץ מְחָרֵף לְנוֹפֵף⁴ אִוּוּי⁵ הוֹבַשְׁתָּ פְגָרָיו בַּלַּיְלָה,⁶

》 by night. 〈 his 〈 You 》 against the 〈 to wave 〈 The blasphemer
corpses disgraced cherished his hand [Sennacherib]
[Jerusalem]; had planned

כָּרַע בֵּל⁷ וּמַצָּבוֹ בְּאִישׁוֹן לַיְלָה,

》 of the night. 〈 in the 》 along with its 》 [The idol] Bel
darkness supporters [the collapsed,
Babylonians]

לְאִישׁ חֲמוּדוֹת⁸ נִגְלָה רָז חֲזוֹת לַיְלָה,⁹

》 of the night. 〈 in a 〈 was the 〈 revealed 〈 of Your delight 〈 To the man
vision secret [Daniel]

וַיְהִי בַּחֲצִי הַלַּיְלָה.

》 of the night. 〈 in the middle 〈 It happened

מִשְׁתַּכֵּר בִּכְלֵי קֹדֶשׁ נֶהֱרַג בּוֹ בַּלַּיְלָה,¹⁰

》 night. 〈 that 〈 was slain 〈 from the holy vessels 〈 He who
very [Belshazzar] caroused

נוֹשַׁע מִבּוֹר אֲרָיוֹת¹¹ פּוֹתֵר בְּעִתּוּתֵי לַיְלָה,¹²

》 of the night. 〈 the frightening 〈 was [Daniel] 〈 of lions 〈 from 〈 Rescued
sights who interpreted the den

שִׂנְאָה נָטַר אֲגָגִי⁸ וְכָתַב סְפָרִים בַּלַּיְלָה,¹³

》 at night. 〈 decrees 〈 and 》 did the Agagite 〈 Hatred
wrote [Haman] maintain,

וַיְהִי בַּחֲצִי הַלַּיְלָה.

》 of the night. 〈 in the middle 〈 It happened

---

(1) Cf. *Judges* 4:2. (2) Cf. *Lamentations* 1:15. (3) Cf. *Judges* 5:20. (4) Cf. *Isaiah* 10:32.
(5) Cf. *Psalms* 132:13. (6) Cf. *II Kings* 19:35. (7) *Isaiah* 46:1. (8) *Daniel* 10:11,19.
(9) Cf. 2:19,28. (10) Cf. 5:30. (11) Cf. 6:21-24. (12) Cf. 5:5-6. (13) Cf. *Esther* 3:5-12.

עוֹרַרְתָּ נִצְחֲךָ עָלָיו בְּנֶדֶד שְׁנַת לַיְלָה,[1]

《 at night. 〈 [Ahasuerus'] 〈 by 〈 over 〈 Your 〈 You began
sleep disturbing [Haman] triumph

פּוּרָה תִדְרוֹךְ לְשׁוֹמֵר מַה מִלַּיְלָה,[2]*

《 [with the long] 〈 What 《 [to save those 〈 You will tread 〈 [As] with a
night of exile?]* [will be] asking the] [on the enemies] winepress
Watchman:

צָרַח כַּשּׁוֹמֵר וְשָׂח אָתָא בְקֶר וְגַם לַיְלָה,[4]

《 night [for 〈 but 《 Morning is coming 《 and said: 〈 like a 〈 [God]
the enemies]! also [for you], watchman shouted back

וַיְהִי בַּחֲצִי הַלַּיְלָה.

《 of the night. 〈 in the middle 〈 It happened

קָרֵב יוֹם אֲשֶׁר הוּא לֹא יוֹם וְלֹא לַיְלָה,[5]

《 night. 〈 nor 〈 day 〈 neither 〈 is 〈 which 〈 the day [of 〈 Bring
the Messiah], near

רָם הוֹדַע כִּי לְךָ הַיּוֹם אַף לְךָ הַלַּיְלָה,[6]

《 is the night. 〈 Yours 〈 and 〈 is the 〈 Yours 〈 that 〈 make it 〈 Exalted
also day known One,

שׁוֹמְרִים הַפְקֵד לְעִירְךָ כָּל הַיּוֹם וְכָל הַלַּיְלָה,[7]

《 night. 〈 and all 〈 day 〈 all 〈 over Your City, 〈 appoint 〈 Watchmen
[Jerusalem,]

תָּאִיר כְּאוֹר יוֹם חֶשְׁכַת לַיְלָה,[8]

《 of the night. 〈 the 〈 of day, 〈 as the 〈 Illuminate,
darkness light

וַיְהִי בַּחֲצִי הַלַּיְלָה.

《 of the night. 〈 in the middle 〈 It happened

---

(1) Cf. *Esther* 6:1. (2) Cf. *Isaiah* 63:3. (3) 21:11. (4) 21:12. (5) *Zechariah* 14:7. (6) Cf. *Psalms* 74:16. (7) Cf. *Isaiah* 62:6. (8) Cf. *Psalms* 139:12.

מַה מִלַּיְלָה — *What [will be with the long] night of exile?* May You tread on those who oppress us. May light shine for the righteous, and darkness enshroud the wicked. Hasten the time of redemption for Your nation, for Your City. Let the darkness of exile be brightened by the light of day.

ON THE FIRST NIGHT CONTINUE ON PAGE 114.
ON THE SECOND NIGHT RECITE THE FOLLOWING.

וּבְכֵן וַאֲמַרְתֶּם זֶבַח פֶּסַח:¹

≪ of *Pesach*. ⟨ [This is] ≪ you shall say: ⟨ And so
the offering

בְּפֶסַח. אֹמֶץ גְּבוּרוֹתֶיךָ הִפְלֵאתָ

≪ on *Pesach*. ⟨ You displayed wondrously ⟨ of Your powers ⟨ The might

פֶּסַח. בְּרֹאשׁ כָּל מוֹעֲדוֹת נִשֵּׂאתָ

≪ *Pesach*. ⟨ You elevated ⟨ festivals ⟨ all ⟨ Above

פֶּסַח. גִּלִּיתָ לָאֶזְרָחִי חֲצוֹת לֵיל

≪ of *Pesach*. ⟨ the [future] midnight ⟨ To the Ezrahite ⟨ You
[Abraham] revealed

וַאֲמַרְתֶּם זֶבַח פֶּסַח.

≪ of ⟨ [This is] ≪ And you
Pesach. the offering shall say:

בְּפֶסַח. דְּלָתָיו דָּפַקְתָּ² כְּחֹם הַיּוֹם³

≪ on *Pesach*; ⟨ of the day ⟨ in the heat ⟨ You knocked ⟨ At his doors

בְּפֶסַח. הִסְעִיד נוֹצְצִים עֻגוֹת מַצּוֹת⁴

≪ on *Pesach*. ⟨ of matzah ⟨ with ⟨ for the spark- ⟨ He prepared
cakes ling [angels] a meal

פֶּסַח. וְאֶל הַבָּקָר רָץ⁵ זֵכֶר לְשׁוֹר עֵרֶךְ

≪ for *Pesach*. ⟨ arrayed ⟨ of the ⟨ — a ≪ he ran ⟨ the herd ⟨ And to
[on the altar] bull reminder

וַאֲמַרְתֶּם זֶבַח פֶּסַח.

≪ of ⟨ [This is] ≪ And you
Pesach. the offering shall say:

בְּפֶסַח. זוֹעֲמוּ סְדוֹמִים וְלוֹהֲטוּ בָּאֵשׁ

≪ on *Pesach*; ⟨ by fire ⟨ and they were ≪ were the ⟨ Recipients of
consumed Sodomites [God's] wrath

(1) *Exodus* 12:27. (2) *Judges* 19:22. (3) *Genesis* 18:1. (4) *Exodus* 12:39. (5) *Genesis* 18:7.

NIRTZAh   hALLeL   BARECh   TZAFUN   shulchAN ORECh   kORECh   MAROR

חֻלַּץ לוֹט מֵהֶם וּמַצּוֹת אָפָה בְּקֵץ[1] פֶּסַח.
Rescued > was Lot > from > — matzos >> he had > at the >> of Pesach.
them baked time

טִאטֵאתָ אַדְמַת מוֹף וְנוֹף בְּעָבְרְךָ בַּפֶּסַח.
You swept clean > the land > of Mof > and Nof > when You >> on Pesach.
[in Egypt] passed through

וַאֲמַרְתֶּם זֶבַח פֶּסַח.
And you >> [This is] > of >>
shall say: the offering Pesach.

יָהּ רֹאשׁ כָּל אוֹן[2] מִחַצְתָּ[3] בְּלֵיל שִׁמּוּר[4] פֶּסַח.
God, > the first > of all > their > You > on the > that is >> on Pesach.
strength crushed night protected

כַּבִּיר עַל בֵּן בְּכוֹר[5] פָּסַחְתָּ בְּדָם פֶּסַח.
O mighty >> — over >> the > who is [Your] > You >> because of > of the Pesach
One son firstborn skipped, the blood offering,

לְבִלְתִּי תֵּת מַשְׁחִית לָבֹא[6] בִּפְתָחַי בַּפֶּסַח.
Not > allowing > the Destroyer > to enter > my doorways >> on Pesach.

וַאֲמַרְתֶּם זֶבַח פֶּסַח.
And you >> [This is] > of >>
shall say: the offering Pesach.

מְסֻגֶּרֶת סֻגְּרָה[7] בְּעִתּוֹתֵי פֶּסַח.
The barricaded > was turned > at the time >> of Pesach.
[Jericho] over [to Israel]

נִשְׁמְדָה מִדְיָן בִּצְלִיל שְׂעוֹרֵי[8] עֹמֶר פֶּסַח.
Destroyed > was > with a > of barley > from the >> of Pesach.
Midyan roasted cake Omer

שׂוֹרְפוּ מִשְׁמַנֵּי פוּל וְלוּד[9] בִּיקַד יְקוֹד[10] פֶּסַח.
Consumed > were the fatted > of Pul > and Lud > in a great >> on Pesach.
[warriors] [Assyria] conflagration

(1) *Genesis* 19:3. (2) Cf. *Psalms* 105:36. (3) Cf. *Habakkuk* 3:13. (4) Cf. *Exodus* 12:42.
(5) Cf. 4:22. (6) Cf. 12:23. (7) Cf. *Joshua* 6:1. (8) Cf. *Judges* 7:13.
(9) *Isaiah* 66:19. The army of Senacharib was destroyed at the gates of Jerusalem, *II Kings* 19:35.
(10) Cf. *Isaiah* 10:16.

קַדֵּשׁ וּרְחַץ כַּרְפַּס יַחַץ מַגִּיד רָחְצָה מוֹצִיא מַצָּה מָרוֹר
MATZAh   MOTZI   RAChTZAh   MAGGID   yAChATZ   KARPAS   uREChATZ   KADDESh

וַאֲמַרְתֶּם זֶבַח פֶּסַח.

》 of 〈 [This is] 《 And you
Pesach. the offering shall say:

עוֹד הַיּוֹם בְּנֹב לַעֲמוֹד[1] עַד גָּעָה עוֹנַת פֶּסַח.

》 of 〈 of the 〈 the 〈 until 《 he [Senachareb] 〈 at 〈 that day 〈 Yet
Pesach. time arrival would have stood, Nob

פַּס יַד כָּתְבָה[2] לְקַעֲקֵעַ צוּל בְּפֶּסַח.

《 on Pesach. 〈 of Tzul 〈 of the 〈 wrote 〈 of a 〈 The
[Babylon] destruction hand palm

צָפֹה הַצָּפִית עָרוֹךְ הַשֻּׁלְחָן[3] בְּפֶּסַח.

《 on Pesach. 〈 was the 〈 and 《 was the 〈 While
[royal] table decked sentinel, watching

וַאֲמַרְתֶּם זֶבַח פֶּסַח.

《 of 〈 [This is] 《 And you
Pesach. the offering shall say:

קָהָל כִּנְּסָה הֲדַסָּה צוֹם לְשַׁלֵּשׁ בְּפֶּסַח.

《 on Pesach. 〈 for three 〈 to fast 〈 by Hadassah 〈 was 〈 A cong-
days [Esther] gathered regation

רֹאשׁ מִבֵּית רָשָׁע מָחַצְתָּ[4] בְּעֵץ חֲמִשִּׁים[5] בְּפֶּסַח.

《 on 〈 fifty 〈 upon a wooden 〈 You 〈 of the evil 〈 of the 〈 The head
Pesach. [cubits high] [gallows] crushed one [Haman] clan

שְׁתֵּי אֵלֶּה רֶגַע תָּבִיא[6] לְעוּצִית בְּפֶּסַח.

《 on Pesach. 〈 upon Utzis 〈 You should 〈 in an 《 These two, [loss of chil-
[Edom] bring instant dren and widowhood],

תָּעֹז יָדְךָ וְתָרוּם יְמִינְךָ[7] כְּלֵיל הִתְקַדֶּשׁ חַג[8] פֶּסַח.

《 of 〈 [as] the 〈 that was 〈 as on that 《 be Your 〈 and let 《 be 〈 Let streng-
Pesach. festival sanctified night right arm exalted Your thened
[against Edom], hand,

וַאֲמַרְתֶּם זֶבַח פֶּסַח.

《 of 〈 [This is] 《 And you
Pesach. the offering shall say:

(1) Isaiah 10:32. (2) Cf. Daniel 5:5. (3) Cf. Isaiah 21:5. (4) Cf. Habakkuk 3:13.
(5) Cf. Esther 5:14. (6) Cf. Isaiah 47:9. (7) Psalms 89:14. (8) Isaiah 30:29.

ON BOTH NIGHTS CONTINUE HERE:

כִּי לוֹ נָאֶה, כִּי לוֹ יָאֶה:[1]

‹‹ it is proper! ‹ to Him ‹ for ‹‹ it is fitting; ‹ to Him ‹ For

אַדִּיר בִּמְלוּכָה,* בָּחוּר כַּהֲלָכָה, גְּדוּדָיו יֹאמְרוּ

‹ say ‹ His legions ‹‹   as is ‹ distinguished ‹‹ in kingship,* ‹ Mighty
     [of angels]   befitting,

לוֹ, לְךָ[2] וּלְךָ, לְךָ[3] כִּי לְךָ[4] לְךָ[5] אַף לְךָ[6],

‹‹ Yours...; ‹ also ‹ Yours..., ‹‹ to ‹ for ‹ Yours..., ‹‹ and ‹ Yours... ‹‹ to
       You...;   Yours...;   Him:

לְךָ יהוה הַמַּמְלָכָה,[7] כִּי לוֹ נָאֶה, כִּי לוֹ יָאֶה.

‹‹ it is ‹ to ‹ for ‹‹ it is ‹ to ‹ for ‹‹   is the ‹ HASHEM, ‹ Yours,
proper! Him   fitting; Him   sovereignty —

דָּגוּל בִּמְלוּכָה, הָדוּר כַּהֲלָכָה, וָתִיקָיו יֹאמְרוּ

‹ say ‹ His faithful ones ‹‹ as is befitting, ‹ majestic ‹ in kingship, ‹ Preeminent

לוֹ, לְךָ וּלְךָ, לְךָ כִּי לְךָ, לְךָ אַף לְךָ,

‹‹ Yours...; ‹ also ‹ Yours..., ‹‹ to ‹ for ‹ Yours..., ‹‹ and ‹ Yours... ‹‹ to
       You...;   Yours...;   Him:

לְךָ יהוה הַמַּמְלָכָה, כִּי לוֹ נָאֶה, כִּי לוֹ יָאֶה.

‹‹ it is ‹ to ‹ for ‹‹ it is ‹ to ‹ for ‹‹   is the ‹ HASHEM, ‹ Yours,
proper! Him   fitting; Him   sovereignty —

זַכַּאי בִּמְלוּכָה, חָסִין כַּהֲלָכָה, טַפְסְרָיו יֹאמְרוּ

‹ say ‹ His officers ‹‹ as is befitting, ‹ mighty ‹‹ in kingship, ‹ Righteous
  [the angels]

לוֹ, לְךָ וּלְךָ, לְךָ כִּי לְךָ, לְךָ אַף לְךָ,

‹‹ Yours...; ‹ also ‹ Yours..., ‹‹ to ‹ for ‹ Yours..., ‹‹ and ‹ Yours... ‹‹ to
       You...;   Yours...;   Him:

---

(1) Cf. *Jeremiah* 10:7. (2) וּלְךָ אֲ־דֹנָי חָסֶד, *Psalms* 62:13.
(3) לְךָ ה' הַגְּדֻלָּה וְהַגְּבוּרָה, *I Chronicles* 29:11.
(4) מִי לֹא יִרָאֲךָ מֶלֶךְ הַגּוֹיִם כִּי לְךָ יָאָתָה, *Jeremiah* 10:7.
(5) לְךָ זְרוֹעַ עִם גְּבוּרָה, *Psalms* 89:14. (6) לְךָ שָׁמַיִם אַף לְךָ אָרֶץ, *Psalms* 89:12; לְךָ יוֹם אַף לְךָ לָיְלָה, *Psalms* 74:16. (7) *I Chronicles* 29:11.

אַדִּיר בִּמְלוּכָה — *Mighty in kingship*. We cannot possibly list all of God's praises for He and His praises are infinite. It has become the practice to used an alphabetical ordering of praise, as if to say, "We praise You in every way which starts with the letter aleph, or beis, or gimmel . . . from the beginning of the alphabet to the end."

קַדֵּשׁ וּרְחַץ כַּרְפַּס יַחַץ מַגִּיד רָחְצָה מוֹצִיא מַצָּ
MATZAh   MOTZI   RACHTZAh   MAGGID   YACHATZ   KARPAS   URECHATZ   KADDESH

לְךָ יהוה הַמַּמְלָכָה, כִּי לוֹ נָאֶה, כִּי לוֹ יָאֶה.

it is ‹ to ‹ for ≪ it is ‹ to ‹ for ≪ is the ‹ HASHEM, ‹ Yours,
proper! Him   fitting; Him   sovereignty —

יָחִיד בִּמְלוּכָה, כַּבִּיר כַּהֲלָכָה, לִמּוּדָיו יֹאמְרוּ

‹ say ‹ His disciples ≪ as is befitting, ‹ powerful ≪ in kingship, ‹ Unique

לוֹ, לְךָ וּלְךָ, לְךָ כִּי לְךָ, לְךָ אַף לְךָ,

≪ Yours…; ‹ also ‹ Yours…, ≪ to ‹ for ‹ Yours…, ≪ and ‹ Yours… ≪ to
You…;   Yours…;   Him:

לְךָ יהוה הַמַּמְלָכָה, כִּי לוֹ נָאֶה, כִּי לוֹ יָאֶה.

it is ‹ to ‹ for ≪ it is ‹ to ‹ for ≪ is the ‹ HASHEM, ‹ Yours,
proper! Him   fitting; Him   sovereignty —

מוֹשֵׁל בִּמְלוּכָה, נוֹרָא כַּהֲלָכָה, סְבִיבָיו[1] יֹאמְרוּ

‹ say ‹ His surround- ≪ as is befitting, ‹ awesome ≪ in kingship, ‹ Reigning
ing [angels]

לוֹ, לְךָ וּלְךָ, לְךָ כִּי לְךָ, לְךָ אַף לְךָ,

≪ Yours…; ‹ also ‹ Yours…, ≪ to ‹ for ‹ Yours…, ≪ and ‹ Yours… ≪ to
You…;   Yours…;   Him:

לְךָ יהוה הַמַּמְלָכָה, כִּי לוֹ נָאֶה, כִּי לוֹ יָאֶה.

it is ‹ to ‹ for ≪ it is ‹ to ‹ for ≪ is the ‹ HASHEM, ‹ Yours,
proper! Him   fitting; Him   sovereignty —

עָנָיו בִּמְלוּכָה, פּוֹדֶה כַּהֲלָכָה, צַדִּיקָיו יֹאמְרוּ

‹ say ‹ His righteous ≪ as is befitting, ‹ the ≪ in kingship, ‹ Humble
ones   Redeemer

לוֹ, לְךָ וּלְךָ, לְךָ כִּי לְךָ, לְךָ אַף לְךָ,

≪ Yours…; ‹ also ‹ Yours…, ≪ to ‹ for ‹ Yours…, ≪ and ‹ Yours… ≪ to
You…;   Yours…;   Him:

לְךָ יהוה הַמַּמְלָכָה, כִּי לוֹ נָאֶה, כִּי לוֹ יָאֶה.

it is ‹ to ‹ for ≪ it is ‹ to ‹ for ≪ is the ‹ HASHEM, ‹ Yours,
proper! Him   fitting; Him   sovereignty —

קָדוֹשׁ בִּמְלוּכָה, רַחוּם כַּהֲלָכָה, שִׁנְאַנָּיו יֹאמְרוּ

‹ say ‹ His angels ≪ as is befitting, ‹ merciful ≪ in kingship, ‹ Holy

(1) Cf. *Psalms* 89:8.

לוֹ, לְךָ וּלְךָ, לְךָ כִּי לְךָ, לְךָ אַף לְךָ,

Yours…; also Yours…, to for Yours…, and Yours… to You…; Him:

לְךָ יהוה הַמַּמְלָכָה, כִּי לוֹ נָאֶה, כִּי לוֹ יָאֶה.

it is to for it is to for is the HASHEM, Yours, proper! Him fitting; Him sovereignty —

תַּקִּיף בִּמְלוּכָה, תּוֹמֵךְ כַּהֲלָכָה, תְּמִימָיו יֹאמְרוּ

say His perfect ones as is befitting, sustaining in kingship, Mighty

לוֹ, לְךָ וּלְךָ, לְךָ כִּי לְךָ, לְךָ אַף לְךָ,

Yours…; also Yours…, to for Yours…, and Yours… to You…; Him:

לְךָ יהוה הַמַּמְלָכָה, כִּי לוֹ נָאֶה, כִּי לוֹ יָאֶה.

it is to for it is to for is the HASHEM, Yours, proper! Him fitting; Him sovereignty —

THOSE WHO DID NOT DRINK THE FOURTH CUP AFTER THE BLESSING AT THE CONCLUSION OF HALLEL DO SO NOW. SEE PAGE 105 FOR THE BLESSINGS BEFORE AND AFTER DRINKING THE CUP, AND FOR חֲסַל סִדּוּר פֶּסַח.

אַדִּיר הוּא* יִבְנֶה בֵיתוֹ בְּקָרוֹב, בִּמְהֵרָה,

speedily, soon; His May He is He.* Mighty House rebuild

בִּמְהֵרָה, בְּיָמֵינוּ בְּקָרוֹב. אֵל בְּנֵה, אֵל בְּנֵה,

rebuild, God, rebuild, God, soon. in our days, [yes] speedily,

בְּנֵה בֵיתְךָ בְּקָרוֹב.

soon! Your House rebuild

בָּחוּר הוּא. גָּדוֹל הוּא. דָּגוּל הוּא. יִבְנֶה בֵיתוֹ

His May He is He. preeminent is He, great is He, Distinguished House rebuild

בְּקָרוֹב, בִּמְהֵרָה, בְּיָמֵינוּ בְּקָרוֹב. אֵל

God, soon. in our days, [yes] speedily, speedily, soon;

אַדִּיר הוּא — *Mighty is He.* A hymn of our fervent desire for the Messianic age and the rebuilt Temple. The Sages teach that the Third Temple will not be built by man but will descend from heaven at the time of the redemption; for this reason we ask that *He rebuild His House soon.*

קַדֵּשׁ וּרְחַץ כַּרְפַּס יַחַץ מַגִּיד רָחְצָה מוֹצִיא מַצָּה
ATZAH MOTZI RACHTZAH MAGGID YACHATZ KARPAS URECHATZ KADDESH

בְּנֵה, אֵל בְּנֵה, בְּנֵה בֵיתְךָ בְּקָרוֹב.

« soon! ‹ Your House ‹ rebuild « rebuild, ‹ God, « rebuild,

הָדוּר הוּא. וָתִיק הוּא. זַכַּאי הוּא. חָסִיד הוּא.

« is He. ‹ pious « is He, ‹ righteous « is He, ‹ faithful « is He, ‹ Majestic

יִבְנֶה בֵיתוֹ בְּקָרוֹב, בִּמְהֵרָה, בִּמְהֵרָה, בְּיָמֵינוּ

‹ in our days, ‹ [yes] speedily, ‹ speedily, « soon; ‹ His House ‹ May He rebuild

בְּקָרוֹב. אֵל בְּנֵה, אֵל בְּנֵה, בְּנֵה בֵיתְךָ בְּקָרוֹב.

« soon! ‹ Your House ‹ rebuild « rebuild, ‹ God, « rebuild, ‹ God, « soon.

טָהוֹר הוּא. יָחִיד הוּא. כַּבִּיר הוּא. לָמוּד הוּא.

« is He, ‹ all-wise « is He, ‹ powerful « is He, ‹ unique « is He, ‹ Pure

מֶלֶךְ הוּא. נוֹרָא הוּא. סַגִּיב הוּא. עִזּוּז הוּא.

« is He, ‹ mighty « is He, ‹ supreme « is He, ‹ awesome « is He, ‹ King

פּוֹדֶה הוּא. צַדִּיק הוּא. יִבְנֶה בֵיתוֹ בְּקָרוֹב,

« soon; ‹ His House ‹ May He rebuild « is He. ‹ righteous « is He, ‹ the Redeemer

בִּמְהֵרָה, בִּמְהֵרָה, בְּיָמֵינוּ בְּקָרוֹב. אֵל בְּנֵה, אֵל

‹ God, « rebuild, ‹ God, « soon. ‹ in our days, ‹ [yes] speedily, ‹ speedily,

בְּנֵה, בְּנֵה בֵיתְךָ בְּקָרוֹב.

« soon! ‹ Your House ‹ rebuild « rebuild,

קָדוֹשׁ הוּא. רַחוּם הוּא. שַׁדַּי הוּא. תַּקִּיף הוּא.

« is He. ‹ powerful « is He, ‹ Almighty « is He, ‹ merciful « is He, ‹ Holy

יִבְנֶה בֵיתוֹ בְּקָרוֹב, בִּמְהֵרָה, בִּמְהֵרָה, בְּיָמֵינוּ

‹ in our days, ‹ [yes] speedily, ‹ speedily, « soon; ‹ His House ‹ May He rebuild

בְּקָרוֹב. אֵל בְּנֵה, אֵל בְּנֵה, בְּנֵה בֵיתְךָ בְּקָרוֹב.

« soon! ‹ Your House ‹ rebuild « rebuild, ‹ God, « rebuild, ‹ God, « soon.

נִרְצָה הַלֵּל בָּרֵךְ צָפוּן שֻׁלְחָן עוֹרֵךְ כּוֹרֵךְ מָרוֹר

NIRTZAh hALLEL BARECh TZAFUN shULChAN ORECh kORECh MAROR

אֶחָד מִי יוֹדֵעַ?*

אֶחָד מִי יוֹדֵעַ? אֶחָד אֲנִי יוֹדֵעַ. אֶחָד
One — Who knows [it]?* One I know: One is

אֱלֹהֵינוּ שֶׁבַּשָּׁמַיִם וּבָאָרֶץ.
our God, Who is in heaven and on earth.

שְׁנַיִם מִי יוֹדֵעַ? שְׁנַיִם אֲנִי יוֹדֵעַ. שְׁנֵי לֻחוֹת
Two — Who knows [it]? Two I know: two are the Tablets

הַבְּרִית, אֶחָד אֱלֹהֵינוּ שֶׁבַּשָּׁמַיִם וּבָאָרֶץ.
of the Covenant; One is our God, Who is in heaven and on earth.

שְׁלֹשָׁה מִי יוֹדֵעַ? שְׁלֹשָׁה אֲנִי יוֹדֵעַ. שְׁלֹשָׁה
Three — Who knows [it]? Three I know: three are

אָבוֹת, שְׁנֵי לֻחוֹת הַבְּרִית, אֶחָד אֱלֹהֵינוּ
the Patriarchs; two are the Tablets of the Covenant; One is our God,

שֶׁבַּשָּׁמַיִם וּבָאָרֶץ.
Who is in heaven and on earth.

אַרְבַּע מִי יוֹדֵעַ? אַרְבַּע אֲנִי יוֹדֵעַ. אַרְבַּע
Four — Who knows [it]? Four I know: four are

אִמָּהוֹת, שְׁלֹשָׁה אָבוֹת, שְׁנֵי לֻחוֹת הַבְּרִית,
the Matriarchs; three are the Patriarchs; two are the Tablets of the Covenant;

אֶחָד אֱלֹהֵינוּ שֶׁבַּשָּׁמַיִם וּבָאָרֶץ.
One is our God, Who is in heaven and on earth.

אֶחָד מִי יוֹדֵעַ — One — Who knows [it]? Although on the surface this song has no connection to either the Egyptian Exodus or the future Redemption, some commentators view the concepts associated with the numbers from one to thirteen as sources of merit by which our ancestors were redeemed from Egypt: They believed in the One God and were eager to accept the two Tablets. God had promised the three Patriarchs — Abraham, Isaac, Jacob — that He would redeem their children. The Israelite women followed the way of modest righteousness taught them by the four Matriarchs — Sarah, Rebecca, Rachel, Leah. They would soon receive the Five Books of Moses, which form the core of the Written Torah, as well as the Oral Torah comprising the six sections of the Mishnah. Even during their period of slavery, they chose the seventh day as their day of rest. Circumcision, usually done on the eighth day of life, was performed en mass on the eve of the Exodus. The Jewish wives were not intimidated by Pharaoh's orders to cast every son...into the river, but conceived and carried for the full nine

חֲמִשָּׁה מִי יוֹדֵעַ? חֲמִשָּׁה אֲנִי יוֹדֵעַ. חֲמִשָּׁה

‹ five are ‹‹ know: ‹ I ‹ Five ‹‹ knows [it]? ‹ Who ‹‹ Five —

חֻמְשֵׁי תוֹרָה, אַרְבַּע אִמָּהוֹת, שְׁלֹשָׁה אָבוֹת,

‹‹ the Patriarchs; ‹ three are ‹‹ the Matriarchs; ‹ four are ‹‹ of the Torah; ‹ the Books

שְׁנֵי לֻחוֹת הַבְּרִית, אֶחָד אֱלֹהֵינוּ שֶׁבַּשָּׁמַיִם

‹ Who is in heaven ‹ is our God, ‹ One ‹‹ of the Covenant; ‹ the Tablets ‹ two are

וּבָאָרֶץ.

‹‹ and on earth.

שִׁשָּׁה מִי יוֹדֵעַ? שִׁשָּׁה אֲנִי יוֹדֵעַ. שִׁשָּׁה סִדְרֵי

‹ the Orders ‹ six are ‹‹ know: ‹ I ‹ Six ‹‹ knows [it]? ‹ Who ‹‹ Six —

מִשְׁנָה, חֲמִשָּׁה חֻמְשֵׁי תוֹרָה, אַרְבַּע אִמָּהוֹת,

‹‹ the Matriarchs; ‹ four are ‹‹ of the Torah; ‹ the Books ‹ five are ‹‹ of the Mishnah;

שְׁלֹשָׁה אָבוֹת, שְׁנֵי לֻחוֹת הַבְּרִית, אֶחָד

‹ One ‹‹ of the Covenant; ‹ the Tablets ‹ two are ‹‹ the Patriarchs; ‹ three are

אֱלֹהֵינוּ שֶׁבַּשָּׁמַיִם וּבָאָרֶץ.

‹‹ and on earth. ‹ Who is in heaven ‹ is our God,

שִׁבְעָה מִי יוֹדֵעַ? שִׁבְעָה אֲנִי יוֹדֵעַ. שִׁבְעָה

‹ seven are ‹‹ know: ‹ I ‹ Seven ‹‹ knows [it]? ‹ Who ‹‹ Seven —

יְמֵי שַׁבַּתָּא,שִׁשָּׁה סִדְרֵי מִשְׁנָה, חֲמִשָּׁה חֻמְשֵׁי

‹ the Books ‹ five are ‹‹ of the Mishnah; ‹ the Orders ‹ six are ‹‹ of the week; ‹ the days

תוֹרָה, אַרְבַּע אִמָּהוֹת, שְׁלֹשָׁה אָבוֹת, שְׁנֵי

‹ two are ‹‹ the Patriarchs; ‹ three are ‹‹ the Matriarchs; ‹ four are ‹‹ of the Torah;

לֻחוֹת הַבְּרִית, אֶחָד אֱלֹהֵינוּ שֶׁבַּשָּׁמַיִם וּבָאָרֶץ.

‹‹ and on earth. ‹ Who is in heaven ‹ is our God, ‹ One ‹‹ of the Covenant; ‹ the Tablets

---

months, placing their trust in God's salvation. The nation would imminently accept the Ten Commandments. The families of Joseph's eleven brothers, represented by the stars in his dream, changed neither their names, language, nor manner of dress in Egypt. (As viceroy, Joseph was given an official name and royal wardrobe by Pharaoh, and spoke the language of the court.) All twelve tribes maintained their familial integrity, for no Jewish woman consented to

שְׁמוֹנָה מִי יוֹדֵעַ? שְׁמוֹנָה אֲנִי יוֹדֵעַ. שְׁמוֹנָה

‹ eight are ‹‹ know: ‹ I ‹ Eight ‹‹ knows [it]? ‹ Who ‹‹ Eight –

יְמֵי מִילָה, שִׁבְעָה יְמֵי שַׁבַּתָּא, שִׁשָּׁה סִדְרֵי

‹ the ‹ six are ‹‹ of the week; ‹ the days ‹ seven are ‹‹ of ‹ the
Orders   circumcision;   days

מִשְׁנָה, חֲמִשָּׁה חֻמְשֵׁי תוֹרָה, אַרְבַּע אִמָּהוֹת,

‹‹ the Matriarchs; ‹ four are ‹‹ of the Torah; ‹ the Books ‹ five are ‹‹ of the Mishnah;

שְׁלֹשָׁה אָבוֹת, שְׁנֵי לֻחוֹת הַבְּרִית, אֶחָד

‹ One ‹‹ of the Covenant; ‹ the Tablets ‹ two are ‹‹ the Patriarchs; ‹ three are

אֱלֹהֵינוּ שֶׁבַּשָּׁמַיִם וּבָאָרֶץ.

‹‹ and on earth. ‹ Who is in heaven ‹ is our God,

תִּשְׁעָה מִי יוֹדֵעַ? תִּשְׁעָה אֲנִי יוֹדֵעַ. תִּשְׁעָה

‹ nine are ‹‹ know: ‹ I ‹ Nine ‹‹ knows [it]? ‹ Who ‹‹ Nine –

יַרְחֵי לֵדָה, שְׁמוֹנָה יְמֵי מִילָה, שִׁבְעָה יְמֵי

‹ the days ‹ seven are ‹‹ of ‹ the days ‹ eight are ‹‹ of ‹ the
circumcision;   pregnancy;   months

שַׁבַּתָּא, שִׁשָּׁה סִדְרֵי מִשְׁנָה, חֲמִשָּׁה חֻמְשֵׁי

‹ the Books ‹ five are ‹‹ of the Mishnah; ‹ the Orders ‹ six are ‹‹ of the week;

תוֹרָה, אַרְבַּע אִמָּהוֹת, שְׁלֹשָׁה אָבוֹת, שְׁנֵי

‹ two are ‹‹ the Patriarchs; ‹ three are ‹‹ the Matriarchs; ‹ four are ‹‹ of the Torah;

לֻחוֹת הַבְּרִית, אֶחָד אֱלֹהֵינוּ שֶׁבַּשָּׁמַיִם וּבָאָרֶץ.

‹‹ and on ‹ Who is in ‹ is our God, ‹ One ‹‹ of the ‹ the Tablets
earth.   heaven   Covenant;

עֲשָׂרָה מִי יוֹדֵעַ? עֲשָׂרָה אֲנִי יוֹדֵעַ. עֲשָׂרָה

‹ ten are ‹‹ know: ‹ I ‹ Ten ‹‹ knows [it]? ‹ Who ‹‹ Ten –

דִּבְּרַיָּא, תִּשְׁעָה יַרְחֵי לֵדָה, שְׁמוֹנָה יְמֵי מִילָה,

‹‹ of cir- ‹ the ‹ eight are ‹‹ of ‹ the ‹ nine are ‹‹ the [Ten] Com-
cumcision; days   pregnancy; months   mandments;

---

the advances of the Egyptian taskmasters. God taught Moses the prayer of the Thirteen Attributes of Divine Mercy, to be followed in word and deed, in times of national distress.

קַדֵּשׁ וּרְחַץ כַּרְפַּס יַחַץ מַגִּיד רָחְצָה מוֹצִיא מַצָּה
ATZAh   MOTZI   RAChTZAh   MAGGID yAChATZ kARPAS urEChATZ kADDesh

שִׁבְעָה יְמֵי שַׁבַּתָּא, שִׁשָּׁה סִדְרֵי מִשְׁנָה, חֲמִשָּׁה

< five are << of the < the < six are << of the week; < the < seven are
Mishnah; Orders days

חֻמְשֵׁי תוֹרָה, אַרְבַּע אִמָּהוֹת, שְׁלֹשָׁה אָבוֹת,

<< the < three are << the Matriarchs; < four are << of the Torah; < the Books
Patriarchs;

שְׁנֵי לֻחוֹת הַבְּרִית, אֶחָד אֱלֹהֵינוּ שֶׁבַּשָּׁמַיִם

< Who is in heaven < is our God, < One << of the Covenant; < the Tablets < two are

וּבָאָרֶץ.

<< and on earth.

אֶחָד עָשָׂר מִי יוֹדֵעַ? אֶחָד עָשָׂר אֲנִי יוֹדֵעַ.

<< know: < I < Eleven << knows [it]? < Who << Eleven —

אֶחָד עָשָׂר כּוֹכְבַיָּא, עֲשָׂרָה דִבְּרַיָּא, תִּשְׁעָה

< nine are << the [Ten] Com- < ten are << the stars < eleven are
mandments; [in Yosef's dream];

יַרְחֵי לֵדָה, שְׁמוֹנָה יְמֵי מִילָה, שִׁבְעָה יְמֵי

< the < seven are << of cir- < the days < eight are << of < the
days cumcision; pregnancy; months

שַׁבַּתָּא, שִׁשָּׁה סִדְרֵי מִשְׁנָה, חֲמִשָּׁה חֻמְשֵׁי

< the Books < five are << of the Mishnah; < the Orders < six are << of the week;

תוֹרָה, אַרְבַּע אִמָּהוֹת, שְׁלֹשָׁה אָבוֹת, שְׁנֵי

< two are << the Patriarchs; < three are << the Matriarchs; < four are << of the Torah;

לֻחוֹת הַבְּרִית, אֶחָד אֱלֹהֵינוּ שֶׁבַּשָּׁמַיִם וּבָאָרֶץ.

<< and on < Who is in heaven < is our God, < One << of the < the Tablets
earth. Covenant;

שְׁנֵים עָשָׂר מִי יוֹדֵעַ? שְׁנֵים עָשָׂר אֲנִי יוֹדֵעַ.

<< know: < I < Twelve << knows [it]? < Who << Twelve —

שְׁנֵים עָשָׂר שִׁבְטַיָּא, אַחַד עָשָׂר כּוֹכְבַיָּא,

<< the stars [in < eleven are << the tribes; < twelve are
Yosef's dream];

NIRTZAh   hALLeL   BARech   TZAFUN   shulchAN oRech   koRech   MARO[R]

עֲשָׂרָה דִבְּרַיָּא, תִּשְׁעָה יַרְחֵי לֵדָה, שְׁמוֹנָה יְמֵי

‹ the ‹ eight are ‹‹ of ‹ the ‹ nine are ‹‹ the [Ten] Com- ‹ ten are
days pregnancy; months mandments;

מִילָה, שִׁבְעָה יְמֵי שַׁבַּתָּא, שִׁשָּׁה סִדְרֵי מִשְׁנָה,

‹‹ of the ‹ the ‹ six are ‹‹ of the week; ‹ the ‹ seven are ‹‹ of cir-
Mishnah; Orders days cumcision;

חֲמִשָּׁה חֻמְשֵׁי תוֹרָה, אַרְבַּע אִמָּהוֹת, שְׁלֹשָׁה

‹ three are ‹‹ the Matriarchs; ‹ four are ‹‹ of the Torah; ‹ the Books ‹ five are

אָבוֹת, שְׁנֵי לֻחוֹת הַבְּרִית, אֶחָד אֱלֹהֵינוּ

‹ is our God, ‹ One ‹‹ of the Covenant; ‹ the Tablets ‹ two are ‹‹ the Patriarchs;

שֶׁבַּשָּׁמַיִם וּבָאָרֶץ.

‹‹ and on earth. ‹ Who is in heaven

שְׁלֹשָׁה עָשָׂר מִי יוֹדֵעַ? שְׁלֹשָׁה עָשָׂר אֲנִי

‹ I ‹ Thirteen ‹‹ knows [it]? ‹ Who ‹‹ Thirteen —

יוֹדֵעַ. שְׁלֹשָׁה עָשָׂר מִדַּיָּא, שְׁנֵים עָשָׂר שִׁבְטַיָּא,

‹‹ the tribes; ‹ twelve are ‹‹ the attributes ‹ thirteen are ‹‹ know:
[of God];

אַחַד עָשָׂר כּוֹכְבַיָּא, עֲשָׂרָה דִבְּרַיָּא, תִּשְׁעָה

‹ nine are ‹‹ the [Ten] Com- ‹ ten are ‹‹ the stars [in ‹ eleven are
mandments; Yosef's dream];

יַרְחֵי לֵדָה, שְׁמוֹנָה יְמֵי מִילָה, שִׁבְעָה יְמֵי

‹ the ‹ seven are ‹‹ of cir- ‹ the days ‹ eight are ‹‹ of ‹ the
days cumcision; pregnancy; months

שַׁבַּתָּא, שִׁשָּׁה סִדְרֵי מִשְׁנָה, חֲמִשָּׁה חֻמְשֵׁי

‹ the Books ‹ five are ‹‹ of the Mishnah; ‹ the Orders ‹ six are ‹‹ of the week;

תוֹרָה, אַרְבַּע אִמָּהוֹת, שְׁלֹשָׁה אָבוֹת, שְׁנֵי

‹ two are ‹‹ the Patriarchs; ‹ three are ‹‹ the Matriarchs; ‹ four are ‹‹ of the Torah;

לֻחוֹת הַבְּרִית, אֶחָד אֱלֹהֵינוּ שֶׁבַּשָּׁמַיִם וּבָאָרֶץ.

‹‹ and on ‹ Who is in heaven ‹ is our God, ‹ One ‹‹ of the ‹ the Tablets
earth. Covenant;

חַד גַּדְיָא,* חַד גַּדְיָא, דְּזַבִּין אַבָּא בִּתְרֵי

⟨ for two ⟨ by father ⟨ that was bought ⟨⟨ little goat, ⟨ one ⟨⟨ little goat,* ⟨ One

זוּזֵי, חַד גַּדְיָא חַד גַּדְיָא.

⟨⟨ little goat! ⟨ one ⟨⟨ little goat, ⟨ One ⟨⟨ zuzim.

וְאָתָא שׁוּנְרָא וְאָכְלָה לְגַדְיָא, דְּזַבִּין אַבָּא

⟨ by father ⟨ that was bought ⟨ the little goat ⟨ and ate ⟨ a cat ⟨ Then came

בִּתְרֵי זוּזֵי, חַד גַּדְיָא חַד גַּדְיָא.

⟨⟨ little goat. ⟨ one ⟨⟨ little goat, ⟨ One ⟨⟨ zuzim. ⟨ for two

וְאָתָא כַלְבָּא וְנָשַׁךְ לְשׁוּנְרָא, דְּאָכְלָה לְגַדְיָא,

⟨ the little goat ⟨ that ate ⟨⟨ the cat, ⟨ and bit ⟨ a dog ⟨ Then came

דְּזַבִּין אַבָּא בִּתְרֵי זוּזֵי, חַד גַּדְיָא חַד גַּדְיָא.

⟨⟨ little goat. ⟨ one ⟨⟨ little goat, ⟨ One ⟨⟨ zuzim. ⟨ for two ⟨ by father ⟨ that was bought

וְאָתָא חוּטְרָא וְהִכָּה לְכַלְבָּא, דְּנָשַׁךְ

⟨ that bit ⟨⟨ the dog, ⟨ and beat ⟨ a stick ⟨ Then came

לְשׁוּנְרָא, דְּאָכְלָה לְגַדְיָא, דְּזַבִּין אַבָּא בִּתְרֵי

⟨ for two ⟨ by father ⟨ that was bought ⟨ the little goat ⟨ that ate ⟨⟨ the cat,

זוּזֵי, חַד גַּדְיָא חַד גַּדְיָא.

⟨⟨ little goat. ⟨ one ⟨⟨ little goat, ⟨ One ⟨⟨ zuzim.

וְאָתָא נוּרָא וְשָׂרַף לְחוּטְרָא, דְּהִכָּה לְכַלְבָּא,

⟨⟨ the dog, ⟨ that beat ⟨⟨ the stick, ⟨ and burnt ⟨ a fire ⟨ Then came

דְּנָשַׁךְ לְשׁוּנְרָא, דְּאָכְלָה לְגַדְיָא, דְּזַבִּין אַבָּא

⟨ by father ⟨ that was bought ⟨ the little goat ⟨ that ate ⟨⟨ the cat, ⟨ that bit

בִּתְרֵי זוּזֵי, חַד גַּדְיָא חַד גַּדְיָא.

⟨⟨ little goat. ⟨ one ⟨⟨ little goat, ⟨ One ⟨⟨ zuzim. ⟨ for two

---

חַד גַּדְיָא — *One little goat.* Lest one feel, God forbid, that the events of the Exodus are overshadowed by the centuries-long night of the present exile, and seek respite in some lifestyle inconsistent with that prescribed by the Torah, the Haggadah closes with the soliloquy of a lost

וְאָתָא מַיָּא וְכָבָה לְנוּרָא, דְּשָׂרַף לְחוּטְרָא,
« the stick, ‹ that burnt « the fire, ‹ and extinguished ‹ water ‹ Then came

דְּהִכָּה לְכַלְבָּא, דְּנָשַׁךְ לְשׁוּנְרָא, דְּאָכְלָה
‹ that ate « the cat, ‹ that bit « the dog, ‹ that beat

לְגַדְיָא, דְּזַבִּין אַבָּא בִּתְרֵי זוּזֵי, חַד גַּדְיָא
« little goat, ‹ One « zuzim. ‹ for two ‹ by father ‹ that was bought ‹ the little goat

חַד גַּדְיָא.
« little goat. ‹ one

וְאָתָא תוֹרָא וְשָׁתָה לְמַיָּא, דְּכָבָה לְנוּרָא,
« the fire, ‹ that extinguished « the water, ‹ and drank ‹ an ox ‹ Then came

דְּשָׂרַף לְחוּטְרָא, דְּהִכָּה לְכַלְבָּא, דְּנָשַׁךְ
‹ that bit « the dog, ‹ that beat « the stick, ‹ that burnt

לְשׁוּנְרָא, דְּאָכְלָה לְגַדְיָא, דְּזַבִּין אַבָּא בִּתְרֵי
‹ for two ‹ by father ‹ that was bought ‹ the little goat ‹ that ate « the cat,

זוּזֵי, חַד גַּדְיָא חַד גַּדְיָא.
« little goat. ‹ one « little goat, ‹ One « zuzim.

וְאָתָא הַשּׁוֹחֵט וְשָׁחַט לְתוֹרָא, דְּשָׁתָא לְמַיָּא,
« the water, ‹ that drank « the ox, ‹ and slaughtered ‹ the slaughterer ‹ Then came

דְּכָבָה לְנוּרָא, דְּשָׂרַף לְחוּטְרָא, דְּהִכָּה לְכַלְבָּא,
« the dog, ‹ that beat « the stick, ‹ that burnt « the fire, ‹ that extinguished

דְּנָשַׁךְ לְשׁוּנְרָא, דְּאָכְלָה לְגַדְיָא, דְּזַבִּין אַבָּא
‹ by father ‹ that was bought ‹ the little goat ‹ that ate « the cat, ‹ that bit

בִּתְרֵי זוּזֵי, חַד גַּדְיָא חַד גַּדְיָא.
« little goat. ‹ one « little goat, ‹ One « zuzim. ‹ for two

soul seeking to identify with a higher truth. "The goat supplies my needs — meat, milk, leather, mohair, tent skins — perhaps it is di-

vine! But the cat can easily devour the baby goat — shall I worship the cat? Or the dog that can overpower the cat? . . ." In like fashion he elimi-

וְאָתָא מַלְאַךְ הַמָּוֶת וְשָׁחַט לְשׁוֹחֵט, דְּשָׁחַט
‹ who ‹‹ the ‹ and killed ‹ of death ‹ the angel ‹ Then came
slaughtered slaughterer,

לְתוֹרָא, דְּשָׁתָה לְמַיָּא, דְּכָבָה לְנוּרָא, דְּשָׂרַף
‹ that burnt ‹‹ the fire, ‹ that ‹‹ the water, ‹ that drank ‹‹ the ox,
extinguished

לְחוּטְרָא, דְּהִכָּה לְכַלְבָּא, דְּנָשַׁךְ לְשׁוּנְרָא,
‹‹ the cat, ‹ that bit ‹‹ the dog, ‹ that beat ‹‹ the stick,

דְּאָכְלָה לְגַדְיָא, דְּזַבִּין אַבָּא בִּתְרֵי זוּזֵי, חַד
‹ One ‹‹ zuzim. ‹ for two ‹ by father ‹ that was ‹ the little goat ‹ that ate
bought

גַּדְיָא חַד גַּדְיָא.
‹‹ little goat. ‹ one ‹‹ little goat,

וְאָתָא הַקָּדוֹשׁ בָּרוּךְ הוּא וְשָׁחַט לְמַלְאַךְ
‹ the angel ‹ and slew ‹‹ is He, ‹ Blessed ‹ the Holy One, ‹ Then came

הַמָּוֶת, דְּשָׁחַט לְשׁוֹחֵט, דְּשָׁחַט לְתוֹרָא, דְּשָׁתָה
‹ that drank ‹‹ the ox, ‹ who ‹‹ the ‹ who killed ‹‹ of death,
slaughtered slaughterer,

לְמַיָּא, דְּכָבָה לְנוּרָא, דְּשָׂרַף לְחוּטְרָא, דְּהִכָּה
‹ that beat ‹‹ the stick, ‹ that burnt ‹‹ the fire, ‹ that ‹‹ the water,
extinguished

לְכַלְבָּא, דְּנָשַׁךְ לְשׁוּנְרָא, דְּאָכְלָה לְגַדְיָא, דְּזַבִּין
‹ that was ‹ the little ‹ that ate ‹‹ the cat, ‹ that bit ‹‹ the dog,
bought goat

אַבָּא בִּתְרֵי זוּזֵי, חַד גַּדְיָא חַד גַּדְיָא.
‹‹ little goat. ‹ one ‹‹ little goat, ‹ One ‹‹ zuzim. ‹ for two ‹ by father

ALTHOUGH THE HAGGADAH FORMALLY ENDS AT THIS POINT,
ONE SHOULD CONTINUE TO OCCUPY HIMSELF WITH THE STORY OF THE EXODUS,
AND THE LAWS OF PESACH, UNTIL SLEEP OVERTAKES HIM.
MANY HAVE THE CUSTOM TO READ שִׁיר הַשִּׁירִים, SONG OF SONGS, AFTER THE SEDER.

nates worship of brute strength (stick, ox), deification of the elements (fire, water), idolization of man (slaughterer), and adoration of angels.

The supremacy of the Holy One, Blessed is he, and the subservience of all the Creation to Him is thus arrived at as the ultimate truth.

NIRTZAh hALLeL BARECh TZAFUN shULCHAN OReCh KOReCh MARO

❧ COMPENSATORY BLESSINGS / ברכות למי ששכח ❧

SEE BELOW FOR INSTANCES WHEN COMPENSATORY BLESSINGS MUST BE RECITED. WHEN THE COMPENSATORY BLESSING IS RECITED AT THE FIRST OR SECOND SABBATH OR FESTIVAL MEAL, ONE CONCLUDES WITH ... בָּרוּךְ אַתָּה ה' מְקַדֵּשׁ. AT THE THIRD MEAL THIS CLOSING BLESSING IS NOT RE-CITED. AFTER THE APPROPRIATE BLESSING, CONTINUE WITH THE FOURTH BLESSING, הַטוֹב וְהַמֵּטִיב, GOD'S GOODNESS (P. 78).

IF ONE FORGOT רְצֵה ON THE SABBATH:

בָּרוּךְ אַתָּה יהוה אֱלֹהֵינוּ מֶלֶךְ הָעוֹלָם, אֲשֶׁר נָתַן שַׁבָּתוֹת
⟨ Sabbaths ⟨ gave ⟨ Who ⟨⟨ of the ⟨ King ⟨ our God, ⟨ HASHEM, ⟨ are You, ⟨ Blessed
universe,

לִמְנוּחָה לְעַמּוֹ יִשְׂרָאֵל בְּאַהֲבָה, לְאוֹת וְלִבְרִית. בָּרוּךְ אַתָּה
⟨ are ⟨ Blessed ⟨⟨ and for a ⟨ for a ⟨⟨ with love, ⟨ Israel ⟨ to His ⟨ for rest
You, covenant. sign people

יהוה, מְקַדֵּשׁ הַשַּׁבָּת.
⟨⟨ the ⟨ Who ⟨⟨ HASHEM,
Sabbath. sanctifies

IF ONE FORGOT יַעֲלֶה וְיָבֹא ON A FESTIVAL:

בָּרוּךְ אַתָּה יהוה אֱלֹהֵינוּ מֶלֶךְ הָעוֹלָם, אֲשֶׁר נָתַן יָמִים טוֹבִים
⟨ Festivals ⟨ gave ⟨ Who ⟨⟨ of the ⟨ King ⟨ our God, ⟨ HASHEM, ⟨ are ⟨ Blessed
universe, You,

לְעַמּוֹ יִשְׂרָאֵל לְשָׂשׂוֹן וּלְשִׂמְחָה, אֶת יוֹם חַג הַמַּצּוֹת הַזֶּה.
⟨⟨ of this Festival of ⟨ — the day ⟨⟨ and gladness ⟨ for ⟨ Israel ⟨ to His
Matzos. happiness people

בָּרוּךְ אַתָּה יהוה, מְקַדֵּשׁ יִשְׂרָאֵל וְהַזְּמַנִּים.
⟨⟨ and the [festive] ⟨ Israel ⟨ Who ⟨⟨ HASHEM, ⟨ are You, ⟨ Blessed
seasons. sanctifies

❧§ **If One Omitted** יַעֲלֶה וְיָבֹא or רְצֵה

1. If he realizes his omission after having recited the blessing of בּוֹנֶה, *Who rebuilds,* he makes up for the omission by reciting the appropriate Compensatory Blessing.

2. If he realizes his omission after having recited the first six words of the fourth blessing, he may still switch immediately into the Compensatory Blessing since the words ... בָּרוּךְ אַתָּה הָעוֹלָם are identical in both blessings. (However, the Compensatory Blessing need not be recited after the third Sabbath meal if *Bircas HaMazon* is recited after sunset.)

3. If the omission is discovered after having recited the word הָאֵל, *the Almighty,* of the fourth blessing, it is too late for the Compensatory Blessing to be recited. In that case:
   (i) On the Sabbath and on a Festival day, at the first two meals *Bircas HaMazon* must be repeated in its entirety; at the third meal, nothing need be done.
   (ii) On Chol HaMoed, nothing need be done except if the day fell on the Sabbath and רְצֵה, *Retzei,* was omitted. In that case, at the first two meals *Bircas HaMazon* must be repeated. But if רְצֵה was recited and יַעֲלֶה וְיָבֹא was omitted, nothing need be done.

IF ONE FORGOT BOTH רְצֵה AND יַעֲלֶה וְיָבֹא ON A FESTIVAL THAT FALLS ON THE SABBATH:

בָּרוּךְ אַתָּה יהוה אֱלֹהֵינוּ מֶלֶךְ הָעוֹלָם, אֲשֶׁר נָתַן שַׁבָּתוֹת
⟨ Sabbaths ⟨ gave ⟨ Who ⟨⟨ of the ⟨ King ⟨ our God, ⟨ HASHEM, ⟨ are ⟨ Blessed
universe, You,

לִמְנוּחָה לְעַמּוֹ יִשְׂרָאֵל בְּאַהֲבָה, לְאוֹת וְלִבְרִית, וְיָמִים טוֹבִים
⟨ and Festivals ⟨⟨ and a ⟨ for a ⟨⟨ with love, ⟨ Israel ⟨ to His ⟨ for rest
covenant, sign people

לְשָׂשׂוֹן וּלְשִׂמְחָה, אֶת יוֹם חַג הַמַּצּוֹת הַזֶּה. בָּרוּךְ אַתָּה
⟨ are ⟨ Blessed ⟨⟨ of this Festival of Matzos. ⟨ – the day ⟨⟨ and gladness ⟨ for
You, happiness

יהוה, מְקַדֵּשׁ הַשַּׁבָּת וְיִשְׂרָאֵל וְהַזְּמַנִּים.
⟨⟨ and the ⟨ Israel, ⟨ the ⟨ Who ⟨⟨ HASHEM,
[festive] seasons. Sabbath, sanctifies

IF ONE FORGOT יַעֲלֶה וְיָבֹא ON CHOL HAMOED:

בָּרוּךְ אַתָּה יהוה אֱלֹהֵינוּ מֶלֶךְ הָעוֹלָם, אֲשֶׁר נָתַן מוֹעֲדִים
⟨ appointed ⟨ gave ⟨ Who ⟨⟨ of the ⟨ King ⟨ our God, ⟨ HASHEM, ⟨ are You, ⟨ Blessed
Festivals universe,

לְעַמּוֹ יִשְׂרָאֵל לְשָׂשׂוֹן וּלְשִׂמְחָה, אֶת יוֹם חַג הַמַּצּוֹת הַזֶּה.
⟨⟨ of this Festival of ⟨ – the day ⟨⟨ and gladness ⟨ for ⟨ Israel ⟨ to His
Matzos. happiness people

IF ONE FORGOT BOTH רְצֵה AND יַעֲלֶה וְיָבֹא ON THE SABBATH OF CHOL HAMOED:

בָּרוּךְ אַתָּה יהוה אֱלֹהֵינוּ מֶלֶךְ הָעוֹלָם, אֲשֶׁר נָתַן שַׁבָּתוֹת
⟨ Sabbaths ⟨ gave ⟨ Who ⟨⟨ of the ⟨ King ⟨ our God, ⟨ HASHEM, ⟨ are ⟨ Blessed
universe, You,

לִמְנוּחָה לְעַמּוֹ יִשְׂרָאֵל בְּאַהֲבָה, לְאוֹת וְלִבְרִית, וּמוֹעֲדִים
⟨ and appointed ⟨⟨ and a ⟨ for a sign ⟨⟨ with love, ⟨ Israel ⟨ to His ⟨ for rest
Festivals covenant, people

לְשָׂשׂוֹן וּלְשִׂמְחָה, אֶת יוֹם חַג הַמַּצּוֹת הַזֶּה. בָּרוּךְ אַתָּה יהוה,
⟨⟨ HASHEM, ⟨ are ⟨ Blessed ⟨⟨ of this Festival of ⟨ – the day ⟨⟨ and gladness ⟨ for
You, Matzos. happiness

מְקַדֵּשׁ הַשַּׁבָּת וְיִשְׂרָאֵל וְהַזְּמַנִּים.
⟨⟨ and the [festive] ⟨ Israel, ⟨ the ⟨ Who
seasons. Sabbath, sanctifies

This volume is part of
THE ARTSCROLL SERIES®
an ongoing project of
translations, commentaries and expositions
on Scripture, Mishnah, Talmud, Halachah,
liturgy, history, the classic Rabbinic writings,
biographies and thought.

For a brochure of current publications
visit your local Hebrew bookseller
or contact the publisher:

Mesorah Publications, ltd

4401 Second Avenue
Brooklyn, New York 11232
(718) 921-9000
www.artscroll.com